CW00525127

Humanistic So

Other titles by Malcolm Payne:

Social Work: Themes, Issues and Critical Debates, 3rd edition (co-editor)*

Critical Practice in Social Work, 2nd edition (co-editor)*

Practising Social Work in a Complex World, 2nd edition (co-editor)*

Social Work in End-of-Life and Palliative Care (co-author)

Social Care Practice in Context*

Globalization and International Social Work: Postmodern Change and Challenge (co-author)

What is Professional Social Work? 2nd edition

Modern Social Work Theory, 3rd edition*

The Origins of Social Work: Continuity and Change*

Anti-Bureaucratic Social Work

Teamwork in Multiprofessional Care*

Social Work and Community Care*

Linkages: Effective Networking in Social Care

*Also published by Palgrave Macmillan

Humanistic Social Work
Core Principles in Practice

Malcolm Payne

© Lyceum Books, Inc 2011

All rights reserved. No reproduction, copy or transmission of this
publication may be made without written permission.

No portion of this publication may be reproduced, copied or transmitted
save with written permission or in accordance with the provisions of the
Copyright, Designs and Patents Act 1988, or under the terms of any licence
permitting limited copying issued by the Copyright Licensing Agency,
Saffron House, 6-10 Kirby Street, London EC1N 8TS.

Any person who does any unauthorized act in relation to this publication
may be liable to criminal prosecution and civil claims for damages.

The author has asserted his right to be identified as the author of this work
in accordance with the Copyright, Designs and Patents Act 1988.

Published worldwide excluding North America, Korea and Japan
2011 by PALGRAVE MACMILLAN

Palgrave Macmillan in the UK is an imprint of Macmillan Publishers Limited,
registered in England, company number 785998, of Houndmills,
Basingstoke, Hampshire RG21 6XS.

Palgrave® and Macmillan® are registered trademarks in the United States, the
United Kingdom, Europe and other countries.

Originally published in the United States by Lyceum Books.

ISBN 978-0-230-29360-1

This book is printed on paper suitable for recycling and made from fully
managed and sustained forest sources. Logging, pulping and manufacturing
processes are expected to conform to the environmental regulations of the
country of origin.

A catalogue record for this book is available from the British Library.

A catalog record for the American edition is available from the Library of Congress.

10 9 8 7 6 5 4 3 2 1
20 19 18 17 16 15 14 13 12 11

Printed in the United States of America.

Contents

Boxes

Acknowledgments

I first presented an earlier version of the case study presented in box 4.2, and the discussion of it in chapter 4, at the Council on Social Work Education's Annual Program Meeting, in Chicago, and it was subsequently published in Payne (2007).

Some of the discussion also draws on arguments first presented at conferences. That presented at the University of Bielefeld, in Germany, was subsequently published as Payne (2009a). That presented at the School of Social Service Administration, University of Chicago, was subsequently published as Payne (2009b).

Some of the material on complexity in chapter 5 was first presented in Payne (2008a). Material on spirituality in chapter 7 is drawn from my book, written with Margaret Reith, *Social Work in End-of-Life and Palliative Care* (Reith & Payne, 2009), and from an article based on a paper presented at the U.K. Primary Care Conference in 2008 (Payne, 2008b).

The author and publisher wish to acknowledge with thanks permission to reproduce:

- The International Humanist and Ethical Union, for the text of the Amsterdam Declaration, reprinted in box 1.1
- Thomas Greening and *Journal of Humanistic Psychology*, for the text of the "Five Basic Postulates of Humanistic Psychology," reprinted in box 1.3

Introduction

HUMANISTIC PRACTICE: THE POSITIVE CORE OF SOCIAL WORK

Humanistic principles are and always have been a core part of social work, in the UK and in most other parts of the world. We can see this in the adoption of many of these principles in recent government reports from the UK, as I show below. This book spells out and interprets humanistic principles for social work practice in the twenty-first century. They are core principles for three main reasons.

First, they are the source of social work's commitment to using the widest possible human knowledge achieved through research and scientific debate. Many writers in social work (for example recently Sheldon and Macdonald, 2008; Gambrill, 2006) have emphasised the importance of an evidence-based, or at least evidence-aware, practice. The Social Care Institute for Excellence and the Institute for Research and Innovation in Social Services (in Scotland), together with organisations such as Research in Practice and Research in Practice for Adults, have all been established to make evidence accessible and useable by practitioners. However, this has not been uncontroversial, as it favours limited forms of evidence (Otto et al., 2009), and critical analyses point out that evidence is interpreted through organisational and political requirements and in social relationships and interactions. Moreover, it tends to accept rather than be critical of existing social and political oppression (Gray, Plath, and Webb, 2009).

Humanistic social work incorporates both stances. Central to its position is the human capacity for rational use of scientific evidence and through this, human control of our environment. But humanistic practice is not limited to rigid "evidence-based" practice, which relies on only some forms of understanding. Humanistic practice wants to use *all* the knowledge, *all* the skills, and *all* the creativity that human beings have achieved. An important part of this book focuses therefore on creativity and spirituality.

A second reason for the importance of humanistic principles in social work is that social work is a human-to-human interaction. There are three points regarding this principle. First, humanistic practice connects with ideas such as self-directed support and person-centred planning that are at the centre of advancements in personalisation and the "putting people first" developments in UK adult services (Payne, 2009). Humanistic social work says, "think about the whole human being you are working with," and it gives practitioners important skills and principles that enable them to be flexible and deal with the complexities that are an inevitable part of seeing and assessing people holistically. It does not deny the negative and chaotic lifestyles that social workers have to deal with in a few people and families, but it says, "this is a human being, in the society that we share, entitled to our best efforts to help them achieve at least some aspect of their aspirations."

Humanistic principles also underlie some of the ideas about a new social work that emerged from the Task Force Report on the future of social work in England. Both the approach of personalisation and the task force developments, instead of implementing bureaucratic procedures and planning within the confines of what exists in services, say that the social workers of the future need to be alongside service users and their carers, advocating for and helping them creatively meet their needs in their own person-centred planning. At the moment, there is probably too much of a focus on independent budgets rather than the full range of creative possibilities for enabling and supporting people to be at the centre of their own planning for future care. An important aspect of humanistic practice is advance care planning, in which people can state their preferences and set the direction for our practice early on in their care careers.

The second point about human-to-human interaction as the centre of humanistic practice is that it brings together individual *and* social care and change. Human life takes place as a part of societies, and human interactions incorporate the social within them. Therefore, in this book I redraw individual social work by making a humanistic connection between individual rights and human self-actualization, and the necessity of making that connection within social relationships that are also moving forward in the same direction. Psychological therapies to facilitate individual development are necessary but not enough. Social work needs to facilitate support of those individuals. These two aspects of practice need to take place at the same time and with relevance to the individual's family and community environment. It also requires advocacy for approaches by other social agencies that support and enable individuals to achieve their best future.

The third point about human-to-human interaction as a central aspect of humanistic practice is the importance of practising in such a way as to sustain as much equality as possible in dialogue and engagement with the service user's own narrative about their lives. There may be some official and oppressive assumption about how lives should be, but to practice effectively social workers need to engage with how the evidence tells us people and their lives actually are, and how they perceive and understand their aspirations and objectives. Social workers in the UK may fear that government priorities for fiscal prudence promoted by the Conservative-Liberal Democrat coalition elected in 2010 will place additional burdens on users of social and other public services. Policy positions such as this are always present in UK society, rising to greater influence from time to time. As a result of these policies, many people with whom practitioners work may receive less from the state and struggle more, and social workers may have fewer resources and less time to help. However, this never needs to mean that practitioners resign from practising within their common humanity in relation to the people they work with.

The source of the importance of relationship in social work lies in psychodynamic theories, and recent debate about relationship-based social work draws on a range of mainly psychological models of practice (Ruch, Turney, and Ward, 2010). Recent social care developments have proclaimed the importance of economic and managerial effectiveness on business language and practices (Harris, 2002). Humanistic practice joins together the individual and social aspects of social work using both psychological and social knowledge, but it also affirms human interaction as the core source of authority to act and the main process of personal and social change in social work. Practitioners must be accountable to society through their agency, yes, but also (and importantly) to service users and carers. That accountability can be part of a resistance to the social and political rejection of the need for social care, because practitioners' engagement with the needs of service users, achieved through true human-to-human contact, can provide the only evidence that can call forth, in the end, a social response to need. If practitioners do not engage with need, society cannot engage with it either.

A third reason for the importance of humanistic practice principles is the way in which they require a social work that expresses the human rights and freedoms that are at the centre of social work values—in particular human equality between all the participants in the social work process. This affirmation of social justice as fundamental to social work aligns with the international definition of social work (see box 2.2) and the responsibilities of most Western governments, including the UK government, to international and European human rights agendas.

I argue in this book that contemporary social work focuses too much on problems and deficits. I am thinking both of practices like cognitive behaviour therapy and of social trends in which social work plays a role (such as increases in surveillance and social control of service users). In humanistic practice we are not addressing human deficits or social problems, but rather aiming at human and social betterment. If we start from someone's problems, we are starting from deficits—the negative aspects of their lives. If we start from social change, our objective is social change—but this does not tell us where the right social change lies. If we start from empowerment, this does not tell us, empowerment for what? Many contemporary social work methods require us to look in detail at someone's problems, defining them in precise behavioural detail, as a way of understanding what people want to rid themselves of, rather than determining where they want to go.

This leads us to emphasize the negative until that is all we see. The only objective we set is to remove the negative. We do not lift our eyes to the horizon to look for the positive. This means that we only define the positive as the absence of the negative, in the way a doctor might claim that removing an illness or its symptoms makes you healthy. It does not; it simply makes you not ill. Similarly, a social worker who only helps people solve problems is not improving their clients' personal well-being or achieving social progress; such social workers are simply reducing the effect of some problems.

Fortunately, recent psychological ideas (including positive psychology) and developing social work practices (such as strengths-based, solution-focused, and social construction ideas) make clear that all people do have capabilities and positives in their lives, and that we can develop these. The aim of this book is to explore a humanistic practice of social work that focuses on such positives in practitioners' shared humanity with their clients.

Many of these theoretical and practice ideas are relevant to other caring professions; they are not exclusive to social work. But I do argue that there are special features of social work, and societies make special requirements of it. Although I draw from humanistic counselling, humanistic psychologies, and humanistic psychotherapies, I argue that social work requires more knowledge and practice than from just these sources, because of the roles of social work services. In particular, I emphasise human rights thinking, microsociology, and social construction thinking as important requirements in fulfilling both individual personal development and the mandate of social agencies. The recent Social Work Task Force for England (2009:5) stated that it:

> . . . believes in the value of good social work and in its importance to society. . . When people are made vulnerable—by poverty, bereavement, addiction, isolation, mental distress, disability, neglect, abuse, or other circumstances—what happens next matters hugely. If outcomes are poor, if dependency becomes ingrained or harm goes unchecked, individuals, families, communities and the economy can pay a heavy price. Good social workers can and do make a huge difference in these difficult situations.

Good social work like this—and like the social work described above by service users who spoke to the task force—depends on confident, effective frontline professionals.

Similarly, the Scottish *21st Century Review of Social Work* (Scottish Executive, 2006: 9) comments on:

> . . . a growing public expectation that services will meet their needs, helping them achieve personal goals and aspirations. This may pose a particular challenge for social work, given the need also to manage growing demand and complexity as well as the need to protect the public by taking measures to control some people's liberty. To be effective in meeting that challenge, social work services will need to engage individuals, families and communities and to work in new ways with other parts of the public sector, focusing increasingly on prevention. [The report] sets out five recommendations that will build our capacity to design and deliver personalised social work services through building individual, family and community capacity; refocusing on prevention and earlier intervention; creating whole system response to problems; and making effective use of the mixed economy of care.

This approach also draws on the same principles as humanistic social work practice in its focus on personalized and interpersonal engagement that integrates family and community needs with individual practice, and creates a 'whole system' that aims to help people achieve their aspirations.

THE PLAN OF THE BOOK

Each chapter starts from important principles in humanistic practice and then outlines some current practice techniques that implement those principles. This section provides a guide to the main focus of each chapter.

Chapter 1 argues for the importance of social workers acting as whole human beings in relationships with their clients, other whole human beings. It draws on three sets of ideas as important bases for understanding what it means to take this holistic view of practice: secular humanism, humanistic and transpersonal psychologies, and human rights thinking. These show us that the social environments of individuals are crucial to our humanity, and that we must therefore also draw on microsociology to understand what it means to be that social animal, the human being. These four sets of ideas are the main sources of humanistic social work. The practical outcomes of understanding and using them enable practitioners to "think humanistically," and therefore to identify ways of empowering clients to develop their humanity, personal identity, and rights.

Chapter 2 argues that social work accountability both makes life intelligible to the people we are involved with and justifies our actions; justify here means to clearly show how they are morally and practically right and just in their effect. All of these conflicting accountabilities show that we have to bring together two main responsibilities: to improve individuals' personal psychological efficacy—the feeling that they can make a difference to their lives through their own efforts—and to empower the social groups around them with the agency to facilitate social changes that allow individuals to use their new-found psychological efficacy.

Combining individual and social accountabilities means working openly and transparently so that these different accountabilities work together. Two techniques by which social workers can achieve those outcomes are:

- Informed consent, which ensures that clients are aware of and agree to social work processes and intended outcomes.
- Advance care planning, which enables clients to participate in setting the objectives of social work with practitioners.

Chapter 3 proposes that equality and diversity are important issues, because if we are all human beings, we are all equal as human beings. It should be the task of any society and any social profession to support that equality. Equality of opportunity is not enough as the outcomes of social relations and of social interventions must be equal. This must include affective equality—that is, opportunities to love, care, and live in solidarity with other human beings. Social workers can enhance equality through how they carry out social work, and by advocacy and empowerment practice that enhances equality among the populations that social workers serve. Practice techniques that enhance equality between practitioners and their clients include:

- Dialogue and narrative practice.

Practices that develop equality and diversity in society include:

- Advocacy and due process.
- Empowerment and macropractice.

Chapter 4 argues that an essential feature of humanistic social work is flexibility in response to the diversity of humanity. Crude, formulaic practices based on simplistic assumptions about human behaviour do not achieve that flexibility. Instead, we must embody a whole range of knowledge and skills, drawn from many different sources, within our person as a practitioner so that we can use them responsively. Practice techniques reviewed include evidence-aware, planned eclecticism, and supporting flexibility in clients' lives.

Chapter 5 argues that it is challenging to understand human behaviour in social situations because of its complex nature. It explores chaos and complexity thinking as ways of understanding and working on complexity.

Chapter 6 argues that caring is an important aspect of social work practice and that promoting clients' creativity makes caring a positive, active form of practice. A communication model of caring which develops from a caring environment calls on people's potential to be caring and identifies caring behaviours. People are able to establish continuing caring relationships as a result, and also to experience some of the risks and positive outcomes of caring. Two particular creative techniques, life review and reminiscence, build on narrative approaches as examples of using creativity in practice.

Chapter 7 points to the importance of self-actualization as a part of the process of building personal identity for clients through practice, including the contribution of spirituality as an element of human identity. Techniques that focus in this area of humanistic practice include:

- Focusing on developing self-identity and self-care.
- Assessing and responding to spiritual needs.

Chapter 8 looks at the importance of developing positive approaches to fostering clients' security and resilience, rather than focusing on the negatives and risk in their lives. Practice techniques include:

- Developing people's sense of security.
- Enhancing dignity and respect as an aspect of security.
- Enhancing resilience as a part of family and community support, rather than seeking to create "rugged individuals."

Chapter 9 reinforces the main arguments for developing a positive practice and suggests research techniques for exploring humanistic practice that will strengthen the future development of social work.

CASE STUDIES AND "PAUSE AND REFLECT" SECTIONS

Throughout the book, I have presented case studies drawn from colleagues' and my own experience, and occasionally press reports and other items of literature. The aim of these is to illustrate the implications and uses of the ideas discussed in practice.

Each chapter also has a number of points at which I offer a task that enables you to "pause and reflect" on the issues as they apply to your own self and experience. As we see in chapter 1, humanistic psychologies argue that the only way to understand other human beings is by comparing the evidence of their experience with that of our own. Therefore, examining and thinking about humanistic social work builds on our understanding of our own experience, and the "pause and reflect" sections are designed to help practitioners with this task. They are designed for sharing, and can usefully be worked on with colleagues, so that you can learn how your experience is similar to or differs from that of others.

CONTACT ME

Please contact me through the publisher or through my blog at www.stchristophers.org.uk.

Malcolm Payne

REFERENCES

Gambrill, E. (2006) *Social work practice: A critical thinker's guide, second edition.* New York: Oxford University Press.

Gray, M., Plath, D. and Webb, S. A. (2009) *Evidence-based social work: A critical stance.* London: Routledge.

Harris, J. (2002) *The social work business.* London: Routledge.

Otto, H-U., Polutta, A. & Ziegler, H. (eds) (2009) *Evidence-based practice: Modernising the knowledge base of social work.* Opladen, Germany: Budrich.

Payne, M. (2009) *Social care practice in context.* Basingstoke: Palgrave Macmillan.

Ruch, G., Turney, D. and Ward, A. (2010) *Relationship-based social work: Getting to the heart of practice.* London: Jessica Kingsley.

Scottish Executive (2006) *Changing lives: The report of the 21st century social work Review.* Edinburgh: Scottish Executive.

Sheldon, B. and Macdonald, G. (2008) *A textbook of social work.* London: Routledge.

Social Work Task Force (2009) *Building a safe, confident future.* London: Department for Children, Schools and Families.

Humanity

CHAPTER AIMS

The main aim of this chapter is to introduce a humanistic practice theory of social work in which practitioners focus on their shared humanity with their clients as a way to manage and develop their practice. Thinking humanistically allows practitioners to keep the empowerment of their clients, and their clients' own objectives, in focus.

After working through this chapter, readers should be able to

- Think about their own and others' humanity
- Identify the main sources of ideas about humanity drawn from secular humanism, humanistic and related psychologies and psychotherapies, and human rights ideas
- Incorporate the idea of being as an aspect of humanity, through awareness of some existentialist ideas
- Review the relevance of the ideas about the nature of human beings to social work practice
- Understand the contribution to humanistic social work of human rights ideas
- Understand the contribution of microsociological ideas, in addition to humanistic psychologies and psychotherapies
- Appreciate that humanistic practice offers a positive approach to social work

INTRODUCTION

This book presents social work practice from a humanistic perspective, and this chapter aims to explain the elements and intellectual sources of a humanistic social work practice. Most social work practice is humanistic, but this is usually not made explicit or explored fully in social work education or practice. Therefore, I see this book as coloring in a pencil sketch we made some time ago that we now want to turn into an oil painting. We were happy with the sketch; it gave us outlines of how we might see and understand the world. But without the oils, we cannot display it proudly as our contribution to understanding and living helpfully and lovingly among human beings.

THE STARTING POINT: HUMANITY

Case Example: The People Involved in a Serious Assault

Early in my career as a social worker, I had to write a pretrial report for the court on an offender who was awaiting trial for a serious physical assault on his wife and a sexual assault on his three-year-old daughter. He was in prison, so while I was arranging to visit him, I went to visit his wife; the child was in day care. The very distressed wife described a horrific event, in which her husband had returned home very drunk after being out for the evening. She had refused to have sex with him; he had beaten her; and then he assaulted their daughter, who had been in the same room, eventually masturbating on her body. His wife called the police, who immediately arrested and charged him with those offenses.

She had mixed feelings. He had been an important and dominant figure in her life, helping her establish her independence from her parents, but she was disgusted by his occasional drunkenness and by this particular event. She felt regretful and guilty about getting him arrested, but she felt she had been right to protect herself and her child. She felt ambivalent about going to see him—she was angry and hurt, yet needed his support in her life.

When I went to see him, I found a man to whom being a "man" was important. He worked out in the prison gym to be physically powerful, and he was proud of earning a good income to be a provider for his family. Hard drinking was part of how he saw himself, but he also saw himself as being in control, of his wife and family as well as himself. He had no recollection of the events of the night of the assault, but they had been described to him, and he was angry with himself for losing control by being so drunk. At the same time, he accepted but was unable quite to believe that he had sexually assaulted his daughter, and in his attitude, there was an element of blaming his wife for overreacting. He was both contrite and defensive.

I was shocked by the event when listening to the wife's story, and I tried to maintain a social worker's professional approach of acceptance. I am sure my sense of shock conveyed itself to her, because she behaved as an experienced woman, used to the evils of the world that were not apparent to a young, middle-class professional. Now, many years later, having heard a number of similarly shocking stories, I would probably find it easier to maintain a professional equanimity. I don't know that this would be any better, because my authentic expression of shock probably created a more equal, empathetic, and sharing relationship with her, and allowed her a sense of control in the discussion through her woman-of-the-world stance. Talking with her, I tried to confirm to her that it was right to call the police to protect herself and her daughter, and I tried to be accepting of her ambivalence and fear of what would happen to her now. Social work with her needed to involve thinking through how she evaluated this experience and at the same time planning and constructing a new direction in her life. However, the reality of providing service to someone unable to afford personal counseling or psychotherapy is that, in this case, it would focus on the protection of the child and helping her only in passing to deal with her feelings.

Talking to her husband, I found myself feeling a lot of sympathy for him, in spite of my shock at his behavior. There was a sense of disaster, of his world being suddenly turned upside down because of something he knew nothing about and found hard to believe in. He saw macho behavior as appropriate to his image of himself, and although I often find myself uncomfortable with that sort of masculinity, I could understand this. He seemed slightly pathetic, downcast, lost, and as with his wife, wondering "What's going to happen now?" My rational social worker's mind tells me that this might have been a style of behavior to gain sympathy, and that style, if it was typical of wider behavior, might have been a source of his wife's ambivalence, but it was nevertheless genuine and understandable. While feeling sympathetic, though, I was aware of forming the professional assessment that here was someone who had not come to accept the reality of his responsibility for a terrible crime and awful behavior. Social workers in the future would need to help him come to grips with the offense as evidence of the need to manage his self-perception of a masculine man, and perhaps to change the behavior that was the consequence of it.

This case example deals with a piece of human experience. As a human being, I found myself being sympathetic with both of these other human beings, feeling their distress, and wanting to help them. At the same time, the rational part of me was noting ambiguities in behavior and reaction, which demonstrated the complexity of any human situation and individuals' responses to experiences in their lives. I was also aware of the social relationships that underlay some of the behavior. This awareness included some understanding of the marriage and what made it work, and of what it is to be male and masculine in some cultures and social relationships. Other factors were the human need and social responsibility to protect ourselves against violence and to protect children. I was aware of being in a particular professional and social role: although I was a helping professional and tried to respond supportively, I had a limited official role of preparing a court report.

Thinking about policy, I was aware of the need to respond effectively to protect women and children from domestic violence, and I was aware of the research that stresses the importance of helping offenders confront the realities of their behavior. I was also concerned with excessive drinking as an exacerbating factor in many violent situations. Many different social factors therefore colored my personal human reactions, and I could see the human reactions of the individuals involved also being tempered by their life experience and social expectations around them. I thought about how these events would have created insecurity for this woman and man in their future relationships, and for the child, who was at risk if her father returned to the home in the future.

Writing this report was among my first experiences in social work that really made me feel the human reactions in my work. I felt disgust and anger about this man's behavior, yet in meeting him, I also felt sympathetic to him and his situation. My training told me to love the sinner, not the sin, as the Christian philosophy has it, but I found it hard to do either. I found in this case that you cannot suppress the human in social work practice by being professional. Perhaps I was naive to imagine that this was possible, but that is what my training told me to do. That experience has been repeated numerous times in small and large ways. Such repeated experiences have led me to conclude that social work requires a focus on the humanity of myself and of the people I work with. We must not compartmentalize the professional, the policy, and the personal—not going with our feelings, but not denying them either. We may limit the expression of disgust or criticism, but we must not deny social responses to evil or difficult behavior either. I have searched for an approach to practice that places priority on that humanity; this book, which formulates a humanistic social work, is the result.

Humanity, then, is the starting point of humanistic social work. Social work is about human beings (practitioners) helping and caring for other human beings (clients, service users, their informal caregivers, families, communities, societies). The practitioners are part of human social groups, a profession, a social agency, and other personal and work-related groups and organizations. They help clients in the context of their relationships with other human beings in social groups, families, communities, and social institutions.

PAUSE AND REFLECT: What Does It Mean to Be Human?

We are human beings, but what does that mean? Think about yourself for a few moments, and note the factors in your makeup that make you human.

Some Suggestions

Among the characteristics of being human that you might have thought about are the following:

- Human beings are alive but different from animals or plants.
- Human beings are flesh and blood, not gods, spirits, or supernatural beings.
- Human beings can use their minds, think rationally, calculate, and so on.
- Human beings can feel emotions and generate creativity.
- Human beings are creatures that exist on Earth; they are not aliens from another planet.
- Human beings are sexual and can mate and reproduce with each other.
- Human beings can communicate, interact, and form relationships with other humans.

You probably found this task rather difficult. Trying to understand the nature of our humanity is hard, even though we experience ourselves as human. This is because we are complex beings, and our rational thought processes find it hard to get at the full implications of being human. Usually, we focus on only particular aspects of being human at any one time: our sexuality or our rational thinking or our appreciation of art or music. If we are going to base our practice on being human with other humans, then we need to explore the ways people have tried to understand being human as a whole. Exploring how different systems of thought have understood humanity gives us some concepts to work with.

SOURCES OF IDEAS ABOUT HUMANITY

There are three main sources of ideas about humanity that inform humanistic social work practice:

- Humanism, particularly secular humanism
- Humanistic and transpersonal psychologies and psychotherapies
- Human rights

In the next seven sections (including four connected sections about humanistic, transpersonal, and existential psychologies), I explore these ways of understanding humanity, some connections between them, and how they are useful in social work practice. After looking at human rights ideas, I consider what microsociology offers social workers when they are thinking about humanity.

HUMANISM

Humanism is a philosophy or system of thought that attaches great importance to the capacity of human beings to use rational thinking to manage their lives and environment. Because it focuses on human rationality, humanism is usually understood to be a secular, nonreligious, philosophy, because it rejects the idea that a supernatural entity such as a god can intervene in human lives. However, there are religious humanists who, within their faiths, emphasize the responsibility of human beings to develop and use their divinely given capacity for rational thought to accept personal responsibility for their environment and way of life. Nevertheless, secular humanism is the most significant organized expression of humanist philosophies.

Boxes 1.1 and 1.2 set out international and American statements of accepted tenets of secular humanism created by important organizations in the field. Humanistic social work practice applies and expresses the basic principles set out in these formulations of humanist ideas. For example, it emphasizes the worth and dignity of human beings, as well as human beings caring for one another as part of a sense of general social responsibility. Human beings all participate together in serving humane ideals in social relationships, and by benefiting society as a whole, they achieve greater personal fulfillment.

According to humanist ideas, every kind of human knowledge, skill and cognition, or way of thinking is important to being a human. Nothing that is human is rejected by humanists; instead, we might hope to learn and develop using all of ourselves. Humanism brings together rational thinking through science with artistic creativity and imagination; one is not more important than another. The aims of that constellation of human skills are the development of thought-out value systems, innovation, and critical evaluation of ideas and actions. Democracy, human rights, and personal liberty go alongside one another in helping us achieve personal fulfillment in our lives.

Box 1.1 Amsterdam Declaration of the World Humanist Congress, 2002

Humanism is the outcome of a long tradition of free thought that has inspired many of the world's great thinkers and creative artists and gave rise to science itself.

The fundamentals of modern Humanism are as follows:

Humanism is ethical. It affirms the worth, dignity and autonomy of the individual and the right of every human being to the greatest possible freedom compatible with the rights of others. Humanists have a duty of care to all of humanity including future generations. Humanists believe that morality is an intrinsic part of human nature based on understanding and a concern for others, needing no external sanction.

Humanism is rational. It seeks to use science creatively, not destructively. Humanists believe that the solutions to the world's problems lie in human thought and action rather than divine intervention. Humanism advocates the application of the methods of science and free inquiry to the problems of human welfare. But Humanists also believe that the application of science and technology must be tempered by human values. Science gives us the means but human values must propose the ends.

Humanism supports democracy and human rights. Humanism aims at the fullest possible development of every human being. It holds that democracy and human development are matters of right. The principles of democracy and human rights can be applied to many human relationships and are not restricted to methods of government.

Humanism insists that personal liberty must be combined with social responsibility. Humanism ventures to build a world on the idea of the free person responsible to society, and recognises our dependence on and responsibility for the natural world. Humanism is undogmatic, imposing no creed upon its adherents. It is thus committed to education free from indoctrination.

Humanism is a response to the widespread demand for an alternative to dogmatic religion. The world's major religions claim to be based on revelations fixed for all time, and many seek to impose their world-views on all of humanity. Humanism recognises that reliable knowledge of the world and ourselves arises through a continuing process of observation, evaluation and revision.

Humanism values artistic creativity and imagination and recognises the transforming power of art. Humanism affirms the importance of literature, music, and the visual and performing arts for personal development and fulfilment.

Humanism is a lifestance aiming at the maximum possible fulfilment through the cultivation of ethical and creative living and offers an ethical and rational means of addressing the challenges of our times. Humanism can be a way of life for everyone everywhere.

Our primary task is to make human beings aware in the simplest terms of what Humanism can mean to them and what it commits them to. By utilising free inquiry, the power of science and creative imagination for the furtherance of peace and in the service of compassion, we have confidence that we have the means to solve the problems that confront us all. We call upon all who share this conviction to associate themselves with us in this endeavour.

Source: International Humanist and Ethical Union Congress (2002). See: http://www.iheu.org.

Box 1.2 American Humanist Association Humanist Manifesto

Humanism and Its Aspirations

Humanist Manifesto III, a successor to the Humanist Manifesto of 1933

Knowledge of the world is derived by observation, experimentation, and rational analysis.

Humans are an integral part of nature, the result of unguided evolutionary change.

Ethical values are derived from human need and interest as tested by experience.

Life's fulfillment emerges from individual participation in the service of humane ideals.

Humans are social by nature and find meaning in relationships.

Working to benefit society maximizes individual happiness.

Source: Main principles excerpted from American Humanist Association (2003). Humanist Manifesto is a trademark of the American Humanist Association. © 2003 American Humanist Association.

Humanist ideals say something very important about personal help and caring and therefore about counseling, social work, and other organized ways of helping. Starting from the position that human beings can develop control of their social environment through the use of human capabilities, particularly our rational mind, those ideals imply that helping and caring for other human beings in an integrated society of human relationships achieves human fulfillment. Social work and other helping and caring professions therefore express humanity. Also, helping and caring enables human beings to develop themselves to the highest level.

PAUSE AND REFLECT: Do Society's Evils Contradict Humanist Ideals?

My experience with the family that I described earlier, struggling with the husband's violent behavior, seems to go against humanist ideals. Most practitioners can think of people exhibiting extremely disturbed, irrational, and unsocial behavior that must be damaging to social relationships. So do the evils that we encounter every day in practice tell us that these ideals are just that—impossibly idealistic? Look again at that family's situation, and see whether you can find any aspects of humanity there. Or examine one of your own experiences in the same way.

Some Suggestions

The first thing to say about the family's situation is that organized social help between human beings responded: the wife protected her child and herself, the police answered the call and removed the violent husband, the criminal justice system swung into action, and I appeared to investigate on behalf of society and try to help. If these social responses fail, such as when a failure in protective services leads to the death of a child or an older person or to violence from a mentally ill person, there is often consternation and political turmoil. Human societies generally expect that organized social responses will deal with such issues.

The second aspect of this case was the human ambivalences in the participants' responses: the man's disbelief, the wife's uncertainties, the tensions in my thinking. These are the assertion of humanity in the face of social evil. These ambivalences always form a dialectic within us, an argument about the pros and cons, and social relationships and social institutions also reflect such dialectics. If we look at how they are organized, we can often see the uncertainties they contain. One example is the tensions in prison management and policy between retribution and rehabilitation of prisoners, and between concern for protecting the public from dangerous offenders but also for the public responsibility to help plan for their future. Humanistic social work focuses on those personal and social dialectics.

The third thing to note is that we cannot assume that these particular social relationships will continue in the same way. For example, this marriage may break up because of the need for society to express its disapproval through punishment and retribution for the man. Equally, it will try to protect his wife and child. The child may be made more secure and better able to develop in a single-parent family with her mother. Or they may repair their relationships and achieve greater human fulfillment as the result of the learning experience of doing this. Either way, there will be greater human development among these people, and if this is achieved, it will be partly because social responses have provided services to enable the man to confront his behavior and change, and the wife and child to learn and progress. In contrast, all or some of them may experience damaged lives as a result of this experience; humanity does not always win out. One of the tasks of social work is to help humanity win.

Thinking through the ideals of helping and caring work in this way tells us that the presence of democracy and liberty in caring social relationships is a crucial part of any society, and practitioners using relationship skills within a thought-through value system are integral to that social responsibility. We can help humanity win.

HUMANISTIC PSYCHOLOGIES AND PSYCHOTHERAPIES

Humanistic psychologies emphasize the capacity and need of human beings to identify and understand their personal identity, or self, as a means of developing their potential. Logically, in helping professions, both practitioners and clients can achieve personal development through better understanding of their self. Humanistic psychotherapies seek to facilitate self-understanding and self-actualization as a way to respond to psychological problems and difficulties in development. Transpersonal psychologies incorporate, within a humanistic framework, cultural and spiritual extensions of a human being as important aspects of understanding emotional and mental life. This emphasis on the self is an aspect of Goldstein's (1984) important interpretation of humanistic practice for social work. He describes three aspects of the self:

- A self-conception, our being, that is, how we see ourselves
- A perceiving self, our knowing, both general knowledge acquired through education and socialization and specific knowledge about our social relationships, which we gain through our perception of the world
- An intentional self, our becoming, that is, what we are aiming for both in our general lives and in particular instances

Box 1.3 Five Basic Postulates of Humanistic Psychology

1. Human beings, as human, supersede the sum of their parts. They cannot be reduced to components.
2. Human beings have their existence in a uniquely human context, as well as in a cosmic ecology.
3. Human beings are aware and aware of being aware—i.e., they are conscious. Human consciousness always includes an awareness of oneself in the context of other people.
4. Human beings have some choice and, with that, responsibility.
5. Human beings are intentional, aim at goals, are aware that they cause future events, and seek meaning, value, and creativity.

Source: Greening (2006, p. 239).

Humanistic psychology explicitly builds on humanism (Moss, 2001); humanistic psychotherapies do so by relying on humanistic psychologies. Therefore, we can see in a statement of the basic principles of humanistic psychology set out in box 1.3, very similar precepts as those in boxes 1.1 and 1.2 that inform humanism. There is a similar concern for human development, for human beings' engagement with the social and physical environment and their capacity to look to the future, to have intentions and objectives. However, the differences reflect a greater concern with human mental and psychological characteristics.

As well as building on humanist ideas, there is a clear historical intellectual development of the ideas that contribute to humanistic social work, which I set out in box 1.4.

Box 1.4 Ideas Contributing to Humanistic Social Work

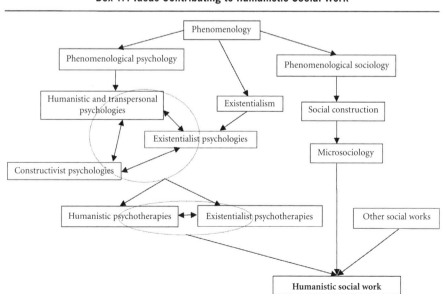

The humanistic psychologies are an important set of ideas, and they are part of a broader group of psychologies that include existential psychologies and constructivist psychologies. These have all influenced one another, and in turn, they have all contributed to the development of psychotherapies based on these ideas. These psychotherapies are an important contributor to humanistic social work ideas. However, humanistic social work incorporates more than these ideas. In this book, I emphasize the important aspects of social understanding and our social environment; these aspects distinguish humanistic social work from humanistic psychology and psychotherapy.

Humanistic psychologies and psychotherapies all derive originally from phenomenology, a set of ideas originating with the philosopher Edmund Husserl, which also contributed to the development of existential ideas and philosophy. I look briefly at existentialism in this chapter in the section on being. Phenomenology also influenced sociology and was crucial to what is now often called microsociology. This has also had an impact on social work. Finally, of course, no social work is separate from other social works, so humanistic practice also draws on mainstream traditions of social work theory and practice.

Because these ideas come from phenomenology, it is useful to have some idea of what this philosophy says. To simplify and focus on the particular concerns of this book, phenomenology suggests that all understanding and knowledge comes from the appearance of things, how we perceive them and process our perceptions in our thinking. The things themselves affect this, of course, but how we see them can be just as or more important than reality in their influence on how we act (Misiak & Sexton, 1973). This distinction implies that we cannot know and experience objects outside ourselves. Therefore, we cannot know and understand fully other human beings. We can only evaluate them from our observation, and we do this by comparing them with our knowledge and understanding of ourselves. Everyone will interpret things and other human beings outside themselves differently, because their perception and interpretation of them will vary according to their observation and experience. Therefore, examining, describing, and explaining our own experience is a crucial part of gaining the evidence for saying what the world is like, because it is only through our own observation, construction, and understanding of our own experience that we can understand the world around us; it cannot be observed and understood from the outside. This leads to the importance of dialogue and narrative as the basis for social work actions, discussed in chapter 3.

Following up on this, humanistic psychologies focus on understanding and exploring people's experiences. They do this in several important ways that have had considerable influence on ideas about helping practice.

First, humanistic psychologies and psychotherapies see themselves as a third force, an alternate, in psychological understanding of human beings. This view is humanistic because it involves seeing and working with human beings as a whole rather than with parts of the person.

Historically, the first force was psychodynamic theory, based on the work of Sigmund Freud and his followers. *Psychodynamic* implies that the mind (the "psycho," that is, psychological) aspect of human beings is dynamic; that is, it moves and affects us. The corollary of this is that we can understand human behavior by understanding the internal mechanisms of the mind and how they move us. If we say that the mind moves us, it must have energy, and that led psychoanalysts to try to understand how the energy (the id) may be directed (or perhaps misdirected) by our conscious planning and thought (the ego), which in turn is influenced by our experiences in life and in relationships with other people who are important to us. The psychodynamic view of psychotherapy suggests that we have to help human beings explore and understand how their minds are working so that they have greater conscious control over their mind. Greater conscious control and understanding of how their mind works will allow them to better manage their behavior.

The second force was behavioral or learning theory, which contests psychodynamic explanations. This view of psychology suggests that people's behavior is all we can actually observe and produce evidence of, and we can also observe and experiment to see how things that happen to a person or that are withheld from them change that behavior. What we cannot see is how the mind actually works. The importance of behavioral ideas is their focus on how we research and investigate the mind. Those ideas show, as humanists would say, that we have to use our rational mind and scientific procedures devised to give us the clearest evidence of the most effective ways to manage our behavior and society.

Therefore, to understand human beings, learning and behavioral ideas posit that it is better to concentrate on actual behavior and the factors that affect it than to try to understand processes that we cannot observe and investigate fully. Psychotherapies in a learning or behavioral view involve focusing on specific behaviors that people want to change and identifying factors in the environment that will lead to the desired change.

According to humanistic psychology, both these psychodynamic and behavioral views are partial; they each emphasize only part of the story of human behavior. Both of these aspects of a human being are relevant to understanding psychology and behavior, so it is important to include both internal dynamics and external behavior and how it affects and is affected by the surrounding environment, thus seeing the human being as a whole, within the social environment. Applying this view to psychotherapies, it would be necessary to focus on and encounter the person as a whole and not look at only some aspects of the person.

Similarly, humanistic psychologies see people as both subjects and objects in their lives (Bugental & Sapienza, 1994). This means that the outside world, and particularly other people, has an impact on people, how they are and how they behave; thus, they are objects of others' influences. But that is not all they are; we have seen that humanism and humanistic psychology see people as having intentionality, the capacity to have their own aims in life and in social situations. In recognizing this, humanistic psychotherapies focus particularly on helping people gain greater impact as a subject, to take control of their lives and to achieve greater self-actualization. This connects with social work's empowerment objectives; humanistic practice seeks to enhance people's personal power, as humanistic psychotherapies would, but also to influence the patterns of power in society in ways that help people use their personal power more effectively. Thus, social workers are concerned both with personal efficacy, helping people feel that they can have an impact on aspects of their life that are important to them, and with the groups they are part of having greater social agency, that is, impact in social power relations.

The second important set of influences from humanistic psychology is the wide range of therapies that have emerged from this. Two formulations stand out as the most influential for social work:

- Person-centered therapy focuses on the whole person, explored through a human relationship with a therapist.
- Encounter groups—in these, a group worker facilitates a group of people who encounter one another in an open way and explore their humanity together.

The third important aspect of humanistic psychologies is therapists' approaches in each of these ways of doing therapy. Openness to experiencing the other person in totality is an important principle. Rogers (1951, 1961) developed and with others subsequently validated through research (Carkhuff & Berenson, 1967; Truax & Carkhuff, 1967) an approach by the therapist that has had wide influence: therapists should be empathetic with the client, who can see that they are genuine or congruent in their behavior, so that what they say and do is consistent. Finally, the therapist greets others with an unconditional positive regard; that is, they see others as capable of making progress towards self-actualization. This research points to the importance of how practitioners conduct themselves in their relationship with the client, so that they together can share openly an experience of the other in a trusting way. In this way, the humanity of the practitioner is an important aspect of developing trust between the practitioner and the client to achieve results in humanistic practice.

TRANSPERSONAL PSYCHOLOGIES DEVELOP FROM HUMANISTIC PSYCHOLOGIES

Transpersonal psychologies and psychotherapies build on humanistic ideas. Although they form a separate tradition, they emerged from and are connected to humanistic psychologies and psychotherapies, often regarding themselves as a fourth force in psychology. They are part of a multidisciplinary movement, mainly within psychological healthcare professions, which suggests that consciousness is broader than the individual's perceptions (hence the prefix *trans*) but that individuals experience and express broader consciousness (Shorrock, 2008). In particular, transpersonal psychology incorporates religious and spiritual experiences, as these are clearly experiences that many, if not all, people have but that lie outside psychological and physical experiences. Transpersonal psychologies, such as Wilbur's (2000) integral psychology and psychotherapies and Assagioli's (1990) psychosynthesis, seek various ways to integrate an understanding of and work with all aspects of human experience, including the shared consciousness that lies outside ourselves.

Accounts of transpersonal psychotherapies often refer to important ideas from early psychologies:

- William James, the early Harvard psychologist interested in religious experience, identified separate elements of the self that included a spiritual, material, and social self, which interacted to form a higher self beyond observable cognitive and emotional processes (Rowan, 1993; Shorrock, 2008).
- Carl Gustav Jung, the Swiss psychoanalyst, broke from loyalty to Freud's ideas and introduced the idea of archetypes, universal myths found in all cultures forming a collective unconscious that we all share. The archetypes in our collective unconscious structure the way we all experience the world and therefore contribute to the way we develop our self (Rowan, 1993; Shorrock, 2008).
- Roberto Assagioli, the Italian creator of psychosynthesis, described a complex structure of the mind, which includes a superconscious, an intuitive sense of awareness of the possibilities inherent in the interaction of a person's self with their environment (Rowan, 1993; Shorrock, 2008).
- Abraham Maslow, the American psychologist, differentiated human needs, proposing a pyramid of needs in which, once basic needs for nutrition and personal relationships were fulfilled, people sought self-actualization, a state in which they achieved a "peak experience" (Maslow, 1971, pp. 162–163). Maslow found that most people could identify occasions when they had a very satisfying experience in their lives, often attained around music, sex, and childbirth. Exploring what people meant by this, Maslow (1971) said: "It looks as if any experience of real excellence, or real perfection, of any moving toward the perfect justice or toward perfect values tends to produce a peak experience" (p. 169). Notice that he says "moving toward"; he is not saying that we can achieve perfect justice or perfect values, but people particularly value experiences that they see are helping them toward moral and personal attainments.

The ideas of these forerunners of transpersonal psychology suggest a focus on something important but hard to express about being a human being. This something might be an energizing experience attained through religion or spiritual experience, or in some way a response to or interaction with people's social environments. Because social work, according to its international definition (International Federation of Social Workers, 2000), works at the interface of individuals and their social environment, these ideas might have something to offer social work practice. They are saying to us, "Think beyond the rational and observable, because there is something there in human experience that you have to take account of, and that sometimes you can work with."

Case Example: A Woman With Dementia and a Musical Experience

As an example of what I mean, one of my colleagues is a music therapist who works with older people in care homes. One day she was working with a group, a member of which had very severe dementia, to the extent that she could barely move. She was unable to feed herself, and care assistants fed her at every meal. All the residents were given percussion instruments, and this woman had a drum and drumsticks. The group provided varying rhythms to a melody, and after some time, the woman with dementia also joined in, drumming in time to the music and singing more or less along with the melody. My colleague and the care staff were very pleased with her unexpected degree of participation. The following day, she arrived for a meal, picked up the fork and fed herself; she continued to do so at subsequent meals. This change stunned the care staff and my colleague. This is an example of a peak experience, attained through music, as Maslow (1971) says it often is, which allowed a client of social care services to get in touch with what Assagioli (1990) might have called her superconscious, her sense of what was possible for her self. This was a self that others saw only as a person with dementia. Perhaps she was in some way aware of that self but in some way also did not accept it. In this case, her self extended her current life experience with an immediate, practical outcome.

All social workers have experienced such sudden movements in situations that seem immovable, in a way that may connect with something we have done, or sometimes that seems to have no connection with anything that we can identify. Even though our typical experience is perhaps that many of our clients experience an unchanging life, hemmed in by psychological and social barriers of all kinds, one of the excitements of doing social work is the possibility and the actuality of, on occasion, making a difference. Transpersonal ideas have also been influential in thinking about spirituality in social work. For example Canda and Smith's (2001) collection of papers about various aspects of spirituality presents a range of connections between transpersonal ideas and social work, suggesting the importance for empowerment of stimulating clients to go beyond ordinary waking consciousness toward inspirational experiences (E. R. Smith, 2001).

Case Example: A Woman's Life

Firman and Vargiu (1980) describe a woman's experience in a more prosaic situation. She is focusing on "getting the children off to school." Relaxing after a hectic time, she thinks about the children in her life now. "I began seeing my life as one flow, a flow which was only one stream in the larger flow of life within the universe. Suddenly, I was unexpectedly overwhelmed by an intense feeling of joy. I felt intensely alive and saw my life filled with meaning and direction. Mixed with the joy was a deep love—a love for my life, my family, and a love for humanity" (p. 104). This sort of experience, which many people have on occasion, connects reflection on a routine part of life with a bigger picture of that life, and then goes on to connect it with a wider view of the world, which might be described as spiritual.

This example describes what we mean by transpersonal experiences. Firman and Vargiu's (1980) discussion makes the point, to draw on Assagioli's psychosynthesis, that psychologically healthy people are able to maintain the link between everyday experience and their experience of moments that transcend that experience, and this enables them to be more resilient in dealing with the difficulties of everyday life. It is not that barriers to fulfillment do not exist; this is true for many people whom social workers help, and at times for all of us. It is more that people can be satisfied in the struggle to make progress that is important to them.

For practice, therefore, it is worth trying to make a connection with the particularity of the directions people are trying to achieve and the positives of their struggles toward them. It is also worthwhile to try to help them to see possibilities in what may be a very unsatisfactory life experience. This is an important aim of humanistic social work, and it is one of the reasons spirituality, the energy gained from this broader sense of ourselves, is an important issue for social workers, as we shall see in chapter 7.

BEING: IDEAS FROM EXISTENTIALISM

Existentialism is another set of ideas that contributes to humanistic psychologies and psychotherapies and, less significantly, to humanistic social work. So far, in talking about human beings, we have concentrated on what humanity consists of. Existentialism concentrates on the other aspect: what a being is.

What does it mean to say that we are a being? The idea of a human being implies that simply existing means something to us, and there is a range of ideas about this, developed during the twentieth century. In humanism and humanistic psychology, we saw that being implies being aware that we are aware and therefore that we are responsible for what we do when we are acting on our awareness. Similarly, we base our understanding of what human beings and the world are like from our constructions, the stories we construct about what has happened to us, narratives as we call them in sociological and psychological jargon, and thoughts about our experience of our own being. So our own understandings about these things are crucial to understanding what it means to be human. One of the important ideas about being in existentialism is our human fear of the unknown, a dread about what might happen to us, including fear of loss and of our own death, which is the ultimate loss of our own identity, our own being. Existentialism points to the possibility that we have an underlying vulnerability or insecurity, that in some way we will not be able to cope with the world or achieve our own self-actualization. Therefore, security is particularly important to us, and I pick this up in chapter 8.

Maslow (1999) distinguishes between deficiency motivation and growth motivation and proposes that when we experience some needs, it is because we lack something, such as food or comfort. When we seek personal growth, we seek not to correct something we do not have but to build on something that we have already achieved. Achieving something pushes us on to get more of something satisfying. This connects with the social work aim of empowerment, because these experiences of achievement motivate people to want more satisfaction in their lives; their moving forward has continuity. One of Maslow's contributions to humanistic psychology is this emphasis on helping people focus on a growth motivation rather than deficits.

Case Example: Marissa

Marissa was a single parent with two children who found it a struggle to bring up her children in very poor housing conditions and poverty. She herself had been brought up in residential care, because her parents were drug addicts. She was part of a child development project in which a worker visited weekly to help her experience successful play with her children. She found, as many parents do, that the children were happy to play imaginatively with everyday items rather than wanting expensive toys. The project worker encouraged her to forget all her troubles for an hour a day and concentrate on playing with the children. She found this distraction very satisfying, and eventually she spent more time with the children, improving their care and development as a result. The worker referred her to a financial help project, and a worker there took her twice to a local store and showed her how to shop economically, and a volunteer helped her learn to cook rather than buying takeout foods. These things also helped with some of the practical problems and again gave her a sense that things were more in her control than she had thought.

HUMANISTIC PSYCHOLOGY IN HUMANISTIC SOCIAL WORK

Humanistic and transpersonal psychologies and therapies bring to humanistic social work the idea of seeking to promote personal growth and self-actualization through our shared human experience.

Although I identify the importance of humanistic psychology as a source of humanistic helping, I do not propose a wholesale transfer of humanistic psychologies or psychotherapies into other forms of helping. This is because psychologies have important disadvantages as a basis for caring and helping practice. They focus only on individual personal development and have been criticized for not recognizing the limitations and barriers that many people face in the societies and communities in which they live. To develop a humanistic social work, we need to balance humanistic psychologies with social ideas about humanity. There are two sources of such social ideas: human rights and microsociology.

HUMAN RIGHTS

Human rights are privileges that all human beings possess arising from their humanity. It is accepted as morally good to accord human rights to everyone in our dealings with them. Human rights are expressed in international codes agreed on among nations through diplomacy and often in constitutions of nations; the U.S. Constitution is one of the earliest and most famous.

In this section, I compare three important charters (see box 1.5), explain some of the problems and limitations of them, and then pick up some of the implications for humanistic social work. I have started from the fifty-four articles of the Charter of Fundamental Rights of the European Union (European Union, 2000) for three reasons. First, it is very recent, produced at the beginning of the twenty-first century. Second, because it is recent, it uses modern language and ideas, expresses the most up-to-date concepts, and can draw on previous experience. Third, because of these factors, it is the most detailed, so it sets out the broadest possible range of human rights ideas. The charter was created as the basis of an agreement between European countries to extend their economic, social, and political cooperation. The second column of box 1.5 summarizes the thirty articles of the Universal Declaration of Human Rights (United Nations, 1948), created in the early stages of the foundation of the UN and reflecting the human rights worries that had come out of the then very recent Second World War and the Holocaust. It is the most international of the charters, claiming support from most nations in the world. The third column of box 1.5 summarizes the main points of the first ten amendments to the U.S. Constitution, the Bill of Rights, which have been the source of all such charters worldwide since they were established. As well as the more general rights, which later charters have copied, the Bill of Rights reflects some of the worries that had led to the American Revolution, which I have set against comparable paragraphs of the more recent and broader charters. The only difficulty I had in aligning the charters—aside from the fact that they order the rights differently—was the Second Amendment of the U.S. Constitution, the right to bear arms. Other charters have not thought this necessary; in fact, gun control is fairly strictly enforced in European countries, where unpleasant experience across the centuries has led governments to maintain control of the means of war. The experience of the Revolutionary War led the people who framed the Second Amendment to include the right to bear arms to resist state control of the means of self-defense. Therefore, I have set it alongside provisions in other charters for freedoms of assembly and association, that is, the right for citizens to come together to pursue their interests collectively. I think the rather specific provision of the American Constitution connects with this right, which other charters express more generally.

One of the limitations of charters is, like all official documents, that their contents come from the circumstances and reflect the historical period of their creation. This means that they also reflect the purposes for which they are created. You can see this in the three charters compared here. They also use legalistic and, particularly the older ones, archaic language.

Looking down the three columns, the first point to make is the extensive social provision of the European charter, which creates positive social rights. This reflects the European social model, in which the state takes responsibility for setting a positive environment of social support for all people, for example, to have a family, but it also focuses on people with potential disadvantages. This includes children, older and disabled people, and people affected by economic insecurity; the social work profession classically focuses on such people. The older UN declaration, which was less concerned with managing

Box 1.5 Human Rights Charters in Comparison

European Charter of Fundamental Rights (2000)	UN Universal Declaration of Human Rights (1948)	Bill of Rights, U.S. Constitution (1791)
1 Dignity		
1.1 Human dignity is inviolable	1 Human beings are free and equal in dignity and rights, and act toward each other in brotherhood 22 Attain dignity and free development of personality 26.2 Education aims at full personal development, tolerance, mutual understanding between groups 29.1 Duty to community to attain free, full development of personality	
1.2 Right to life, no death penalty	3 Right to life	
1.3 Respect for individual physical and mental integrity; in medicine/biology ■ free, informed consent ■ no eugenics ■ no using bodies as a source of money ■ no reproductive cloning of humans		
1.4 No torture or degrading treatment	5 No torture, inhuman, degrading treatment or punishment	8 No cruel or unusual punishment
1.5 No slavery, forced labor, or trafficking in human beings	4 No slavery or servitude	

Box 1.5 Continued

European Charter of Fundamental Rights (2000)	UN Universal Declaration of Human Rights (1948)	Bill of Rights, U.S. Constitution (1791)
2 Freedoms		
2.6 Right to personal liberty and security	3 Liberty and security of person	4 Freedom from search and seizure of person
2.7 Respect for private and family life	12 No arbitrary interference with privacy, family, home, or correspondence	2 Freedom from compulsory quartering of soldiers
	16.3 Family protected as the natural basis of society	4 Freedom from search and seizure of private residence
2.8 Right to protect personal data; to fair processing, by consent, and right to correct; to independent authority to control personal data rights		
2.9 Right to marry and start a family	16.1–2 Right to marry and start a family with full, fair consent of spouses	
2.10 Freedom of thought, conscience, religion; right to conscientious objection (to participation in war)	17 Freedom of thought, conscience, and religion, and to practice them	1 Freedom of religion
2.11 Freedom of expression, opinion; a free, plural press	19 Freedom of opinion and expression; right to seek and impart information with no frontiers	1 Freedom of the press
2.12 Freedom of assembly and association, especially in trade unions and political and civic groups; political parties of union to express people's will	20.1 Freedom of assembly and association 20.2 No compulsion to join associations	2 Right to bear arms

Box 1.5 *Continued*

European Charter of Fundamental Rights (2000)	UN Universal Declaration of Human Rights (1948)	Bill of Rights, U.S. Constitution (1791)
2.13 Free, unconstrained arts, science, and research; academic freedom	27.1 Free participation in arts and culture	
2.14 Right to education, including vocational and continuing; right to free, compulsory education; right to found educational institutions conforming to parents' principles	26.1 Right to education, free at basic levels; available technical or professional education; equal access to higher education 28.3 Parental right to choose education	
2.15 Right to choose occupation freely and to work; to seek work in any member state; authorized nonnationals have equal rights	23.1 Right to work and choose employment	
2.16 Freedom to conduct business		
2.17 Freedom to own, use, dispose of, bequeath property; intellectual property	17.1 Right to own property 17.2 Right to not be arbitrarily deprived of property 27.2 Protection of rights in scientific and artistic production	
2.18 Asylum	14 Asylum	
2.19 No collective expulsions; no removal to a state at risk of death penalty, torture, or inhuman or degrading treatment		
3 Equality		
3.20 Equality before the law	7 Equality before the law, and no discrimination	

Box 1.5 *Continued*

European Charter of Fundamental Rights (2000)	UN Universal Declaration of Human Rights (1948)	Bill of Rights, U.S. Constitution (1791)
3.21 No discrimination; no discrimination on grounds of nationality	2 Rights and freedoms available without distinction 15 Right to nationality	
3.22 Respect for cultural, religious, and linguistic diversity	22 Economic, cultural, and social rights	
3.23 Men and women are equal	23.2 Equal pay for equal work	
3.24 Child's rights to protection, care, to express opinions, and to have them considered; public or private actions respect child's best interests; right to maintain contact with both parents	25.2 Children receive equal protection whether born in or out of wedlock	
3.25 Rights of the elderly: dignity, independence, and social and cultural participation		
3.26 Rights of people with disabilities: measures to ensure independence, integration, and participation		
4 Solidarity		
4.28 Workers' rights to information and consultation		
4.29 Right to collective bargaining and action	23.3 Just, favorable pay to achieve family dignity 23.4 Right to form and join trade unions	

Box 1.5 *Continued*

European Charter of Fundamental Rights (2000)	UN Universal Declaration of Human Rights (1948)	Bill of Rights, U.S. Constitution (1791)
4.30 Right to access free placement service		
4.31 Protection from unjustified dismissal		
4.32 Working conditions respect health, safety, and dignity; maximum work hours, daily and/or weekly rest, and annual leave	23.1 Just and favorable conditions of work 24 Rest, leisure, and limited work hours	
4.32. No child labor; young people protected at work		
4.33 Legal, economic, and social protection of families; no dismissal for maternity; right to maternity and parental leave	25.1 Adequate standard of living for family 25.2 Special protection for motherhood, childhood	
4.34 Right to social security; combat social exclusion, decent existence even with lack of resources	22 Social security 25.1 Social security in circumstances beyond individual control	
4.35 High level of preventive health care and medical treatment		
4.36 Services to promote social and territorial cohesion	28.2 Rights exercised in ways that meet general morality and social welfare	
4.37 High level of environmental protection		
4.38 High level of consumer protection		

Box 1.5 Continued

European Charter of Fundamental Rights (2000)	UN Universal Declaration of Human Rights (1948)	Bill of Rights, U.S. Constitution (1791)
5 Citizens' rights		
5.39 Right to vote and stand as a candidate for European Parliament; universal suffrage by free, secret ballot	21.1 Participate in government 21.3 Government authority by equal, universal suffrage by secret vote	
5.40 Right to vote and stand as a candidate at all levels where resident		
5.41 Right to good administration, impartiality, fairness, and with reasonable time, to be heard before adverse decisions, access files, know reasons for decisions; right to restitution; right to receive reply in own language	21.2 Equal access to public services	
5.42 Access to EU documents		
5.43 Refer to ombudsman of EU		
5.44 Petition European Parliament		
5.45 Free movement and residence throughout EU; also for legal residents from third countries	13.1 Freedom of movement and residence 13.2 Freedom to leave and return to country	
5.46 Diplomatic and consular services in third countries from any member state		
6 Justice	6 Right to recognition as person before the law	
6.47 Effective remedy, fair trial	8 Effective remedy 10 Equal, fair, and public hearing	5 No trial without indictment; due process 6 Speedy trial, ability to confront witnesses 7 Trial by jury

Box 1.5 *Continued*

European Charter of Fundamental Rights (2000)	UN Universal Declaration of Human Rights (1948)	Bill of Rights, U.S. Constitution (1791)
6.48 Presumption of innocence; right to defense	9 No arbitrary arrest, detention, or exile 11.1 Presumption of innocence	
6.49 Criminal offenses specified legally or by international convention; punishments are proportionate	11.2 Criminal offenses specified by law or international convention; punishments are proportionate	
6.50 Right to not be tried twice		5 Right to not be tried twice
7 General provisions		
7.51 Subsidiarity (EU does not take on member states' rights)		10 States and people retain rights unless specified in the Constitution
7.52 Scope of guaranteed rights (limited only where consistent with charter principles)	28 International order that respects rights 29.3 Rights exist only within broader UN principles	
7.53 Level of protection (human rights should not contradict law)		
7.54 No abuse of rights (freedoms do not confer rights to abuse others' rights)	29.2 Exercise rights only where they do not conflict with others' rights	9 Enumeration of rights in the Constitution does not entitle people to disparage others' rights

Source: European Union (2000); United Nations (1948); United States (1791).

economies and more with dealing with conflict over international issues, spells this out less fully. This idea barely appears in the U.S. Constitution, which mainly emphasizes limitations on the power of government. A focus on seeing social support and social cohesion as a right is an important attitude that underlies European welfare states. The argument is that, to be fully human, you must have positive rights to support from other citizens within the boundaries of shared citizenship in a state, and that other citizens have the right to the satisfactions that come from helping and supporting their brothers and sisters in humanity.

Humanistic social work, therefore, must see giving and receiving social support as a fundamental part of being human. Therefore, it must aim to enable people to give support to others by being good parents and good citizens and to help people build connections in social relationships so that they can receive support. This is important in humanistic social work as a basis for helping people in relationship skills and in seeing groupwork and community and social development as integral to social work practice.

A second striking difference between the columns is the extensive discussion in the UN declaration of human dignity, with the assumption that this is attained by the full development of personality. Other articles point to a right to education and to community support to achieve this. This is present in the European charter and was present also in the ringing tones of the U.S. Declaration of Independence, but it is not incorporated into the Bill of Rights. This tells us that human dignity does not just mean feeling that we are treated well and courteously, although that is important. For the values of humanistic social work, we can take the point that fulfilling personal development is a key aim of any practice that seeks to maintain humanity and individual humans. Important tenets of humanistic psychology and psychotherapies tell us the same thing, as we have seen, and were created at much the same time that the UN declaration was being written.

An important similarity among the charters, though, is the importance given to all kinds of freedoms, of speech, faith, and belief; the right to the means of expressing those through the freedom of the press; and the right to a reasonable level of education as the basis for being able to develop ideas. The charters also provide the means to enforce those freedoms in the courts. These ideas are important to people feeling secure in their social environment.

Another shared feature of the charters is the various freedoms from oppression, for example, torture or inhumane or degrading treatment of various kinds, and the right not to be oppressed and to have equal access to legal representation if accused of a crime. This is about being able to protect yourself against unfairness or oppression, to achieve a feeling of security, and it expresses a duty of states and other citizens to help you achieve that security.

Such provisions may seem fairly distant from rich Western societies, until we think about the way Muslim people have been treated with suspicion after terrorist attacks in Western countries. Also, outsiders, such as aggressive working-class young men or people from minority ethnic groups, have been more likely to be treated unfairly by the authorities and in the courts of many countries. Physically disabled people, people with intellectual disabilities, and older people have sometimes been discriminated against in various ways, and many countries have enacted legislation to protect them. Some treatment in residential care might well be regarded as inhumane and degrading. These protections have therefore been important to many of the people whom social workers work with, and at times, we have perhaps been guilty as a profession of treating people unfairly. Picking these ideas up in later chapters, particularly chapters 2 and 3, I emphasize the importance of equality and accountability to our clients, as well as to the social agencies that provide our mandate to practice. This requires openness, participation, and fair processes in the decisions that we make as social workers.

In this way, humanistic social work incorporates into its thinking from human rights ideas the idea that we have a shared human right to freedom and equality in our social relationships, which enables us to pursue human well-being.

MICROSOCIOLOGICAL IDEAS

I have already suggested that humanistic social work incorporates important sociological ideas from microsociology. What does this mean? When we think about sociology, we often think of large-scale social trends and discourses. One example is the twentieth-century conflict between socialist and capitalist economic and social organization. Others might be the impact of social movements such as feminism, environmentalism, or consumerism on our culture and the way we think. We also think about understanding how large-scale social institutions work: discrimination and oppression through class and race, families, communities, the police, government, social agencies. Many social workers find this knowledge a useful context for their interpersonal practice and in explaining how things that happen in their clients' lives have occurred. However, when they think of ways to intervene, they tend to turn mainly to psychological ideas derived from psychotherapies or concerned with interpersonal social influence or persuasion.

However, Barbalet (2001) points out that the behavioral reactions and emotions of individual human beings are the channel of such broad social movements. Human beings and the social groups around them have to experience and act on resentment about inequalities, shame to feel that they need to conform, fear if they are to change, and confidence in themselves and others if they are to take action. This is an important set of ideas for social workers if they are to understand why individuals, families, groups, and communities do or do not react to wider social forces, and if they are to help people take action.

Many social workers feel that psychological knowledge and psychotherapeutic techniques give us ways to change individuals' lives. Looking at social explanations often makes the factors that affect us feel like a whole set of complex social interactions that are a context for personal behavior, a series of social structures that form a social order. These are hard to understand and seem impossible to change. The argument in this book is that microsociology helps us understand the personal effects of complex social factors, and thinking about individual and group emotional and cognitive responses to social change and social order help us work with the personal consequences of social issues and the social consequences of individual feelings and thoughts.

A range of sociological ideas have also been developed that can help us with understanding interpersonal relations in a sociological rather than a psychological way. Roberts (2006) summarizes several important sociological ideas that we can recognize as a basis for practice. I have set these out in box 1.6, with some examples of their relevance to social work.

Box 1.6 Ideas from Microsociology

Idea	*Source*	*Social work relevance*
People are part of groups in a social environment; group relations and environmental barriers create social distance; group and environment form an ecological setting for interpersonal relations.	Chicago school emphasized social planning of communities as a basis for improving social relations.	Idea of the person-in-environment as the focus of practice; importance of group, community, and organizational contexts as part of intervention.
Symbolic interactionism—our minds construct a generalized "other," a social audience of our life and our self; we create and test out roles against our understanding of that audience; the roles connect our individual way of being with society's expectations of us.	Mead (1934); Blumer (1969)	The importance of the family, community, ethnic group, and/or local culture as constructing the roles we take in work, leisure, and education.
Interaction order is a socially established way of interacting with others individually and in groups, allowing us to manage our relationships and present our self to others, through rituals, games, and performances in life.	Goffman (1968a)	Managing the stigma of poverty or disability, presenting a positive front to people outside our usual social environment; roles and behaviors in residential and day care established through institutional expectations.
Studies of social rules show what people in social groups agree on and understand as appropriate behavior, and how they hold people accountable to those rules.	Ethnomethodology; Garfinkel (1967)	Hidden rules of behavior typical of ethnic and social groups.
Personal and local experience is affected by inequalities and barriers associated with how cultures have been formed, and social categories are used in daily life.	Feminism, empowerment, and antioppression (see Payne, 2005)	Discrimination against or oppression of both minorities and less powerful people.
Social relations are formed and continued through exchange, rational choice, networks, disciplinary power, and structuration.	Especially Foucault (1979) and Giddens (1979, 1991)	People negotiate caring roles in family but may be oppressed by social expectations; people develop support networks.
Individual and group experience is informed by how people experience their body, time, community, and place.	Recent social theorists; Adam (1990)	Understanding how physical characteristics of the world contribute to human functioning.

Source: Developed from an analysis by Roberts (2006).

These ideas emphasize how individuals' identities and way of life come from their social environment, and this creates both barriers and things that can help them in their lives. This picks up from humanistic psychologies the importance of personal identity and self, but it shows how that identity interacts with social experience and relations and the oppressions that human rights ideas use to defend human beings against inequalities. Some of these ideas are postmodernist, and that term will be familiar because there has been a debate in the social sciences about the impact of postmodernist ideas on research. In social work, the importance of postmodernist ideas is that they show how social processes enable practitioners to help people understand where the issues come from that are important in their personal identities. Postmodernist ideas also help us understand how people can overcome barriers and develop their identities toward a feeling of self-actualization. A social work approach does not just focus on the individual's personal strengths and cognitive abilities, as counseling, psychology, and psychotherapy do, but it adds in interventions to make the social environment more supportive.

Case Example: Claudette

Do these ideas really make a contribution, or are they too generalized to be helpful? Claudette is an example of how these ideas can contribute to the richness of our thinking. She was the daughter of African refugees who, although middle class, had been housed in a very poor area when they had come to a new country. They had tried to give Claudette a good start in life, but she had formed a relationship with a local gang leader, became pregnant, and then was abandoned by him—to her parents' relief. However, she struggled in poorly paid jobs to cope with her new life as a single parent. Eventually, a refugee family project offered her counseling, using person-centered techniques, a humanistic counseling approach. This involved helping her review her life and think through the skills and support she had in her family relationships, and it aimed to make her feel empowered by being more positive about her achievements, for example, as a successful mother. The hope was that she would feel more positive about herself and have more self-confidence, thus developing her personal power to make improvements in her situation.

This was beneficial to her, and with her newfound self-confidence, Claudette found a better job as a classroom assistant in a local school. But because of her minor criminal record and the fact that she lived in a poor area, she was unable to get a loan to improve her situation and still felt she was struggling against impossible barriers. Eventually, she was referred to a children's center attached to a neighborhood project. Here, there was a social work approach, which valued the psychological development that she had already achieved and intervened in her situation to develop better social networks and to remove some of the barriers that were holding her back. She took part in group meetings with other mothers in her own situation; received financial advice on how to present herself when making loan applications and seeking new accommodation; and received training in effective child care and help in improving her relationships with her estranged parents, who gave her better support.

The social work interventions built on the developing person because, using the Chicago school ideas that our social context can limit the person, they identified and worked on the barriers of community and place that were holding her back. They emphasized to Claudette how her role as a successful mother, which she had drawn from the expectations of her minority ethnic culture, had contributed to developing the classroom assistant role and the possibility of moving on eventually to teacher education. She began to see herself as in a different social place, with a more positive social audience. She learned how to present herself more effectively, recognizing that the stigma of the area she was reared in limited the progress that she could make but that there were cultural strengths there also, which she could draw on. There was an emphasis on building her social networks, first with other mothers in her own situations but later with reconnecting her with her family and regaining their support.

In this example, I have tried to show how help based on humanistic psychological ideas and social help complement and strengthen each other and create a social work that includes both the psychological and the social—a whole social work for whole human beings in their social environments.

PREVIOUS FORMULATIONS OF HUMANISTIC SOCIAL WORK

Humanistic ideas have been influential in social work, in all the ways that I have brought together in this chapter. Among the most important contributors are the following:

- Rogers's (1951, 1961) person-centered practice and its three conditions of effective therapeutic relationships
- Goldstein's (1984) attempts to bring together cognitive and humanistic psychologies in the 1980s
- Krill's (1978) and Thompson's (1992) explicit use of an existential approach to practice
- Brandon's (1976, 2000) and Canda's explicit use of spiritual ideas to underpin practice approaches (Canda & Furman, 1999; Canda & Smith, 2001)
- Encounter groups and Glassman and Kates's (1990) humanistic groupwork

THINKING HUMANISTICALLY

Practitioners can use the ideas presented in this chapter to think humanistically. This means the following:

- Practicing in ways that facilitate clients' experience of using their own knowledge and skills
- Looking for personal growth and development for clients, their families, and communities in everything you do
- Maintaining a focus on securing human rights for clients

PAUSE AND REFLECT: Practicing by Thinking Humanistically

In box 1.7, I present in column 1 a list of client groups that social workers typically deal with; I repeat this process in later chapters. For each client group, use your own experience to suggest, in columns 2–4, a humanistic social work approach that you could use with that client group. I have filled in a few examples. You can add to these, fill in the blanks, and think in the same way about client groups that are important to you.

Box 1.7 Thinking Humanistically About Social Work Client Groups

Client group	Clients using their own experience	Growth objectives	Secure human rights
People with fertility concerns	Reviewing fears and wishes for having children or remaining childless from past discussions	Thinking about how having children or remaining childless might enhance or build new skills	Thinking through rights to have children or remain childless
Children			Identifying situations where adults ignore their views
Families			
Physically disabled people		Improving fitness through new activities	
People with learning disabilities	Helping the client and family make their own Social Security claims		
Mentally ill people	Rebuilding relationships with estranged family members		
Older people			
Dying people			

CONCLUSION

This chapter introduced the main outlines of the thinking that underlies humanistic practice, humanism (particularly secular humanism), humanistic and transpersonal psychologies and psychotherapies, human rights thinking, and microsociological ideas. In doing so, I have identified three main principles of humanistic practice, each drawn from one of these sources:

- The emphasis of secular humanism on developing the capacity of human beings to manage and take control of their life and social environment through their human abilities in rational thinking and through their mutual responsibility to one another as human beings

- The emphasis of humanistic psychologies on personal growth and self-actualization through understanding shared human experience
- The emphasis of human rights ideas on promoting the freedoms associated with our shared human nature and responsibility to one another, which leads to social rights to equality and well-being

To sum up humanistic social work, it is a practice that seeks human and social well-being by developing human capacities; personal growth; and social relationships of equality, freedom, and mutual responsibility through shared social experience. I have emphasized the social aspects of practice for social work as part of a broader range of humanistic helping practices. Later chapters pick up these ideas in filling out the picture of humanistic helping and social work practice.

FURTHER READING

Rowan, J. (2001). *Ordinary ecstasy: The dialectics of humanistic psychology* (3rd ed.). New York: Taylor and Francis.

A thoughtful and well-informed account of humanistic psychology and psychotherapy, which has stood the test of time for more than thirty years of publication.

Shorrock, A. (2008). *The transpersonal in psychology, psychotherapy and counselling.* Basingstoke, UK: Palgrave Macmillan.

Roberts, B. (2006). *Micro social theory.* Basingstoke, UK: Palgrave Macmillan.

The two preceding works are more recent guides and commentaries to the ideas discussed in this chapter.

Schneider, K. J., Bugental, J. F., & Fraser Pierson, J. (Eds.). (2001). *The handbook of humanistic psychology.* Thousand Oaks, CA: Sage.

Cain, D. J., & Seeman, J. (Eds.). (2001). *Humanistic psychotherapies: Handbook of research and practice.* Washington, DC: American Psychological Association.

The two preceding works are comprehensive and authoritative guides to enable you to explore humanistic psychologies and psychotherapies.

Readers who would like to explore an important source of humanistic psychology may like to explore any of the writing of Carl Rogers. There is a good collection of these in this work:

Rogers, C. (1990). *The Carl Rogers reader* (H. Kirschenbaum & L. Henderson, Eds.). London: Constable.

Accountability: Psychological Efficacy and Social Agency

CHAPTER AIMS

The main aim of this chapter is to help practitioners develop relationships of accountability to their clients and other people that they serve, to their agencies, and to the law and social policy.

After working through this chapter, readers should be able to

- Understand how humanistic practice links individual empowerment, aiming for psychological efficacy, and social agency within clients' environments
- Understand and debate the consequential importance of two different meanings of accountability in practice: first, the wish and need of human beings to account intelligibly for and make sense of what is happening to them in their social relationships; second, human and organizational accountability for their standards of practice
- Ensure that appropriate people in the client system give informed consent for interventions
- Practice advance care planning

ACCOUNTABILITY CONNECTS THE INTERPERSONAL AND THE SOCIAL IN PRACTICE

If social work means a practitioner as a human being helping another human being, an important part of a social worker's accountability is to the person he or she is helping. It is not the only accountability, however, because social work is not just individual help. Oppressed women trying to be good parents without family and community support, people with disabilities struggling with a society that limits their options, mentally ill people trying to fight their personal demons while a stigmatizing society excludes them, older people hoping to retain a satisfying lifestyle in poverty and fear of frailty—all these people may receive our services and individual help and support. But the fact that they feel helped or empowered to make a particular choice counts for little if the community and society that they live in place barriers in the way of their efforts and the efforts of people similar to them. Moreover, as we saw in chapter 1, we are able to give them our help because social structures and institutions empower us and mandate that we do so. This chapter is about squaring those individual and collective responsibilities.

PAUSE AND REFLECT: Seeing Others Like Yourself

Reflect on a situation in which you were helped with something difficult in your life but could see that other people in the same position needed similar help but did not get it. Or reflect on a situation in which you helped someone but were not able to help others in that person's same position. Make a note of how you felt; what did you do about how you felt? If you can, share this with other people.

Some Suggestions

Perhaps you felt relief that you had gotten out of a difficulty or were pleased when you made progress with your own difficulties or with other people. Perhaps you had a sense of satisfaction at seeing people move on. Humanistic psychology argues that motivation to make things better for ourselves, personal growth or self-actualization, is an important human characteristic.

But what about the other people in the same situation? Perhaps relief or the progress you made was so overpowering that you did not feel the responsibility to help others. Perhaps you would have helped your sister, brother, or a good friend in the same situation. However, you did not feel a personal connection with someone you did not know across the street or people in a poorer neighborhood than yours; they were not in the same position as you. Perhaps your life was too busy or your workload was too high to help them too, or they lived in a neighborhood that your agency did not cover. Perhaps people you helped did not make progress, so you felt you were wasting your time and gave up.

These situations point to a difficulty of helping other people. We know and we can see that there are groups of people who have similar problems, so we can see that there are social problems, in the sense that the existence of these problems affecting a large number of people affects how our society works and social relationships among people. An issue may similarly affect social groups of people. For example, the people who live in a particular neighborhood with old, poor-quality housing may all have problems with health because damp affects their lungs, or people who share a particular characteristic, such as being from a minority ethnic group, even if they live in a variety of districts, may all be affected by discrimination in employment, so they have unreliable employment and low incomes.

You might expect a general reaction to that; they might all complain or protest. Why does this not happen very often? In some cases, it is because they are not aware that other people share the same problems. Political and social activists and macropractitioners argue that mutual assistance, consciousness raising, and similar techniques should be used to enable people to see that they have shared problems and can work together to support one another and take action to improve the position of them all. In other cases, people do not see that they share something with others, or they do not feel that they are part of a social group that includes others. Barbalet (2001) has shown that individuals in groups with shared concerns and interests may have different emotions about the issue that affects them all. Some may be depressed or anxious, some may get angry, some resentful. In contrast, by sharing their experiences, others may gain confidence.

This reminds us of the humanistic principle that all human beings are different, even though they are mostly part of social groups, and they share the same social and physical environments. Therefore, we cannot work only with the individuals, because their connections with social groups and their social and physical environment will affect their individual reactions, but nor can we work only with social groups, because the individual reaction to the social group and social environment will affect how the group moves on. Kondrat (2002) talks about how to understand the traditional ecological systems theory social work perspective of the person-in-environment. She argues that we should do this by focusing on people as actors in social situations who have agency, that is, the power to operate through social relationships in ways that help them achieve their objectives. This connects with, but is different from, the psychological concept of efficacy. Efficacy proposes that people will be more effective in achieving their objectives if they believe that they can have some influence over the issues that they are trying to deal with.

An important struggle for all social work is its need to achieve social objectives, including general social change, through interpersonal work. I have shown elsewhere that this has been a continuing and essential discourse throughout the history of social work (Payne, 2006). It is part of our daily work experience: we are constantly frustrated because social structures made up of patterns of social relationships in society establish barriers to some people achieving their potential. However, the same social structures help other people. Some social work at the macro level involves advocacy on behalf of individual clients and social groups in communities to achieve social change that removes those barriers. But for the social worker who practices mainly with individuals and families, this possibility seems distant.

How does humanistic practice deal with this important issue for practitioners? The humanistic ideas that we examined in chapter 1 proposed that human beings have rights. Among them is the right to achieve progress toward personal growth that they want, toward self-actualization, and they achieve this through using their own personal capacity, in particular their capacities for rational thought, forward-looking planning, and creativity. These ideas also propose that human development can be achieved only in interaction with communities and societies of human beings caring for and supporting one another. When that care and support do not exist or there are barriers to using it, social workers and other helping professionals provide experience of it so that people can move forward with confidence. They also work to ensure that people who lack support or opportunities can build social relationships and participate in social structures as a foundation for their human rights. Where structures are exclusionary, practitioners also seek to change those structures so that they are more accommodating.

Kondrat (2001) uses concepts from Giddens's (1979) structuration theory (see box 1.6, chapter 1) to explain how interventions through the interpersonal and the social may be used together. Social life is recursive; that is, patterns of social interaction constantly recur. They do so because people have been raised in a particular culture and social milieu. In many social situations, such as school, leisure facilities, or workplaces, people become socialized into patterns typical of their culture. Patterns of social power in turn reinforce those cultural patterns. So, for example, people learn in childhood how to behave within social relations between different ethnic groups in their society. Some groups are oppressed as part of a pattern of power relations between groups, and people learn how to behave within the expected patterns. For example, they may learn not to speak out to officials with power over them because they learned in school that teachers reacted badly when their teaching was questioned. This can be changed only by helping individuals learn alternative patterns of behavior and at the same time helping them become part of social groups that have enough power to achieve some degree of social change. If they speak out to officials and are put down, then what they learned in school is reinforced. So if we are going to encourage people to speak out about their needs, we have to make sure first that there will be a reasonable reaction to their requests. This involves helping them express their needs in ways that people with power can accept, but it also means influencing the people with power to take the trouble to be positive about the points of view that oppressed people are expressing. Beginning that change facilitates further social changes.

Box 2.1 sets out in a diagram humanistic practice methods for achieving these practice aims; this chapter explores them more fully. The downward arrow shows that people are always in their social environments and that they always want to move forward from past life experiences through their present life situation toward future aims. To intervene,

Box 2.1 Humanistic Practice Aims

Person-in-environment
Past experience

Social work interventions

Current life experience

Working with the person
• Increase **psychological efficacy**
• Increase participation in environment
• Improve environmental response

The person moves forward within a social group, which also moves forward

Movement forward

Working on patterns of power in the environment
• Empower to move forward
• Increase **social agency**

Future aims

so that this movement forward is toward positive personal growth, means simultaneously engaging the following:

- Development of personal psychological efficacy, the person's capacity to act to take their personal development forward.
- Recognition that people do not move forward on their own; they have to do so within social groups that are also moving forward in the same direction, or they have to move into social groups that accord with the direction that they want to move in. If clients are not part of a social group that can help them, we need to help them make connections with another social group or influence their present social group to help them.
- The development of strength in the social agency of their environment; the groups within which they live support and motivate them to use their increased personal efficacy to remove barriers interfering with personal growth. These barriers are a consequence of persisting patterns of power within broader social structures. If the social groups available to clients are hemmed in, we need to help the whole of the group make progress, not just individual clients.

Humanistic practice, therefore, as we saw in chapter 1, focuses first on the individual human being. But we cannot just focus on individual human action, because all human beings express their humanity and increase their efficacy through social relationships in their social environment. Those social relationships are interpersonal, but they are also structural, so therefore, both the individuals and their social environment need to be empowered to use their human social agency within broader structural relationships. The International Federation of Social Workers (International Federation of Social Workers [IFSW], 2000) defines social work as using both psychological and social knowledge and processes together, and it positions social work at the interface of the personal and the social (see box 2.2, discussed in more detail later). Thinking about practice as bringing together psychological efficacy and social agency implements these widely accepted ideas about social work.

ACCOUNTABILITY: TWO HUMAN AND ORGANIZATIONAL ASPECTS IN PRACTICE

Now we can return to accountability. We sometimes think of accountability as responsibility for work to an organization, but it is more than that. Some of the examples that we looked at in the previous reflection suggested that agency factors such as high workloads or limited responsibility for particular geographical areas might affect whether we respond to a need for help that we can see. It is clear, then, that the agency's responsibility affects what work we do and how we do it. This may limit our professional responsibility, or our professional and human duties may override it.

Case Example: The Child in the Corner

A practitioner was developing a management plan for the care of an older woman. As part of doing this, she visited the woman's daughter, who, although she suffered from immense poverty and was living in very poor-quality housing, was trying to help her mother. In the corner of the room, the practitioner noticed a bundle of rags moving and feared rodent infestation. However, after a while, she realized she was looking at a very young baby, awake but unnaturally quiet. She encouraged the woman to allow her to look at the "new baby" and discovered that it had several bruises on its body and was in very poor physical condition. Abandoning her work on helping the mother, the practitioner persuaded the woman to seek emergency medical help. As a result, the child was removed from its mother's care, who then refused to work with the practitioner on her own mother's care.

This is a situation in which the practitioner's employing organization was not responsible for overseeing the care of the child, and this limited her own mandate. However, social work organizations accept a social responsibility for participating in arrangements for child protection, and the practitioner had a personal professional responsibility to notice that something was wrong and to take action to safeguard the child's well-being.

Accountability has two meanings, which connect the personal and interpersonal and the social and collective. The first refers to the need and wish of practitioners and clients to make sense of what is happening both in the practice of social work and in their lives. Giving an account of what is happening as we work with someone, or as we try to understand events in someone's life, or in our own lives, involves turning it into an account, a narrative or story that makes sense to someone else and to us. A lot of people feel helped by understanding the story of what is happening to them; it often helps them feel more in control.

This view of accountability comes from the work of the ethnomethodologist Harold Garfinkel (Roberts, 2006; see box 1.6, chapter 1), who emphasized that an aspect of accountability was making sense of the world so that we could operate in social relationships. We all develop a sense of reasonable explanation of what the world brings us, an understanding through sharing reports, information, and records that create a reasonable narrative about the events we are dealing with and the social environment, culture, and history that explain them. Therefore, accountability is partly about creating a reasonable account of the world and testing it to see whether it accords with a shared view of intelligible behavior. This is an important assessment technique; practitioners elicit accounts of a situation and observe whether the accounts accord with what they can see. They talk through inconsistencies and, as a result, understand the situation better and can be more effective in their work.

This also connects with social workers' tasks to prepare assessments for services, as well as social histories and reports for colleagues, other professionals, or decision-making bodies such as courts and agencies that need a social perspective to decide on placement of people in need. Practitioners make the social aspect of people's lives intelligible to decision makers.

The second meaning of accountability refers to the duty to give an account of ourselves, our actions, and our thinking. We usually exercise this kind of accountability through the organization that we work for, and perhaps also through education and accreditation for our professional standards. I argued at the outset of this chapter that humanistic thinking emphasizes a sense of accountability to the people we serve for meeting their objectives. Justifying ourselves in this way may not be a daily occurrence, but it is always in the mind of any practitioner with a concern for ethical or values-based practice: are they seeking appropriate aims and meeting appropriate standards for the way in which they meet those aims? Practitioners who see a baby at risk while carrying out some other task accept this ethical responsibility in addition to their accountability to their employing organization.

Accountability in both senses implies social relationships. This is because to make sense of something inevitably involves making sense of the relationships between people and between them and their environments. To have a duty to give an account requires us to have a relationship with another person. It is impossible to have a relationship with an organization, only with a person within that organization. It is only a convenient shorthand to say that we are accountable to our professional body or the organization that employs us. This also means trying to make ourselves and our actions intelligible or understandable to others. A duty implies a power relationship; the person we are accountable to has some kind of right, conferred by human rights, by the law, by professional standards, by organizational requirements, or by force of personality.

How practitioners justify their practice connects with the idea of justice. When practitioners justify what they do, they are saying, in the context of the employing organization, of social policy, of professional standards, and of the client's needs and wishes and the expectations of the community and culture around them, "What I am doing in my practice is right, fair, and just." How they justify their practice is concerned with both the argument that they put forward that what they are doing is right and the processes through which they put that argument forward. Going further, "right" implies that what they are doing is both morally right and right in the sense of being socially effective in achieving outcomes for the agency and for the client, their family, caregivers, community, and others that form the social system around them.

Accountability is an important issue for any kind of social work, for four main reasons. Practitioners' accountability is about the aims of their work, so it sets their strategy, focus, and priorities for practice. Thinking accountability through therefore has to come before any discussion of how they practice. I refer to this as the accountability strategy for our work.

Second, accountability always takes place in human relationships, so we have to think about the human aspect of rendering our account. For example, a trusting relationship with our manager can help us gain support when we have made a mistake, whereas a less trusting relationship might lead us to conceal the problem, which may be more stressful for the practitioner and may lead to less good service for clients. This is why I argue that organizational relationships are always interpersonal. Pithouse's (1998) study of social workers with families and children suggests that a "making sense" is going on in much social work supervision. Another example is that describing a well-worked-out intervention supported by research evidence can convince a client to accept our help and work on an issue, whereas being vague about why something will help, or relying on the authority of our professional role, may be less convincing and motivating for the client. This connects with the making-sense meaning of accountability: if clients and managers can make sense of what practitioners are doing, then that work seems more human and also more humane.

Third, systems of accountability make sure that our practice fits within legal and organizational frameworks. Some practice with clients is involuntary, either because official systems or legal requirements force them to accept our help or because social pressures have pushed them to come to us for help, even though they are skeptical.

Keeping within what the evidence tells us is effective, within legal and professional boundaries, codes of practice and ethics—all these protect clients' rights to fair and competent care and treatment. Complying with human rights objectives means aligning our practice with the aim of achieving justice and equality for everyone, including our clients. This is implicit and sometimes explicit in the human rights codes and constitutions that underlie many government social services and nongovernmental professional value systems. We saw in chapter 1 how these are also interpersonal, because people negotiating the right outcome to deal with a current social issue produce them. After the Second World War, the worry was the experience of the Holocaust and oppressive political regimes, so the result was the UN Universal Declaration of Human Rights that focused on legal rights. For European countries setting up a shared economic system, the aim was to ensure that every country was on an equal social footing, so the European Charter of Fundamental Rights focuses more on social rights.

Fourth, achieving accountability, in the second sense, can help people toward self-actualization because they feel more in control of their lives and more motivated to act if they can make sense of what is happening to them and ensure that it meets agreed-on standards and accepted processes.

Making sense in this way can often be achieved by psychological theories, such as psychodynamic ideas, which describe how behavior results from internal processes in our minds, and sociological ideas such as role, which describe how expectations from different people interact to put pressure on us to behave in socially accepted ways. Although it may be hard to confirm these ideas by clear scientific research or experiment, developing accounts that make sense of how things happen in our lives can be satisfying and help motivate us to move forward.

Case Example: Miya's Family Review

A social worker and psychologist were helping a family because Miya, a teenage daughter, had eating difficulties and had become anorexic. Miya built up a good rapport with the social worker, and she was prepared to talk about many different aspects of her relationships with brothers and sisters and parents that she had not discussed with anybody else. Both the social worker and the psychologist managed to develop different styles of relationship, with varying levels of openness with different members of the family.

After several individual sessions with Miya, with her parents, and with the whole family, the practitioners received permission to share several different points of view about family relationships over the years at a family meeting. It would be hard to say that putting together different perceptions of relationship difficulties in childhood provided any explanation for Miya's difficulties or problems affecting other members of the family. However, after this open session, Miya and her mother said to the social worker and the psychologist, respectively, that they had not understood so much about how communication had developed in the family and how family members saw that as causing difficulties for them and for others. Family members clearly found it satisfying and gained a sense of progress from their greater breadth and depth of understanding. It helped them make sense of what was going wrong. This enabled both practitioners to plan cognitive-behavioral techniques for working on specific aspects of the problems.

ACCOUNTABILITY AS STRATEGY: PROBLEM SOLVING, EMPOWERMENT, AND SOCIAL CHANGE

A useful way to think through accountability strategy is to focus on the main aims of social work, as expressed in the IFSW definition of social work, set out in box 2.2; it is internationally accepted as an appropriate representation of social workers' responsibilities. The definition says that social work is of three kinds: social change, problem solving in human relationships, and empowerment and liberation of people to enhance well-being. In my study of definitions across the ages (Payne, 2006, chapter 2), I argue that social work is a constantly developing discourse about the interaction of those three aspects of social work. However, my analysis of these three aspects of social work is more complex, as I explain here.

Humanistic social work focuses mainly on the empowering, liberating aim of social work, so humanistic practitioners have some difficult questions to answer. In following humanistic social work, are we naively rejecting the other two aspects of social work? Does humanistic practice fail to seek social change where it is necessary and evade responsibility for dealing with important individual problems that clients face? Or in adapting humanistic ideas to meet the requirements of social work to work on social problems and social change, are we perverting the humanistic focus on individual human identity and the responsibility to help people achieve their highest human capacity? The answer might be to stick to humanistic psychotherapy and avoid social work's

Box 2.2 The International Definition of Social Work

The social work profession promotes social change, problem solving in human relationships and the empowerment and liberation of people to enhance well-being. Utilising theories of human behaviour and social systems, social work intervenes at the points where people interact with their environments. Principles of human rights and social justice are fundamental to social work.

Source: International Federation of Social Workers (2000).

wider responsibilities for intervening with the social. This might be fine for a counselor or psychologist, but not for a social worker, because, as we have seen, social work connects individual psychological efficacy with collective social agency: the agency supports the efficacy and people have to progress in social groups that are also progressing in the same direction.

PAUSE AND REFLECT: Accountability in Typical Social Work Cases

Select one or more commonplace social work tasks, and decide where your accountability lies if you take a problem-solving approach, a personal empowerment approach, and a social change approach. You may like to choose an area of practice typical of your present work or to test out your ideas on several client groups:

- A child with behavioral problems
- A young person who has become addicted to cocaine
- A person with intellectual disabilities whose parents are growing older and are less able to care for him or her
- A man with a long history of mental illness who has become isolated from his family
- A middle-aged woman with multiple sclerosis who has experienced several recoveries and relapses and now has to use a wheelchair for most of her days at work
- An older woman who has had several falls at home, with a daughter worried that she may be unable to live on her own any longer

Some Suggestions

If we take a problem-solving approach to these cases, most of the people concerned will see that they have a difficulty in living day to day, which they might value your help in resolving. But there may be ambiguities: the child and the addict may not see that behavior as problematic; the practitioner may be involved because other people see the behavior as a problem. Similarly, the people with intellectual disabilities or mental illness may not be able to appreciate the possibilities or the need to take action about them. The disabled and older women may resist thinking through the consequences of their changing life; they might hope to get better and not have to face continuing problems. There will also be people around these clients, parents, friends, relatives, caregivers, and other services who may see and understand the problem differently, or they may identify a problem that causes them difficulties where the client is not so concerned. Finally, the society and community surrounding the client will also have views. These social entities will be concerned with ensuring that the child and the addict do not worsen, perhaps moving on to a criminal lifestyle. The people with intellectual disabilities and mental illness might become social nuisances to neighbors; the disabled or older person may be at risk and unable to care for themselves. Some of these clients may therefore become involuntary clients, or there may be social pressures that force them into contact with social care services. Our accountability is not solely to solve the problems that the clients see; it also is to the people around them and often to a wider social mandate to maintain the social order. Where they want different things from the client, we may need to resolve conflicts of opinion about what we should do.

Taking an empowerment approach with accountability mainly to the client and perhaps people who are concerned that the client should lead a happy life may not meet accountability to the wider community. Aiming for the self-actualization for such clients may lead to difficulties for their caregivers, relatives, and local community. We may help them toward greater independence and self-fulfillment, but this may not remove all the risk to the community. Also, the humanistic view that self-fulfillment is achieved only through human relationships means that if they, and we, do not take into account the views and needs of the people around them, we will not be helping our clients' self-fulfillment either.

A social change approach, similarly, may help facilitate a better life for these individuals and give them better resources to live in the community. This may benefit their independence and lead to improved support in the community and a richer community life for all. So thinking about social work's general accountability to the community and society, this approach may be both positive and personally helpful; it may also be more facilitative and not impose interventions on involuntary clients. However, this may not help them with individual problems or achieve individuals' personal growth, so accountability to the individual may be more limited, and we may also not deal with difficult issues where some members of the community might disagree about what is good progress.

These examples draw attention to the complexity of accountability in the three apparently simple aims of social work set out in the IFSW definition, which is why I argue (Payne, 2006) that it is important to see these aims in a more complex way. First, simply describing the first aim as "problem solving" is inadequate. A more accurate account includes providing and organizing services, as well as helping people find their way through the complexity of other services, for example, housing, health care, and Social Security. "Problem solving" also misses out the advocacy and mediating functions of social work, where practitioners make a case within their own agencies and with other agencies for resources to be provided for their clients. All these activities solve problems for and with people, but the definition leads us to focus on problem solving to meet their personal objectives. Humanistic social work points to the importance of maintaining people's human rights and the interaction of clients' rights with the rights and interests of other people, such as their caregivers, family, and community.

The second issue about a focus on problem solving is that it emphasizes deficit rather than growth motivation: we met this idea of Maslow's (1999) in chapter 1. Because we start from someone's problems, we start from something that they do not have. Using cognitive-behavioral practice approaches emphasizes deficit even more, because we concentrate on specifying and defining that problem so that we can resolve it. The result is that we often come to see the deficit as defining the person. Goffman (1968b) emphasized this in his sociological research on how stigmatizing conditions overwhelmed other identities in people's lives. In other people's eyes, a disability can become the most important thing about them. Many physically disabled people feel quite strongly that other people often do not look beyond their physical disability to see the person underneath and fail to appreciate how much that person might achieve. Many parents of people with learning disabilities similarly feel that the many attractive personality traits of their child are underestimated and that they do not achieve things they might manage to do because services do not take enough trouble to give the maximum possible help. Older people and younger people both feel at times that their frailty or lack of experience, respectively, mean that they do not receive credit for their intelligence, motivation, and skills. I have put older and younger together in one sentence to emphasize that we discriminate against both groups at different times for opposite reasons. The older person is assumed to be inflexible because he or she has too much experience, the younger person to be incapable because he or she does not have enough. We are not looking at the capability of the person in front of us when we make these generalized assumptions.

Connected with this, the third problem with problem solving is that it encourages social work to be very individualistic, or at least family and group centered. Practitioners are presented with a problem and work hard to define it so that it can be tackled. Most models of social work that we are encouraged to use because evidence shows that they have good outcomes for clients focus on precise behaviors that we can change through recognized and researched techniques. This means that social work does not do anything about the unchanged poverty or power relationships that will create another generation of the same difficulties for social workers in the future. Such unchanged social relationships will also put barriers in the way of someone learning and using the new knowledge or social skill that we have helped them with.

The fourth problem is the failure of a problem-solving perspective to incorporate social roles of social work, such as managed care or care management. These roles include organizing packages of care services for clients, such as arranging for people to be admitted to residential facilities, care homes, day care, or social and clinical services. This problem also ignores the role of social work in managing and caring within such settings. Much social work focuses on arranging or facilitating long-term caring, and this requires a focus on caring tasks rather than on problem-solving interventions.

However, the examples examined in the previous Pause and Reflect draw attention to similar weaknesses in the other aims for social work. This returns us to the inevitable conclusion that social work needs to incorporate and balance all these objectives and provide for accountability for all of them. This is indeed what the IFSW's definition of social work says. Each social agency in each welfare system needs policies about the balance that it wants to pursue, and social workers need to work out a balance in their practice, and they need to do it with each client, in each social work act that they carry out.

In doing humanistic social work, therefore, we face important questions about what social work practice is about, what it aims to achieve, and the people it aims to work with. My answer to these questions is that the full range of social work responsibilities can and should be tackled through humanistic practice. The main reason for this is that the human includes the social. We saw in chapter 1 that human relationships always interact with the environment. Therefore, intervening in the interpersonal inevitably must always involve social relationships and social structures, and intervening in the social inevitably must respond to personal needs.

Dealing with this issue of the interaction of the three aspects of social work—social change, problem solving, and empowerment—is a universal aspect of social work, because all social work practice involves balancing them. All agency organization involves deciding on the balance among them in the services the agency offers, and social policy involves deciding on the right balance in service provision in a state or nation. The result of this constant discourse among the three aspects of social work means that we are always accountable to different individuals and groups in society.

ACCOUNTABILITY, EVIDENCE, AND HUMAN EXPERIENCE

If social workers focus on working with other human beings, where does their professional accountability lie? Humanism argues that it lies first in science, that only the rational human mind can give us the capacity to understand and take control of our environment, that our practice must be evidence based. This leads us to an evidence-based practice that seeks to use the best information to achieve the best results. And it leads us to want to strengthen clients' mental strength to manage their own affairs, because therein lie stronger, more developed human beings better able to deal effectively with their environment.

But humanistic psychology affirms that science is enacted in human relationships. Evidence-based practice is crucial, but it looks only at the rational, cognitive part of the whole human being, which can be evidenced using positivistic research methods; random controlled trials and single-case research designs are preferred. Humanistic social work says we should look at evidence about all aspects of human beings and their interactions with other people in social relationships and in the context of their social and physical environment. This will include creative, complex, and flexible interventions that are not so easily testable in positivist research designs. The research design of choice for dealing with flexible complexity is a qualitative assessment of a range of personal responses to a constantly changing balance of social and human factors; because it is constantly changing, it must be constantly reassessed. Therefore, practitioners must participate in those relationships to be accountable through evidence-based research to multiple interests in the social work process. These interests include clients, informal caregivers, social work colleagues, paraprofessional caregivers, multiprofessional colleagues, managers, and political and social debate. A psychological evidence-based view that we are responsible only for achieving specific outcomes that we define with the client is not acceptable for many social work aims.

This chapter argues that practitioners must represent the variety of evidence bases relevant to all these interests, for example, respecting clients and informal caregivers' perceptions of their roles and interests while representing agency and social policies and professional evidence. This is a lot to ask, and I take up in chapters 4 and 5 how we become flexible enough to deal with the complexity of this. In chapters 6–8, I examine practice that incorporates those complexities and is concerned with identity, spirituality, caring, creativity, security, and resilience. Practice must humanize knowledge and evidence through the relationships that carry out the social work process. Humanistic social work argues for acting in a transparent, open way that enables others to understand and evaluate how practitioners are doing their jobs, so that there can be a democracy among practitioners, clients, and society.

Case Example: Psychological Efficacy and Social Agency in Going Home From the Hospital

Mrs. Truman was a frail older woman, living alone, who broke bones in her foot when she had a fall in her apartment. She had a complex series of fractures pinned in hospital and was ready to go home, but she was not fit enough to go back to her own home immediately, so it was planned that she would stay with her daughter, Erin. Mrs. Truman was depressed about her circumstances and received some cognitive-behavioral treatment from a psychologist to help her think more positively about the opportunities and to lift her mood. This was effective and improved Mrs. Truman's psychological efficacy; she believed that she would be able to regain her independence and move back to her own home.

Catherine, the social worker attached to the ward, was responsible for making the practical arrangements for the move to Erin's home. She talked to Mrs. Truman in the ward and was surprised, in view of the apparent success of the cognitive-behavioral treatment, to find her despondent again about the difficulties she would face. Catherine visited Erin's home with an occupational therapist to see whether adaptations were required and to assess any issues for Erin's family. Discussing the plans with Erin, her husband, and their teenage children, she found that they were gloomy about having Mrs. Truman in their home and worried that the arrangement would be permanent until Mrs. Truman's death. This, in turn, had been affecting Erin's talk with her mother; she had tried to prepare her mother for some of the family's doubts and probable hostility. A factor in the teenagers' views was the difficulties that several families had experienced in the neighborhood with similar arrangements and their teenage children had experienced a lot of restrictions on their opportunities and leisure. The local rumors were of a hospital that washed its hands of the family's problems and left them to cope with increasing difficulties. Listening to this made Catherine realize that there were many social barriers within the family supported by community attitudes and fostered by the hospital's policies. These meant that Mrs. Truman could not use the psychological efficacy that she had achieved, which in turn reduced her motivation. The skepticism might be a self-fulfilling prophecy, thus preventing her from achieving what should be possible.

Catherine's interventions included laying out the plans, together with the occupational therapist, for ensuring that Mrs. Truman was able to move on. The family, though still skeptical, could see that these were well worked out. She held a meeting with Mrs. Truman, Erin, and Erin's husband to set some boundaries about arrangements in the home. Also, Catherine reported back to the team so that they were more aware of the difficulties, both in this case and in general.

Therefore, four ideas from the discussion in chapter 1 are important in understanding social workers' accountability:

- Human beings think and act according to evidence and rational analysis, drawing on human thinking skills—they use evidence-based practice, but they use all the evidence derived from many different human senses and understanding brought together in a complex way. Evidence derived from the rules of positivist scientific research may offer specific techniques for focusing on particular problems, but this is part of a broader practice.

- Accountability arises in human social relationships and the meaning that people give to them—therefore, another aspect of accountability has to take place through how practitioners treat the people that they work with and the impact of their work on the human environments that they work in.

- Human beings have intentionality, choices, and responsibility—therefore, there are always choices to be made. Practitioners have to plan and use rationally researched evidence, human understanding of relationships, and the environment as part of their accountability.

- Human beings interact with an environment—accountability therefore takes into account the impact of what a practitioner does on the physical and human environment as well as on the main person or group they focus on.

Each of these factors is relevant to social work's accountability, but together they also balance and interact. Examples of the need to balance these different factors are that people do not always behave rationally in their human relationships and choices and that human rights thinking says that they are free to do so. Therefore, pursuing only rational modes of practice is impossible, and environments may affect a human being's degree of choice and responsibility.

Moreover, recent psychological research suggests that babies and young children use an inborn sense of intuition as they investigate the world, and they build on these using "rational thought" as they test out their intuitions in new experiences. Hood's (2009) account of extensive cognitive research with children suggests that all human beings may have a supersense, a form of unlearned, inborn reasoning based on whether things fit with our expectations. Children exhibit this cognitive sense in extensive experiments. This accounts for the widespread existence of religious and superstitious beliefs, and for a widely shared sense of moral rightness. Thus, if we look back at the case of the assault in chapter 1, most people anywhere in the world would react with a similar feeling of the social and moral wrongness of the man's behavior. Reading on through the case study, they might accept the information there as a reasonable argument for a more nuanced view of the situation, as I came to do, but we still mostly share the same moral revulsion. This is not reasoned, although it might be rationalized. We could, for example, talk about the human rights of the other people involved. But Hood (2009) quotes Steven Pinker as saying that the conscious mind, our self or soul, is the spin doctor, not the commander in chief: in many instances, it justifies and organizes what we have already decided to do.

Case Study: The Mother-in-Law and the Child of a Former Partner

If we think about our practice in this way, our evidence-based and rational thinking helps us test out what we decide intuitively; we may alter it by realizing that the evidence tells us something different from our intuition. But intuition guides us as we first react to a situation.

I learned this very early on in my career. As a student social worker, I was sent to make an appointment to see a young man and his new wife, to discuss the adoption of the illegitimate child he had had by a previous relationship. I knew that they both supported this move, and my task was to begin the formal arrangements. I knocked at the door, and it was opened by a Mrs. White, the right name at the correct address. It flashed through my mind that she was older than I expected, but with the right name at the correct address, I started on my inquiry, only to discover that this was the new wife's mother, the mother-in-law, at the house looking after their new baby. She was devastated to find that her newly married daughter had hitched up with a man who had a previous child by another woman. After this, I have always gone with what I feel first and tested it out with my formal knowledge afterward. I should have made sure who I was talking to. Hood (2009) would say, I think, that my natural intuition was asserting itself against the limitations of my structured knowledge base and anxiety to comply with agency procedures.

I think this is one of the reasons some members of the public find social workers' reactions to difficult situations inappropriate or scandalous, as when things go wrong and social workers are criticized. There is evidence that social workers generally are more liberal than most members of the public in their attitudes, for example, about criminal behavior or lifestyle choices. This is probably because they are accustomed to seeing things in a more nuanced way, having learned from experience that there are very often more complexities in many situations than we can see at first glance. However, most people have an inbuilt intuition about what is right. For example, as we have seen, if you see a very distressed child, you step in, especially if you are a social worker and that is your job. Public opinion cannot understand compliance with assessment criteria or thinking about parental rights: you should have saved the child.

I take these points up again in chapter 4, where I argue that practitioners incorporate into their whole human being their trained knowledge and skills, the evidence-based understanding that they gain from their education and socialization into professional practice. This adapts and channels social workers' intuitive response to situations. Thus, evidence contributes to the whole, but it is the humanity that uses the evidence in human activity—in this case, social work interventions.

ACCOUNTABILITY AS JUSTICE

I have suggested that accountability is one of the ways social work ensures that its practice is just. If social workers' acts are intelligible to their agencies and clients, it is easier to see that they are fair, for example, that a husband and wife or children in a family are treated appropriately, so that their interests are equally met. Transparency helps with accountability, because people can see and understand what is involved. Also, there is evidence that many social arrangements are unfair, because they lead to inequalities that evidence and reasoned argument cannot justify. One example is the way minority ethnic groups in many countries, such as African Americans in the United States, are disproportionately arrested and imprisoned as compared to similar people from the majority or white populations. This may come about because minority ethnic groups often experience greater poverty and lack of access to education in childhood than does the majority population. Another example is the worldwide impact of health inequalities. In most countries, there is a gradient in health; the wealthier you are, the healthier you are. This is also true between countries; poorer countries usually have a greater burden of ill health than do richer countries.

Inequalities of this kind are the reason for the IFSW's emphasis on social justice. These examples make clear, however, that widespread injustices remain a part of the patterns of power relations in many countries and between countries. However, social workers are dealing with the detailed personal experience of those injustices rather than the broader social consequences. Our sense of what is just may come from a feeling or intuition or from a reasoned analysis of situations that we face. The feeling aspect of justice develops from empathy with other people (Hoffman, 2000); for example, we are upset when we lose out, and we come to understand that others feel the same. We have seen that research suggests that we are born with innate views of the world that we start from and then develop reasoned principles from. Over time, therefore, we might understand that people who make a fuss because they were not given a piece of cake may deserve our sympathy because they are upset, but they do not deserve more of the cake if they make no effort to clean up their bedroom.

Considerable psychological research and controversy has examined how an idea of what is just or fair develops in children. Among the factors that affect children are the following:

- Caring elements, looking after other people ("I must look after my little sister").
- Need elements, providing something that is missing ("He isn't very good at this, so I must encourage and help him more").
- Effort elements that reward effort and achievement ("She has worked very hard to make our meal, but he only read the paper, so I will give her a kiss").

Developmental research shows that people take different factors into account and develop a more complex way of seeing what is fair as they grow toward adulthood (Hoffman, 2000). They do this as they gain experience of different situations in life, both as an observer and as a participant. Eventually, they realize that they have choice and control over many situations that they are involved in and can juggle multiple claims and complex situations. In doing so, they internalize a number of moral principles about fairness. The ethics-of-care view of ethics, which I discuss in relation to caring in chapter 6, emphasizes the caring and need elements of this.

These ideas about justice on a small scale have been developed into principles of justice that refer to the way we organize matters in society, for example, in political or legal processes. There are two fundamental ways to think about this:

- A process view, which emphasizes being fair in how we do things
- An outcome view, which emphasizes achieving fair outcomes

Both views are relevant to many situations. For example, there are two frail people, Joan and May, applying for a place in a care home: who should be chosen? One way to think about this is to carry out a full assessment of their needs and allocate the place to the person who has the most needs. But what if Joan is a very relaxed person who copes much better than May with more severe physical needs, whereas May is overanxious about her less serious problems? How can we equate the physical and psychological needs? Someone who follows utilitarian views might argue for admitting May, on the grounds that the overall sum of human happiness is increased. If May is admitted and Joan later falls and injures herself, the outcome in the longer term might lead to a different view of what would have been a just decision.

Rawls (1971) starts from an "original position" (p. 171) in which we have no knowledge of any of the circumstances and then develop consistent rules in a rational way but connecting with a sense of fairness that human beings share about the human condition. There's that idea of intuition again. Political and legal institutions are just if they maintain principles that lead us to be satisfied according to this shared human sense of fairness. A process view leads us to say that the decisions we make should be impartial between those affected, and therefore not affected by our own interests, and the outcome view says that the outcomes should meet reasonable objectives set by fair processes.

Accountability comes from this. Human beings feel that we should set up institutions in society, such as social work agencies, so that they meet both process and outcome standards of fairness, and practitioners are accountable through the agencies to the social structures that have been established to decide on fairness. In humanistic social work, justice and justifiability partly come from the idea we explored in chapter 1 that all behavior, and therefore our practice, is informed by the fact that human beings are aware, self-aware, and responsible for their actions in the social and physical environment that they inhabit. If we are responsible, we must have mechanisms for that responsibility, and these come from our social relationships and our participation in social institutions and structures.

What mechanisms help us achieve these different sorts of accountability? In humanistic social work, this has to be done through processes that aim to achieve transparent decision making, because this is the only way others can exercise their self-responsibility; if they are not aware, they cannot be responsible.

One important mechanism, therefore, is the idea of informed consent, which means that people are well informed about what we are doing and able to understand and work out rationally whether they agree to and accept both the aims and the processes that we will go through. This means that people can participate in deciding our strategy for helping them: this is a process form of justice leading to accountability.

Another important mechanism is advance care planning. This facilitates people in expressing their intentions and wished-for outcomes so that we can incorporate their preferences into our practice. This is an outcome form of justice, also leading to account-ability. Both these mechanisms are important in humanistic social work because they operationalize people having greater rational control over what is happening to them.

INFORMED CONSENT

Making sure that workers gain informed consent to interventions is an important way to signify accountability to clients. In medicine, it is a well-established requirement that physicians get informed consent before treating or intervening with patients. This origi-nates from the fact that medicine often involves physical contact with patients, which is an offense unless the patient gives permission. Moving on from that, using physical treat-ments such as medication has meant that patients need to be aware of side effects and dangers in the treatments they receive. This idea of informed consent has influenced other professions, including social work. Box 2.3 reprints the paragraphs on informed consent from four important English-language codes of ethics.

As we found when looking at human rights charters in chapter 1, there is also some variation in the ethics codes. For example, the British code is absolute, implying that all social workers will work on the basis on informed consent, whereas the U.S. code is more nuanced, requiring that only where it is appropriate. However, all focus strongly on making sure that information given is appropriate to the individual and that the individual is free to make decisions rather than being put under pressure. A humanistic approach sees this as an important principle of due process in practice. As with all codes of practice, the various statements are sometimes vague and generalized. A useful sum-mary of informed consent in health care, from the American Medical Association (2009), helps with this, because medicine has experienced many of the practical prob-lems; I have adapted this to apply to social work. It starts from building an understand-ing of informed consent:

Informed consent is more than simply getting people to sign written consent forms. It is a process of communication between clients and the people around them and practitioners that results in authorization or agreement to participate in specific interventions. In the communications process, the practitioners carrying out inter-ventions should disclose and discuss:

- The issues the practitioner is trying to tackle
- The nature and purpose of the proposed intervention
- The risks and benefits of the intervention
- Alternates (regardless of cost or availability)
- The risks and benefits of the alternates and
- The risks and benefits of not participating in the intervention

Box 2.3 National Ethics Codes on Informed Consent

Australian Association of Social Workers (2002)	British Association of Social Workers (2002)	Canadian Association of Social Workers (2005)	U.S. National Association of Social Workers (1999)
4.2.3(1) Informed consent a) Social workers will ensure that clients understand informed consent and the circumstances in which it may be required. b) Where clients have limited capacity to comprehend or grant informed consent, social workers will provide information in accordance with clients' level of understanding, restricting their freedom of decision and action as little as possible. c) When informed consent is required and the client cannot grant informed consent, social workers will, with the client's permission if applicable, obtain informed consent from a party empowered in accordance with relevant State legislation to provide consent on the client's behalf.	**4.1.4 Informed consent** Social workers will not act without the informed consent of service users, unless required by law to protect that person or another from risk of serious harm. Where service users' capacity to give informed consent is restricted or absent, social workers will as far as possible ascertain and respect their preferences and wishes and maintain their freedom of decision and action, whether or not another person has powers to make decisions on the service user's behalf. Where the law vests the power of consent in respect of a child in the parent or guardian, this in no way diminishes the social worker's duty to ascertain and respect the child's wishes and feelings, giving due weight to the child's maturity and understanding.	**1.3 Promote Client Self-Determination and Informed Consent** **1.3.1** Social workers promote the self-determination and autonomy of clients, actively encouraging them to make informed decisions on their own behalf. **1.3.2** Social workers evaluate a client's capacity to give informed consent as early in the relationship as possible. **1.3.3** Social workers who have children as clients determine the child's capacity to consent and explain to the child (where appropriate), and to the child's parents/guardians (where appropriate) the nature of the social worker's relationship to the child and others involved in the child's care (see section 1.5.5 regarding confidentiality). **1.3.4** Social workers, at the earliest opportunity, discuss with clients their rights and responsibilities and provide them with honest and accurate information regarding the following: ■ the nature of the social work service being offered;	**1.03 Informed Consent** (a) Social workers should provide services to clients only in the context of a professional relationship based, when appropriate, on valid informed consent. Social workers should use clear and understandable language to inform clients of the purpose of the services, risks related to the services, limits to services because of the requirements of a third-party payer, relevant costs, reasonable alternatives, clients' right to refuse or withdraw consent, and the time frame covered by the consent. Social workers should provide clients with an opportunity to ask questions. (b) In instances when clients are not literate or have difficulty understanding the primary language used in the practice setting, social workers should take steps to ensure clients' comprehension. This may include providing clients with a detailed verbal explanation or arranging for a qualified interpreter or translator whenever possible.

Box 2.3 Continued

Australian Association of Social Workers (2002)	British Association of Social Workers (2002)	Canadian Association of Social Workers (2005)	U.S. National Association of Social Workers (1999)
d) Depending on their maturity and level of understanding, children should be given the opportunity to indicate their assent or otherwise to services/treatment when consent is required from their parents or guardians.		■ the recording of information and who will have access to such information; ■ the purpose, nature, extent and known implications of the options open to them; ■ the potential risks and benefits of proposed social work interventions; ■ their right to obtain a second opinion or to refuse or cease service (recognizing the limitations that apply when working with involuntary clients); ■ the client's right to view professional records and to seek avenues of complaint; and ■ the limitations on professional confidentiality (see section 1.5 regarding confidentiality). 1.3.5 Social workers provide services to clients only on valid informed consent or when required to by legislation or court-ordered (see section 1.4 regarding involuntary clients). 1.3.6 Social workers obtain clients' informed consent before audio taping or video taping clients or permitting observation of services to clients by a third party.	(c) In instances when clients lack the capacity to provide informed consent, social workers should protect clients' interests by seeking permission from an appropriate third party, informing clients consistent with the clients' level of understanding. In such instances social workers should seek to ensure that the third party acts in a manner consistent with clients' wishes and interests. Social workers should take reasonable steps to enhance such clients' ability to give informed consent. (d) In instances when clients are receiving services involuntarily, social workers should provide information about the nature and extent of services and about the extent of clients' right to refuse service. (e) Social workers who provide services via electronic media (such as computer, telephone, radio, and television) should inform recipients of the limitations and risks associated with such services. (f) Social workers should obtain clients' informed consent before audiotaping or videotaping clients or permitting observation of services to clients by a third party.

In turn, the people involved should have an opportunity to ask questions to elicit a better understanding of the intervention, so that he or she can make an informed decision to proceed or to refuse a particular intervention. (Adapted from the original: AMA, 2009)

What this account makes clear is that getting informed consent is a process that takes place in a human relationship between the practitioner and others involved; it is therefore a humanistic process. It also involves due process; it is designed to make clear what clients are getting involved in and to ensure that they consent to it.

Informed consent is an issue in research as well as in professional practice. We can learn from research, because informed consent has been extensively worked out in this field. Wiles, Heath, Crow, and Charles (2005) review helpfully the issues that researchers have faced, and I have added to their analysis some practice examples. They identify two main approaches to research issues in health-care research:

- Rights-based approaches, which focus on respect for individuals, which involves protecting them from harm and encouraging participation
- Principles-based approaches, which focus on people being free to make their own decisions, not doing harm, doing only what brings benefit to people, and treating people equally in the process

The social sciences often require a broader approach, because the social context of research affects and is affected by the research itself, as follows:

- Rules-based approaches sometimes mean that imposing the rules makes the research impossible; we need to balance the rules against the benefits of achieving useful outcomes and devise flexible approaches that protect people. This argues for leaning toward a rights-based approach.
- There are often issues about participants' rights, such as privacy; respect; the right to know, for example, about organizational practices; and respect for the research field, as by not annoying people with insignificant research so that they will not cooperate with future studies that might be more important.

From this analysis, practitioners can balance their response between principles and rights. It is important to avoid being oversensitive about particular principles when a broader consideration of people's rights will better meet their needs. Researchers have also looked at many practical issues that can help practitioners keep this balance:

- Do people—for example, children, people with learning disabilities, people with mental illness, or older people with impaired mental capacity—have the mental and physical capacity to understand the information and express their consent? This question forces us to look at how we give information in ways that avoid putting pressure on people. This is particularly an issue when people think we might withdraw our services if they do not cooperate with us or where clienthood is involuntary. This is sometimes obvious to people involved with practitioners. For example, a parent might easily think, "Unless I cooperate with this practitioner's involvement in helping my family, he will have my children taken away from me." It is important to be clear when you are and when you are not saying something like that.

- What are the rules for withholding information? For example, if we are observing a situation to see whether children or older people are being abused, how much do we explain about what we are doing, and how do we do it? We might lose the opportunity to observe, or we might see only a performance put on for our benefit if we are open about what we are doing when we are observing.

- Connected to this, when do we provide information? A lot of complex information may be hard to take in, but if we do not give people the full picture, are we misleading them?

- Should we use incentives? For example, is it reasonable to get people's cooperation by promising them rewards or punishments? This is integral to some treatment systems that use behavioral approaches.

- Should we require written consent? Some treatment systems, such as task-centered practice, encourage written contracts, but does this put people off from receiving help because it makes the social work process too formal or official?

- Do you need consent from everyone who is likely to be involved? For example, if a mother and child consent to some family work, how far should we also get consent from the child's brothers and sisters, father, or grandparents, all of whom may come to be involved or might be indirectly affected?

- Do we get consent from other people who might be involved? For example, neighbors of children or mentally ill people whose behavior is causing problems in the community may expect action from the social worker to protect them rather than helping treatment of a family that they regard as a nuisance.

- To what extent and how do people have the right to withdraw from interventions once they have started, particularly if they are not the focal client? For example, if a father unwillingly agrees to involvement in family work but then decides that it is not for him, do we continue with other members of the family because this may still affect him? And what rights do other family members have to put pressure on him if they are benefiting from the intervention?

In many practice situations, these complexities are negotiated informally as the process unrolls. However, humanistic social work suggests to us that we should maintain a careful balance between treatment or intervention and openness, between human responsiveness and due process. An astute and defensive client or family often understands the implications of our approach to them and manages their response according to what is acceptable to them. They control information according to what they want to achieve and obstruct actions that they do not want. Being open works better and accords them their rights appropriately because it develops trust and includes them in decisions: trust means that their defensiveness is less necessary. People who are less aware of the implications of practitioners' involvements may accept engagement without really consenting to or understanding what is going on, and it is unfair and usually unnecessary to deceive them. Doing so also fails to engage them and treat them as equal human beings with ourselves.

Box 2.4 sets out a useful framework on informed consent, which can help practitioners ask themselves the right questions repeatedly as they move through a social work process.

Box 2.4 Framework for Informed Consent Planning

An informed consent plan	*Commentary and examples*
Who? Who is the focal client? Who else is likely to be involved in assessment, intervention? Who is affected by the issues that the practitioner is working with?	It is useful to identify the focal client and the role of others. For example, a child or person with intellectual disabilities may be the client, but much of the work may be done with their parents or carers. Consent to involvement by family or community members cannot be taken for granted.
Interests What are the interests of each person involved in the assessment and intervention process? What conflicts and continuities of interest exist among potential participants?	It is important to be clear whom the practitioner is responsible for and whose aims and needs are paramount. Is it the referrer or the public (e.g., in changing an offender's behavior)? Do parents' or carers' interests differ from those of the focal client? If so, separate but transparent information and consent processes may be needed.
The intervention Consider the assessment and intervention: What stages will it go through? At what stages will information and consent be required and renewed? What general information and consent resources and processes are available? How should they be adapted to promote participation by the people involved?	People may be prepared to give information, but not to engage in interventions. For example, if family members think a child is at fault, they may not be prepared to engage in or may not understand a family therapy approach. Does the therapeutic approach mandate explicit consent, for example, in cognitive-behavioral practice? Will information and consent be better if staged, or do earlier stages commit people to later interventions that they cannot withdraw from?

Box 2.4 *Continued*

An informed consent plan	*Commentary and examples*
Rights What rights to information and participation will each individual have? What forms of information and consent giving are appropriate to each person?	Focal clients and others involved may need different information and consent processes. Some people may be better able to deal with or may prefer written or verbal information or consent.
Resources What existing print, audio, video, electronic, intranet, and Internet information is available? What consent forms or documents are available and required by agency processes? What additional information and consent processes are required?	The agency or other organizations may have official information, but this may need to be adapted, explained, or used repeatedly. People with intellectual disabilities or older people may need to be reminded constantly of information or to have their consent redetermined if they appear uncertain.

ADVANCE CARE PLANNING

Advance care planning (ACP) is the process of finding out and recording people's wishes for how they want to be cared for or treated in the future. It is important in humanistic social work because it is an example of how to protect human rights to freedom of decision making through openness, particularly about difficult issues that some people try to avoid. Another aspect of its importance for social work is that it focuses on the reality that much so-called problem-solving social work is mainly concerned with arrangements for and provision of long-term care rather than counseling or personal problem solving. It is a process, so that the record is continually updated. The Canadian Hospice Palliative Care Association (2009) provides a particularly good definition:

> Advance care planning is a process of reflection and communication in which a person who is capable, makes decisions about future health and personal care in the event that they become incapable of giving informed consent. It involves:

- Thinking about what gives life meaning
- Talking to health care providers, family and friends about future health care wishes
- Thinking about who a person would like to speak for them, when they cannot speak for themselves
- Recording goals and wishes

Because this definition comes from a palliative care service, it emphasizes decision making when mental capacity is impaired, but a transparent ACP process also helps individuals think about and plan decisions of their own. Advance care planning connects with care planning, a stage in managed care or care management that involves discussing with clients and their caregivers the various options and putting those together in an agreed-on written plan. It also connects with planning as part of practice generally. However, Henry and Seymour's (2008) excellent guide to ACP focused on older people makes an important point: "The difference between ACP and planning more generally is that the process of ACP is to make clear a person's wishes and will usually take place in the context of an anticipated deterioration in the individual's condition in the future, with attendant loss of capacity to make decisions and/or ability to communicate wishes to others" (p. 3).

I would add to this that, when we use ACP with other client groups, for example, mentally ill people or people with intellectual disabilities, their capacity to make their own decisions about their care may vary over time. Also, it may take a good deal of effort to elicit their views about their care, so it is important to start early and take time and trouble to obtain and record their views. Another important point is that some groups, such as children in care, offenders, and people with intellectual disabilities, may be stigmatized to the extent that their views are not sought or that people think that their capacity to think through their preferences is not well developed. Most practitioners working with people in such groups know that they may extract from them considerable information about their preferences, and they often have well-formed views about their care, but people often fail to ask or take notice of what they say. People with disabilities may also suffer from others' assumptions that their disability means that they cannot have a good quality of life, and plans for positive options are given less importance than they would be for other adults (U.S. Department of Health and Human Services, 2008). Also, most ACP focuses on people whose capacity is deteriorating to the point of incapability, whereas many people with disabilities or mental illness may need to prepare for periods of illness rather than continuous deterioration in later life.

In end-of-life and palliative care, ACP connects with the process of creating advance decision, advance directives, or living wills, that is, legally enforceable statements of the patient's wishes not to receive particular treatments (Csikai & Chaitin, 2006). In the United States, the Patient Self-Determination Act of 1991 requires health-care facilities receiving Medicare and Medicaid funds to provide information about making advance directives and ask on admission whether patients have made one. Many U.S. states have a process for people to be able to appoint proxies to make treatment decisions on their behalf (U.S. Department of Health and Human Services, 2008). Many other countries have similar provisions. For example, in the United Kingdom, the Mental Capacity Act of 2005 makes provision for people to give others lasting powers of attorney to make decisions about their financial affairs and their personal welfare (Department of Constitutional Affairs, 2007). Advance directives or decisions are particularly an issue for people who have progressive diseases such as amyotrophic lateral sclerosis or multiple sclerosis, in which the physical condition deteriorates and the mind remains active. Many people in this position, once they lose most physical capacity, do not want to be treated for infections that may lead them to die earlier than they might if doctors did everything possible to keep them alive. However, doctors have a duty to provide treatment if they think it is in the best interests of their patients, so the advance directive refuses permission for a treatment. An advance directive is a negative; it says "don't treat me for this." The 2008 report from the U.S. Department of Health and Human Services to Congress, in its extensive review of practice and the literature, reflects international developments when it argues for a shift from "formal written advance directive forms to a developmental discussion process [and support for] a variety of models that recognize advance care planning as fundamentally a process rather than a product" (p. 41).

Henry and Seymour (2008) present this process as a series of building blocks (see box 2.5), starting from a record of people's wishes and feelings, and moving on to ACP and then later to formally constructed advance decisions, if they are required. However, helping people with positive advance planning for their care is not usually about large intervention decisions; it requires a concern for the minutiae of everyday life: the small things count in good care. If we keep giving people the ability to make everyday decisions and, I would say, support them in making the decisions and then implementing what they decide, we enhance their lives because they retain and develop the ability to make these decisions.

Advance care planning focuses on clients' preferences, not on practitioners' professional assessments. Talking with clients about what they want is a crucial part of any professional assessment, but practitioners' own judgments about needs color the outcomes. Assessment of needs is an important professional responsibility, and practitioners have a duty to carry it out comprehensively, so that full evidence and information is available to inform decision making. Comprehensive assessment also gives clients and their caregivers confidence that all their circumstances have been considered. In ACP, practitioners separate the process of helping people identify their preferences and wishes, in the

Box 2.5 Advance Care Planning Processes

Advance directives, formally recorded — Influence practitioners' care, intervention, and treatment decisions

Advance care planning, repeated discussion process — Influences choices and decisions

Preferences and wishes, formally recorded — Influence care options considered

Source: Diagrammatic representation of Henry and Seymour's (2008) analysis.

same way that we would separate the informal caregiver's wishes and needs from those of the client. Similarly, with children, practitioners distinguish a child's wishes and feelings, parents' views, and professional assessments of their needs.

So ACP involves focusing on clients' preferences and recording them clearly. This makes them more clearly available so that practitioners can compare clients' views with their own. This in turn provides for a transparent path along which the client's view may influence what practitioners think. Having a separate format for this is important, because most professional records systems or assessment forms focus on needs according to legislation or the agency's priorities.

Many people are not accustomed to thinking about the kind of issues that arise in ACP. A very good Australian format for ACP (Austin Health, 2007) grounds the process by starting with people's actual experience. It asks whether they have experienced or have seen with other people "a positive or difficult experience" (n.p.) with care, what could have been done better or differently. It then moves on to ask clients about current healthcare needs and any values or preferences that affect their views about it, future health, or care needs. Finally, it moves toward advance decisions by asking who should contribute to decisions about care needs in the future or who might make those decisions for people. This open approach is important because it starts from clients' perceptions of their situation; in the terminology of chapter 3, it starts from their narrative.

The U.K. Mental Capacity Act process, mentioned previously, which allows people to make a "lasting power of attorney" for personal welfare and separately for property and financial affairs means that another person (a proxy) may take over an individual's decisions if that person loses the capacity to do so. It may be registered with a national official, the public guardian (Office of the Public Guardian, 2009). The *Code of Practice* for the Mental Capacity Act (Department of Constitutional Affairs, 2007) suggests guidelines for helping people make decisions if they find this difficult as a preliminary to taking more formal action:

- Make sure they have all the relevant information and access to alternatives.
- Communicate appropriately.
- Help people feel at ease.
- Support them while they go through the process of making decisions.

There are a number of other formats for helping with the process of discussion. Box 2.6 shows one template for use at the very early stage of care planning. It is called thinking ahead. This is a neat phrase to use when introducing it to clients. One problem with this format is that it may be too vague to stimulate clear decisions, and I have found some of the alternative questions useful. Even the most articulate people may have trouble thinking about what particularly is good about their life. However, this use-it-early format illustrates how the whole process is intended to be integral to talking with clients at every stage.

Box 2.6 Advance Care Planning: Thinking Ahead

Thinking ahead . . .

1. At this time in your life, what is it that makes you happy?

Alternatives: Can you tell me about the major positive things in your life at this time? Can you tell me about three aspects of your life that are really important to you?

Examples: Seeing my grandchildren regularly. Being able to see my friends at the local bar. Being able to look at the family photographs.

2. What elements of care are important to you, and what would you like to happen in future?

Alternatives: If you were to need help with personal care in the future, can you tell me what aspects of care are especially important to you?

Examples: I would prefer to stay at home if at all possible. Having good food is very important to me. I like to be able to get out into the open air regularly.

3. What would you not want to happen? Is there anything that you worry about or fear happening?

Alternatives: If you were to need help with personal care in the future, can you tell me three important markers that would tell you when your care was going wrong?

Examples: I like to be clean, neat, and well dressed. I feel the cold very badly. I fear being in a lot of pain.

Source: Developed from Gold Standards Framework (2009).

      Box 2.7 shows another format that I have found useful and developed from the original. It is more highly specified, and the original was developed for people coming into a care home for the first time. It is a useful checklist to remind practitioners of the sort of issues that may be important to people when they are experiencing a major change in their lives.

      Henry and Seymour (2008) suggest that discussion about preferences should be documented and constantly updated. This might then focus on a formal statement of wishes and preferences. Finally, a political point: expressing preferences is not necessarily about making choices; it is a further step to say that clients can be in control of care decisions. Often this is not so, either because they are involuntary clients, such as offenders or children in care, or because there are not enough resources to meet their needs or because practitioners judge that alternate interventions are required. However, expressing their views clearly means that their preferences are more transparent, and, with respect to informed consent, practitioners can take people through understanding why they cannot have what they want and direct them toward any appeals process that is available. This enhances both justice and clients' security that practitioners are looking after their interests.

Box 2.7 Advance Care Planning: Detailed Checklist

Diet

Do you have any special dietary requirements?

Is there any food that you particularly dislike?

What are your regular mealtimes? Do you like to have snacks or refreshments at other times?

Do you drink alcohol?

  Never, sometimes, or regularly?

  Before meals, with meals, in the evening, or on special occasions?

  Beer, wine, or spirits?

Other diet preferences:

Dress

What style of dress do you prefer to wear? Around the house or in public?

On a special occasion? When going to bed?

Other dress preferences:

Grooming

How often do you have your hair cut and/or styled?

Do you use makeup?

Do you get manicures or pedicures?

Do you wear glasses for distance or reading, or other glasses?

Other grooming preferences:

Bathing

Do you prefer to shower or take a bath? How often?

Do you shave or have hair removal?

  Women (legs, armpits, and other):

  Men (frequency and wet/electric razor):

Health Care

Do you visit the dentist regularly?

Who is your regular doctor?

If you have no regular doctor, do you have a preference for a male or female doctor?

Do you have a flu vaccination annually?

Do you have particular fears or issues about your health?

Religion

Do you have any important religious beliefs or faith?

Do you regularly attend a place of worship?

Source: Developed from English Community Care Association (2007).

Therefore, expressing preferences helps with due process: we have clearly listened to, recorded, and given ourselves the best chance of being influenced by clients' wishes. It also permits clarity about when we are going against clients' wishes, and it allows us to plan toward meeting their wishes in the future rather than just accepting a status quo that they feel is unsatisfactory. Also, ACP helps with equality, the focus of the next chapter, because it gives everyone the chance to be listened to. Finally, it helps practitioners make good decisions and interventions, because they can base their judgments on a clear expression of clients and informal caregivers' wishes.

Case Example: Mrs. Truman's Return Home

Picking up on Mrs. Truman's return home, we can see a number of factors discussed here at work. First, if there had been advance care planning prior to Mrs. Truman's fall, the family would have had a previously discussed and agreed-on plan in mind. This does not require a fraught discussion of possible disasters but more of a family discussion on some suitable occasion about what would happen in the event of a temporary period of dependence, like Mrs. Truman's fall. Such a discussion also needs to look at a range of scenarios; it requires a different approach if she seems to be becoming permanently more frail. This might also involve some financial planning. When Mrs. Truman came into the hospital, family members would already be aware of possible routes for the future.

Second, the hospital staff had not achieved truly informed consent. They had held a meeting at Mrs. Truman's bedside with Erin present, when they discussed staying with her. Erin, sitting with her worried mother, accepted the proposed plan, and the hospital staff had taken for granted that Erin could work out the family and community consequences and that Mrs. Truman would behave in a reasonable way and so would facilitate a positive family response to her needs.

Third, they had failed to look at the human consequences in seeing the plans they were making as a routine practical arrangement. Their answer to an adverse emotional reaction was psychological; they provided effective cognitive-behavioral therapy. But a human and humanistic response is to look at social agency alongside psychological efficacy—what social barriers and expectations would affect the outcome?

Fourth, it is important to understand patterns of power relations. The hospital has the power here to define the situation: "we have done our job, the treatment, now it's over to you." General social expectations put pressure on the family. Community experiences led the family to fear that the hospital would abandon them to cope. In all social situations, we must expect that there will be pressure, experiences, and expectations of this kind to be worked out.

When Mrs. Truman went to her daughter's house, there was a breakdown in relationships after a few days. Mrs. Truman was critical of her daughter's home arrangements and her teenage children's behavior. This led to interpersonal tensions, which Catherine helped to defuse by holding a family conference: how can we hold on here? Part of the answer was her having some tactful discussions with Mrs. Truman about managing her feelings about her daughter's family. Another part of the answer was a family plan for more leisure time together, some to involve Mrs. Truman, so that she did not feel excluded, and some just for the teenagers and Erin and her husband. Again, here, humanistic practice assumes that attention to both broader social relationships is required simultaneously with individual work. One will be ineffective without the other.

A final point: the hospital's attitude that it is discharging a cured patient is part of power relations here. Its definition of its role is part of the power relations that have created problems for this family. That definition has probably also contributed to community perceptions of the hospital. In humanistic practice, no institution can operate only according to its own internal assumptions; it must also be aware of its own place in the social environment. We should not talk about the hospital in this way; it is a collection of social groupings affected by social expectations, for example, funding and resources. Catherine cannot change this on her own; nor can the social work team. But it would be possible to change this, over the long term, by a strategic combination of demonstrating human realities to professional colleagues, carrying out professional audits of practice and outcomes, participating in professional and multiprofessional research and publications, and facilitating expressions of community attitudes through participatory machinery and political action. A complete humanistic response to Mrs. Truman's human situation would include such actions, because it would facilitate more effective social agency by families and groups in the community.

CONCLUSION

In this chapter, I have focused on accountability in the dual sense of making sense of our lives and of accepting responsibility to other. I have pointed to the importance of accountability to the people practitioners serve, as well as to agency and organizational accountability. We have explored many situations in which personal accountability to clients connects with organizational accountability. One often cannot be achieved without the other. Clear thinking about accountability to the professional objectives of our practice enables us to balance the three main objectives of social work in our practice. I have introduced social work practice on informed consent and advanced care planning as important techniques that may be widely applied for ensuring accountability to clients and agencies in practice.

FURTHER READING

Sen, A. (2009). *The idea of justice*. London: Allen Lane.
A recent inspiring discussion of justice, focusing on economic and political justice.

WEB SITES

To follow up on advance care planning, you may find the following documents and Internet sites useful:

Canadian Hospice Palliative Care Association. (2009). *Advance care planning in Canada: A national framework and implementation (ACP Project)*. Ottawa: Author. Retrieved from http://www.chpca.net/projects/advance_care_planning/advance_care_planning _index.html.

U.S. Department of Health and Human Services. (2008). *Advance directives and advance care planning: Report to Congress*. Washington, DC: Author. Retrieved from http://aspe.hhs.gov/daltcp/reports/2008/ADCongRpt.pdf.

Achieving Personal and Social Equality

CHAPTER AIMS

The main aim of this chapter is to establish the importance of pursuing equality in social work practice. Practitioners' relationships and interactions with people involved should display equality. Also, enhancing social equality is an important part of the social work role.

After working through this chapter, readers should be able to

- Understand different meanings of equality in social work. This means distinguishing promoting equal opportunities practices from equal outcomes practices that also enhance affective equality.
- Enhance quality in human relationships between practitioners and clients.
- Understand and overcome power differences between practitioners and clients.
- Use narrative approaches to permit clients' voices to have impact on intervention and care decisions.
- Develop empowerment through humanistic practice.

EQUALITY AND SOCIAL WORK PRACTICE

Humanistic ideas recognize that all human beings are equally human, so humans must treat other humans as equal to them. In tension with this idea, our humanity means that we are all different as individuals. When we are presented with many diversities, how do we see and treat people as equal? Social work practice must recognize and sustain equality and at the same time value and promote diversity. Chapter 2 focused on balancing interpersonal work on individual psychological efficacy and group social agency. Incorporating this into thoughts about equality, humanistic practitioners need to practice interpersonally in ways that promote equality, and they need to enhance equality between social groups so as to empower people to use any individual gains in their lives more generally. This connects with the process and outcome forms of justice that we examined in chapter 2. By acting transparently through such processes as informed consent, social workers enable people to take up their personal responsibility for themselves.

By facilitating clients' participation in planning social work practice interventions, social workers enable clients to influence the outcomes of their practice. Practice like this demonstrates that clients are coequal in social work practice; that is, they are together with practitioners in the actions that they take together.

We can take these ideas forward into our thinking about equality. They mean that we must do equality, not just aim for it. Attaining equality is central to leftist thinking and a Marxist policy objective (Fitzpatrick, 2005), and this sometimes leads people to think that concern with equality is only a communist or socialist objective that requires macropractice aimed at social equality. Fitzpatrick (2005) argues that equality as a policy aim cannot be dealt with only as a stand-alone policy objective; it needs to be part of other aims as practitioners put policy into action. However, equality is also a widely accepted principle inherent in the human rights charters that we examined in chapter 1. The humanist and humanistic psychology principle of equality is that, in their humanity, all people are equal; however, does that mean that they are equal in every way, and particularly in their personal capacities, social backgrounds, and luck?

Case Example: Harry and His Family

Harry grew up in a loving family with a strong paternal role model, and in turn, he became an active, responsible man. He stuck with his education, and he gained work skills and a well-paid job in a factory. He married and had a daughter and a son. His wife worked also, and they saved enough money to get a mortgage on a house, and they built a good home for their family. Then Harry had an accident at work that caused a brain injury. It was partly the fault of the employer, who paid compensation, but partly was caused by Harry's momentary inattention. Although he tried to return to work after treatment, he was unsafe in the factory and had a long period of unemployment. A disability pension sustained the family, but eventually their home was repossessed, and the family moved into rented housing and eventually public housing. I came into contact with the family because Harry's brain damage had led to a personality change that resulted in relationship problems in the family. There were fears of domestic violence, difficulties for the children at school, and a need for child protection.

Looking at equality issues in Harry's life story, you could say that his family support had enabled him to have a good start, though this had led to industrial work, where there is a higher risk of workplace injury than in office work, for which you need a different, more academic education, which some people regard as better than vocational skills training. Because office work would have been safer, Harry's job choice increased the risk of destabilizing the family. The accident was partly the employer's fault and partly Harry's fault—was it "bad luck," or was it Harry's responsibility? Even if it were his fault, should the family have to suffer because of it? But their relationships, which include Harry, are important to them, so there is a mixture of good and bad for him.

In many case situations, practitioners are likely to face a number of complex issues like this. It is, therefore, important to think about what equality means and the values we bring to issues of equality.

PAUSE AND REFLECT: What Kinds of Equality?
_____

Review several situations in your life or cases in your practice in which you have been concerned about inequality. List the factors in the situations that you think may have led to inequality. List the people whom inequalities adversely affected, then who gained from the inequality. Last, think about people other than the main people involved who may have benefited or lost from the inequality.

Some Suggestions

Among the situations you looked at, you may have felt that someone did not get the chances in life that most people get, and so that person did not do as well as intelligence or ability suggested that he or she might. Or you may have thought about people who failed to receive a service that someone else in the same position may have received easily. Or, again, you may have thought of someone who was treated badly or excluded from participation in an enjoyable activity because of some character trait or family constraint—perhaps participation cost money that the person could not afford. We saw in chapter 2 that we learn through experience to juggle complex elements of fairness, thus building on innate fairness judgments. We refine these judgments over time with reasoned arguments that we turn into principles of justice. Humanistic practice calls on our intuitive sense of fairness and backs it up with ethical principles in practice.

Particularly if you were thinking about your own practice, you may have thought of people who were unequal because of race or ethnic identity, a physical disability, an intellectual disability, a mental illness, or age. You may have identified someone who was discriminated against because he or she came from a poor part of a city or practiced a religion different from Christianity—perhaps they were Jewish or Muslim—or who had a criminal record or a history of drug or alcohol addiction. Among the factors you may have thought about were stigma because of a particular characteristic, which is the contribution to discrimination of what some people might have thought of as deviant behavior in the past. You may also have thought of situations in which people lost out because of assumptions about them—that a young person was not mature enough to be trusted, for example, or an older person was thought to be at risk.

Who was affected? The individual who was treated unequally may have been adversely affected, although some might claim that he or she had also been protected. The individual's family and people around him or her may also have been affected. Someone did not receive a scholarship or a job, so the family was poorer and had to struggle more as a result. More indirect losses might have occurred: a lot of unemployed people in one area makes the whole population less wealthy, and then businesses cannot be sustained and the quality of the environment may deteriorate because people cannot maintain their house and yard. People in society may be affected more broadly, too, because a society does not make good use of all the talent and resources it has. Excluded people may be dissatisfied and more likely to become angry, cause conflict, or become depressed or anxious about their position and need more medical or social help.

Who benefited? People who were preferred benefited. People may also have bene-fited because they did not have to take trouble. For example, employers could have given people with disabilities or mental illness a job if they had spent a bit of additional money to make it possible for them to work in that job, but there was less hassle and expense in not giving them the job. Whole communities also benefit from the poverty and exclusion of others. If a poor part of the city has many unemployed people, drug addicts, and alco-holics, then home prices and shopping and leisure may improve somewhere else because that is where there are people to spend money on using the facilities. People who are doing OK also benefit, because there is less competition for the things that benefit them, and they can gain more influence. Well-educated young people, given many benefits by their better-off families, have less need to struggle to find and stay in jobs. When an older person in a well-off family progresses toward more serious Alzheimer's disease, the fam-ily can afford a better care package or care home and can make more time or employ more support, so they experience less adversity and feel less guilt and stress than a poorer family who has to do more itself and cannot afford good facilities.

Another factor in some of these experiences is the response of the service providers and practitioners who work in those services. A good response to the poorer family with a frail older person in their midst can reduce the stress and equalize the quality of the older person's life up to the level attained by an older person from a well-off family. However, knowing about stigma and exclusion can also exclude someone from help. For example, someone with serious depression or anxiety may be a real problem for local services but refuse to get help. The reason is that, by getting treatment for a mental ill-ness, that person is labeled with a condition that might exclude him or her from being a valued person, which results in that person being in a more unequal position in other situations.

People affected by several factors that may lead to inequality may therefore find their inequality doubled, tripled, or even more. For example, if they come from a black minority ethnic group, discrimination against them may be worse if they are also elderly, mentally ill, or have intellectual disabilities.

Humanistic social work responds to all of these issues in two ways:

- Humanistic objectives focus on clients' human rights alongside therapeutic and organizational objectives, as we saw in chapter 1.
- Humanistic methods link individualistic practice with personal and inter-personal objectives and social change in how the individual's environment moved forward; this was the focus of chapter 2.

Recursive patterns in power relations, that is, patterns that are forced to recur by social structures that we cannot easily overcome, mean that there will always be tensions between individual objectives and external objectives. Those tensions are expressed in barriers to achieving personal needs through interpersonal psychological help. Therefore, the interpersonal benefit of being involved in personal help through social work connects to social benefits of raising issues to achieve more general social changes that will facili-tate the social agency of groups and communities in clients' social environments.

PRINCIPLES OF PRACTICING EQUALITY

Thinking through our ideas about equality and diversity makes clear that we deal with complex phenomena. It is hard to identify what issues we should seek to deal with, if we want to aim at equality. Also, as time goes on, we seem to face demands for more action with more and different inequalities. Perhaps we started by being worried about inequalities between ethnic groups or gender difference, and then we came to think about many other inequalities between social groups. Baker, Lynch, Cantillon, and Walsh (2004) usefully distinguish two positions, which can help us disentangle some of these complexities:

- Equal opportunities practice derives from liberal egalitarianism. It assumes that inequality will always be present, and thus our aim should be to make fairer how inequality operates within our societies. We achieve this by universal citizenship, which accords everyone the same rights; this goes alongside toleration of minorities and individual freedom of action. Because liberal egalitarianism considers inequalities in resources and poverty to be inevitable, competition should be regulated so that there is equal opportunity to access resources, particularly in employment and education, as these are the route to poverty reduction. People have civil and personal rights; democratic institutions limit the power of elites to control their lives.

In an equal opportunities approach, we say, in effect, this: "We make sure we give you the opportunities, so that you can step up to the plate and achieve what you want." We can implement this sort of view through the human rights ideas we looked at in chapter 1. If we take this position, we would be careful of people's rights; work hard to treat them with due process, such as using informed consent; and make sure that people have fair access to the resources that we are responsible for. We would fight for their rights, and we would support democratic institutions that provide services for people. Part of this we would do as citizens, but as professionals, administrators, and officials, we would also make sure to pursue people's rights.

The problem of an equal opportunities approach is that some people are so disadvantaged by their life experience that they are unable to take up the opportunities that come to them. This suggests that we must go further.

- Equal outcomes practice derives from equality of condition ideas. It seeks to eliminate or reduce major inequalities—ideally to put everyone in the same position, but at least to move toward this. In addition to according rights to citizens, equal outcomes practice celebrates and encourages diversity and recognizes alternative behaviors and preferences. We do this so that people who are different are sure that we value their difference. In addition to reducing poverty, resources are targeted at disadvantaged groups, particularly through public services, to nullify their initial disadvantage. Societies should recognize and support people's needs for affiliation, love, and support. Persistent patterns of power that sustain inequalities are challenged and dismantled. Undervalued work, such as unpaid or low-paid caring work, is given more resources and support, and alternative work-life balances are promoted to support the value of human self-actualization outside education and work that focuses on achievement within conventional business and political success.

We can see some of the ideas we associate with secular humanism and humanistic practice coming through in ideas of equality of condition. They tell us that all human beings should have the same conditions of life, even though, of course, they are diverse and do not share many personal characteristics. As a consequence, we try to create conditions of life that are equivalent but appropriate to the differences in people.

It may seem hard to work for differences that we do not experience ourselves, but there are experiences of life that we can all share, even though we experience them differently than people who do live those differences. In particular, being an active part of society, being accepted by the people around us, being loved and supported, and having the opportunity to love and support others recognizes important basic needs that all people experience. This "affective inequality" (Lynch, Baker, & Lyons, 2009) suggests that an important objective should be affective equality.

People need love and caring in their lives, and to offer love, affection, and caring to others. In this way, human beings build solidarity and sharing with the people around them, and they create families, communities, and other social groups. This support is crucial for their personal identity. The ideas of equality of condition and affective equality emphasize that justice is not just about the allocation of resources in society or mutual respect. Inequality in being able to participate in an emotional life also connects with the inequalities experienced by many people who are part of socially excluded groups.

Case Study: The Refugee in Later Life

Phuoc was a refugee from Vietnam. He had left as part of the "boat people," who made dangerous sea journeys to escape from Vietnam after the war of the 1960s and 1970s. He had traveled with his wife, but she had died quite young, and he now lived alone. They had one son who went to college and was now married and working in a distant city. Work as a builder had taken Phuoc to different parts of the country, and he had settled in an attractive suburb of the town where he and his wife had started their new life. However, this was a long way from the local Vietnamese community near the center of the city. He maintained some contacts with old friends, but he developed diabetes and eventually lost his sight suddenly as a result of the disease. This made getting around much more difficult. The local association for blind people helped him manage his blindness, and he was living a comfortable life. However, he increasingly was feeling homesick for his mother country, he only rarely saw friends and family, and he missed his wife. Although all the practical needs for living were taken care of, he did not want to spend his time with other blind people. An effective social work service would also look at how he can maintain relationships and give and receive support from people with whom he feels personal connections.

Having a concern for affective inequalities draws attention to the ways in which our society may prevent individual people from pursuing human love, affection, support, and solidarity and cast them into social groups in which our society does not facilitate people's experiences of these important human emotions. For example, arranging for people with mental illnesses to drop in regularly at a day center may cut them off from other supportive relationships in their local community because their main connections are with a broader group of people who share their stigmatizing illness. Putting people in the same position as others, therefore, means thinking not only about their financial resources or their equality before the law but also about their emotional experience of the society around them. This is a particularly important part of working on equality for social workers, whose role is to connect the personal with the social.

PAUSE AND REFLECT: Affective and Social Inequalities

Think about one or more of the following groups: migrants moving to another country, where they form a minority ethnic group; women suffering domestic violence from their partners; lesbian, gay, transgender, and bisexual (LGTB) people who want to parent children. How might they experience affective inequality?

Some Suggestions

Migrants may be isolated from other people who share their background, and experience racial discrimination because of their ethnicity and difficulty in establishing a family relationship in accordance with both their traditions and the cultural expectations of their new country. Women who experience domestic violence in their relationships may be fearful and lonely in their family relationships and may not have opportunities to parent their children alongside their partner as they would wish. Some LGTB people may be excluded from parenting by former sexual partners or from adoption and foster care, or they may not have opportunities to form relationships that permit parenting. In all these situations, and many more, opportunities to receive support from others and to have loving relationships may be limited or unavailable.

Taking an equal outcomes approach that also incorporates a concern for affective equality would press us to promote diversity in our services, so that they provide for the greatest possible range of diversity in the population we serve. We would also work for the development and secure funding of services, particularly in the public sector, if this would secure consistent collective support from the community for our clients. We would try to question and remove barriers to our clients' self-actualization and full participation and inclusion in their communities. We would particularly emphasize support for informal caregivers and well-balanced lifestyles, appropriate leisure, and good care for children and vulnerable adults. We would support fruitful family life rather than long working hours or personal obsessions. We would promote affective equality, the chance to love and to be loved, to support and to be supported; to be part of social relationships that mean something to us. An emphasis merely on providing services to deal with problems and not on addressing affective losses is not good practice in humanistic social work.

Seeking people's well-being requires, according to Gough (2004), a sense that there are universal needs that everyone should be able to attain. He argues that human beings have a propensity to adapt to individual and collective misfortunes and gains. He also argues that we should not rely just on individuals' subjective sense of well-being, because in adapting, they may come to accept oppressions that an independent observer would say are inappropriate. Giving people knowledge about unfairness in their lives is not enough to counteract the tendency to adapt; instead, people need a degree of autonomy, competence, and relatedness. That is, they have to be sufficiently free to make their own decisions; they have to have and be able to interpret and understand the knowledge that will enable them to do so, and they need a sense of connection with others so that they can have support in changing or managing their life in ways that are right for them. For affective equality, they need to be free to express mutual love and support. This can be particularly important for older people or people with disabilities, because others might assume, for example, that they cannot have or renew sexual relationships or that they are bound to be lonely or isolated. The idea of the organization Phab (physically handicapped and able-bodied; http://www.phab.org.uk/index.php), for example, in which disabled and able people take the trouble to participate in activities together, often focuses on young disabled people, but such activities that provide a setting for disabled and nondisabled people to share social activities can be equally beneficial for older people. These ideas, again, connect people's personal experience of inequality with the responsibility of any society to ensure that its citizens can incorporate important freedoms in their lives.

For practitioners, therefore, there are different kinds of equality to focus on:

- Equality between practitioners and clients as human beings in the interpersonal relationship through which we do our work. Humanistic social work handles this through a dialogue and narrative approach to engaging with clients and the people around them. Social workers do this because it allows others to bring into practice and express their own conception of the issues that they face and the meaning of those issues for their personal growth.

- Equality of client access to the services we provide or organize. Humanistic social work handles this through effective assessment, due process, and advocacy in its dealings with clients and agencies.

- Enhancing people's personal and institutional power toward self-actualization for themselves and the people around them. Humanistic social work handles this through empowerment practice in interpersonal relationships and social groups.

- Contributing to changes in the patterns of power so that greater equality is available to everyone in society. Humanistic social work handles this by focusing on advocacy for human rights, in agency interventions and macropractice.

DISCOURSE, DIALOGUE, AND NARRATIVE

Social work mainly works through interpersonal relationships. When we start to learn social work, we focus on interviewing skills and questioning styles that enable us to focus on issues that are important for our agency and its job and to pull out the information that will be useful for our task. Humanistic ideas suggest that this is only a beginning. Those techniques should be used to build an interpersonal relationship between whole human beings, people operating as whole persons who have a body and therefore a physical presence when they are with other people, not just a set of tasks set by an organization to carry out with a set of problems that are relevant to those tasks. The practice involves interpersonal interactions in which people influence one another; some of the interaction is unspoken, some spoken. The influence affects the participants' minds through emotion and intuitive reactions, as we have seen in chapter 2, but also, in humanist thought, crucially through reasoning. Therefore, social work operates through the language of the bodies, the minds, and the spirits of the people engaged together in the interaction. Language develops from and within the cultures of the people involved. So mind, body, spirit, culture, interaction, influence—all these are expressed in a social work intervention and work together in a complex way. These aspects of the interaction recur throughout this book.

The starting point of this interaction in humanistic practice is to influence people in their humanity through their reasoning mind. We can gain access to that reasoning only through the use of language, because reasoning can be expressed only through talking in a human relationship. Therefore, to understand and pursue social work, we have to understand influencing people through human spoken interaction. Extensive empirical study of human communication through speech and behavior was an important development of the last part of the twentieth century. However, language and its use in literature and cultures has been a fascination of human beings probably since language developed.

An important recent development has been to see human interaction as a discourse. There are many different definitions and interpretations of the meaning of discourse, and it connects with the idea of being discursive, that is, discussing the issues that arise around a topic as well as the specific topic itself. Howarth (2000) has identified three main historical elements to the idea of discourse:

- The starting point is the idea of investigating "language in use" and "talk in context" as part of linguistics, particularly social linguistics. This means looking at how people use language and how their social environment and personal development influence that use.
- Phenomenological sociologists, ethnomethodologists, and poststructuralists, in particular Foucault (1972), used the idea of discourse to investigate wider social practices, which at least in Foucault's later work, include how discourses shaped by social practices in turn shape social institutions. In particular, Foucault was interested in how we use power in human relationships. Power in human relations becomes established in social patterns and social institutions that allow people who gain power to exercise social control through social institutions. They do this by using social influence to discipline others and by using surveillance to control what people do. For Foucault, discourse has a special meaning; it is looking at social relations to identify where and how power is expressed in them.

■ This idea in turn has been extended in investigations such as Fairclough's (1992) "critical discourse analysis" (p. 12) to nondiscursive practices in a wider range of social relations. A nondiscursive practice is evidence of human relationships that is accumulated in nonhuman forms. For example, analyzing a social work textbook tells you something about how social workers think and act; analyzing a comprehensive set of textbooks gives you evidence about the debates among social workers about their practice. This could show you the differences of opinion within social work and different forms of practice; you might not see these by just watching social workers or asking them about their practice, because they appear to do similar things. But the texts could tell you how the apparently similar things have a variety of aims. Bringing this point closer to practice, we can look at social workers' aims and methods in influencing their clients in their practice by critically examining their records. This would enable us to see consistencies and inconsistencies in how they react to events in clients' lives. Do they always seem to defuse aggressive behavior only when it adversely affects, for example, powerful people, whereas they do not try so much to control aggression toward powerless people?

The first approach focuses on and limits itself purely to linguistic practices, and it tells us that we should examine carefully how people use language. This helps us in social work because we express both our individual ideas and thinking in what we say and how we say it and patterns of relationships, power, culture, and other aspects of the social environment. Foucault's approach and others like it still emphasize the importance of texts and talk, but they go beyond those things. Texts are pieces of language, writing, or action that demonstrate social relationships in some way, and because they do this, by deconstructing what people say and do, you can understand the social relationships and influences that have affected them. Critical discourse analysis and similar techniques look at debates and arguments among people with different interests, to see how the discourse between their points of view reveals broader truths about the nature of the issues that those people face.

Case Study: Discourse in the Care Home

These are complicated ideas, and a case study may help explain them. I once worked with a care home for older people. I was responsible for managing the assessment of people for admission to the home, and I chaired the residents' committee, which planned social events and took up issues that residents were concerned about. The care home was managed by a female manager and a male deputy. The aim of having my external involvement, from the point of view of the operators of the home, was to have an external person who could stimulate more interesting and worthwhile activity for the residents (hence the committee). It also allowed me to have a closer knowledge of the home and the consequences of admissions that I might be considering on the workload and management of the home. I was an outsider not only in my job but also in the culture of the area; most residents were local people and the managers had also always lived in the area.

One linguistic difference was that I had a different accent and way of speaking from everyone else involved, and this reflected class, cultural, and status differences. Our different ways of talking would show to anyone that I was a higher-status outsider. This is an example of the first kind of linguistic analysis—you can identify social patterns from speech and how people interact. We tend to use knowledge and experience of this kind of analysis unthinkingly, and perhaps without formal knowledge.

When I visited the home to see the managers or to chair the committee, it was polite to stop by the office and notify the managers that I was in the home; by contrast, visitors from the locality came in and out to visit their friends and relatives by meeting people in the residents' lounges or rooms. I would chair the committee meetings, and they were set up as fairly formal affairs. By looking at those arrangements and the topics discussed, you could see that, although I had responsibilities in the home, the home's operators benefited from my external "surveillance." The fact that I would visit, see residents, and discuss issues of concern with them was one of the ways the operators exercised control over the ways the managers ran the home. It was a discipline that they had to accept that residents might complain to me about things that the care home managers might not want the operators to hear about. This is the second kind of discourse analysis, to look for power relations, which are often unstated but are readily apparent from the processes that are openly going on.

The managers and I would often discuss among ourselves the people waiting or applying to come into the home. Often, residents would have something to say about this, because as local people, applicants were mostly well known to them. However, managers and residents were concerned with the manageability and congeniality of the home, and I also had to be concerned with the management of frail older people in the community if they were not admitted. So debates would take place about the consideration of particular people. In some cases, the debates represented personal views about the individuals concerned. Often, though, they also represented different ideas about what the home represented. For example, it was the residents' home and the managers sought to make it homelike, domestic. For me, it was a way of managing need in a population of frail older people; if I admitted people whose need was greatest, it might become more problematic for the domesticity of the home. There was also an element of surveillance in this discourse, too, because if the managers found my decisions unreasonable, they could complain to the operators. This was a discipline of me in my job role. Negotiations about admissions were often barely concealed power struggles about the role of the home in the community and in the wider services of the area.

Analyzing those discourses is an example of deconstruction; I am taking apart the language and debates and looking beneath the surface to power relationships, discipline, and surveillance. If human linguistic interactions represent power relationships, it will be obvious that, if we wish to maintain a sense of interpersonal equality in our relationships with clients, we also have to deconstruct the spoken interactions that we have as we practice and adapt how we speak to equalize power in our interactions with our clients. Spoken interactions are important, but actions can speak power just as effectively as words, and so part of our conversations are how we act, as well as what we say. This connects with the importance of congruence in practice, that is, that clients perceive practitioners to behave in ways that are consistent with what they say. I discuss this in chapter 4.

Conversations between people are typically an exchange, and people take turns interacting. If more than two people are present, there may be a shared conversation, among the practitioner, a wife, a husband, and a child, and several dialogues going on at the same time. We are all familiar with situations in which some conversations are shared with children while others are reserved *pas devant les enfants*; this is a representation of parental power over the children. There may be leakage, because they may overhear what parents talk about, and alongside overhearing, power leaks, too, because the parents cannot maintain the power of their secrecy.

Using dialogue, people exchange parts of their minds. They offer and test out with the other person information and interpretation about the world; in this way, they come to know and understand in their own way what the other person has experienced. Because the practitioner manages the dialogue to assist in the helping process, he or she will choose how to respond to the conversational offering.

Case Example: Katya's Interpretation of Her Husband's Behavior

In a part of an assessment interaction, Katya said, "I was angry that my husband seemed to ignore our daughter," and conveyed information about her own feeling response and about her perception of her husband's behavior. The practitioner might say, "How did he ignore her?" seeking information about the husband's behavior that had sparked Katya's perception of his attitudes and her emotional response. It is always useful in an assessment dialogue to secure information first before going into interpretations and responses, because having concrete information allows different possible interpretations and responses to be explored. With the information, the practitioner might say, "Perhaps he was trying to give her space to learn by exploring." Katya might not have thought of that: it might reframe her perception. Or she might say "No, I don't think so, because . . ." and the practitioner will understand more of her thinking. If the reply describes other typical husband behavior, she might also learn something about the relationship context of Katya's perception. She can come back to Katya's reaction later, perhaps by saying, "What do you think made you react so angrily?" This puts some responsibility for a conflict about the husband's behavior with Katya's interpretation of it. However, in an intervention interaction, the practitioner might ask about the reaction first, because working on the present relationship is more important in intervention than understanding the development of the relationship, which will already be shared between them. Going back through the feelings to the informational basis of them maintains the focus of the intervention.

The practitioner needs to maintain and improve the dialogue. Among the difficulties that arise in dialogue is the situation in which people are either very talkative or say little or nothing. Priestley and McGuire (1983), partly based on psychological research have guidance for both of these situations, presented in box 3.1.

Box 3.1 Talkative and Quiet Clients

Too talkative?	*Too quiet?*
Ask lots of questions.	Talk less—use silence.
Cut them off if they stray.	Ask open-ended questions.
Tell them they are talking too much.	Focus on things that interest the other person.
Offer a quick end if they are more concise.	
Repeat the aims of the dialogue.	Reward the person with interest and focus on what he or she says.
Ask someone to join you to keep the dialogue on the rails.	Look at the techniques to deal with people who are too talkative: many of these also apply to people who are too quiet.
Deal with anxieties and fears.	
Offer a different session to separate issues.	
Get someone else to take on some issues.	
End the session and start again at a different time.	

Source: Priestley and McGuire (1983).

Looking at these practical techniques draws attention to the value of focusing on the client's interests rather than on those of the practitioner or agency. This leads to the importance of taking a narrative approach to practice.

Narrative is the process of asking clients to present information and interpretations as a story. This helps in several ways. First, it feels natural to clients to do this, and storytelling is a part of traditional life in any community. The oral tradition of storytelling has been a central way to pass on knowledge and understanding for generations. It continues to be an important part of modern entertainment, in books, cinema, and television, so it is familiar and acceptable as an approach. Using a narrative approach may helpfully contrast with what other professionals do. For example, in a medical interview, doctors often focus on diagnosis, so that rather than listening to a story in their patient's own words, doctors often elicit an initial concern and then ask specific questions to identify symptoms of concern and eliminate possible diagnoses. Although this is efficient for its purpose, it does not feel to the patient like a listening process, which is what social work practitioners are after.

Second, in creating a narrative, people identify explanations that they think are important. This is because narratives are linear. Their sequence of events describes how they think of a linear sequence of events and the factors that, in their minds, explain what happened. By being clear about what happened, practitioners can build on this to pull out of the narrative why a particular sequence of events happened and whether there are alternate perceptions or stories about it. This begins the process of making the narrative nonlinear; it has alternate structures. We look at this in chapter 5, on complexity.

Third, constructionist psychotherapies use narratives as ways to intervene with psychological and personal problems (White & Epston, 1990). The basic approach here is to create space for alternative stories by drawing on how literature approaches narrative. By "re-storying," clients may identify alternate narratives about their experiences, which can lead to changes in their attitudes. They may also see different ways forward. An important aspect of this is that they see themselves as active and able to make a difference in the story of their lives rather than as having things done to them. Practitioners do this by asking questions that assume people's active involvement, and they help develop clients' awareness of their own explanations and possibilities for future actions. Some of the kinds of questions that might help are set out in box 3.2. I am referring to the book on narrative therapy by Martin Payne (2006); this is not me. Many

Box 3.2 Some Questions That Help in Re-storying

Types of questions	*How they might help*
Landscape of action: by understanding the landscape in which things happened, you can see how things might be different now or in the future	Helps focus on the environment affecting clients, in which they take action rather than on their behavior or decisions
How did you make preparations to do that?	Emphasizes that the client would have planned rationally and taken action; things do not just happen to you
What went on at the time that this happened? Who contributed to what happened and how?	Gets clients to think about factors and people other than themselves that contributed to what happened; they are not responsible for everything
Have you or other people you know experienced or seen things in the past that gave you a hint that something like this might happen?	Emphasizes that reactions to events usually come from past experience or from what other people have told us; you might have thought about it differently
Landscape of consciousness: by understanding how you and others thought about the situation, you can see the possibility of alternate ways forward	Helps focus on thinking about a different future
In what ways have these events showed you what you might want to do in the future?	Gets clients to think realistically about their own preferences
What do other people's reactions to what happened tell you about their beliefs and plans?	Gets clients to think realistically about how other participants may have been affected and possibilities for dealing with their reactions
Experience of experience: understanding how people experience events and might experience them in different ways helps to change perceptions	Helps focus thinking on how people might see their experience differently

Box 3.2 *Continued*

Types of questions	*How they might help*
If I had been able to see what happened to you in the past, what would I have seen that would help me understand how you have developed in the way that you have?	Encourages clients to think about the environmental factors that have influenced what has happened
Of the people who know you, who would be most surprised, pleased, and so on, about what has happened?	Uncovers people who have been important in the development of the issues you are dealing with
Who could we talk with who would be well placed to give us another view of what happened?	Uncovers people who could be engaged in the assessment or interventions processes
Deconstructing patterns of power: thinking about who has power in a situation helps in understanding how to change it	Helps focus on how people have taken up or accepted the assumption of power by others
Where does that idea, action, or practice come from?	Identifies when people have picked up others' assumptions
If you started (or stopped) doing that, what would other people say?	Uncovers the influence of other people's assumptions

Source: Adapted and generalized from Martin Payne's (2006) account, based in turn on categories originating in White (1995).

writers, including White (1995), the originator of this analysis, talk about deconstruction. This concept—we met it above as an aspect of discourse and I now take it further—is drawn from literary theory and has a range of meanings. In the context of narrative, the idea is that actions and thoughts in the narrative are expressed in language that expresses power relationships. Looking at how people express power in their use of language helps you understand how they see the influences on them of people in their social environment.

Fourth, research also often uses narrative techniques, which enables researchers to explore the complexities and interactions between humans and their environments that have created both the situation people are in and the people that they have become. For example, Barnes's (2006) study of informal caregivers' biographies makes clear how their life histories have placed them in positions that limit their ability to control their lives. They generally saw caring as situated within sets of relationships, in many cases, in gendered roles; giving and receiving caring was part of long-standing connections among people. Caregivers and care receivers saw caring as part of political relationships and human relationships: caring was a right in a shared human relationship and an expression of citizenship that should be offered to and received by people as part of society. The informal caregivers in this way demonstrated an expectation of affective equality in their lives, sometimes over a period of time.

Narratives are often biographical; they tell stories about people's lives. We tend to think about biography as a simple account of the story of someone's life. But in telling such a story, it is impossible to include everything. This is for two reasons: we forget things and we select things. Logically, that also means that we remember some things and we deselect others.

The information contained in a biography is a series of selected connected points. A practitioner listening to a biography tries to define the points being made. The story may meander, but it contains points that biographers want to make about themselves. Sometimes they are clear about this; they say, in effect, "I'm telling you this because it says something about my personality or an important point that contributed to how I am today." In this way, biography interweaves past and present: it is the present interpretation of the past. Moreover, if the practitioner has asked about how something happened to affect a client, it will show an interpretation of how the past might have affected the present. I take up biography again in discussing life review as a creative technique in chapter 7.

Narratives therefore lead us toward the way that social factors have influenced the development of the present situation, at least in the narrator's view and perhaps more broadly. They also suggest that we must take action on those social factors if we are to respond adequately to the personal position and interpersonal experience of clients and the people around them.

SOCIAL AGENCY AND MACRO PRACTICES

Practice that is interpersonally human must also respect rights. The discussion of human rights in chapter 1 drew attention to the importance of many different aspects of equalities between peoples. Chapter 2 suggested that the role of social work includes facilitating the social agency of the groups and society within which clients are trying to achieve their personal development. The starting point is thinking about what we want to achieve in seeking equality between people to the extent to which we see the social position of human beings as generated by their own efforts or by circumstance. If we see people as mainly the products of their own efforts, our task in securing equality is to train, educate, and develop people's efforts to afford them the maximum opportunities. However, if we see people as attaining their position by fortune, misfortune, or inheritance or because of the social position of their family, personal and interpersonal help will be insufficient, because the environment in which they live will present barriers to their personal achievement.

Case Example: Gandhian Practice with Oppressed Women

Gandhian practice is a form of humanistic social work emerging from social and political development in India; it is based on the philosophy of the political leader Mahatma Gandhi (Kumar, 1995). Holopainen (2009), describing the work of an atheist center in Andhra Pradesh, India, gives an example of interpersonal work with girls and families affected by *jogini*, a social system in which low-caste girls are considered married to local gods and are therefore unable to be married to a man. They become village property to be "used by males of the locality at their will" (n.p.). He draws attention to the way British colonial authorities historically failed to challenge such practices, which continued until 1986. Thus, the failure to use administrative power to contest an oppressive tradition in some ways reinforced it. The practitioners who sought to challenge this system had to engage with government and seek local support to intervene in village meetings, as well as offer interpersonal interventions, such as counseling; literacy programs; children's education (for the children born to *jogini* women); rehabilitation; and a range of personal services for the women, including education in family life. This example of what may seem an extreme situation shows that intervention in an established cultural practice requires both the interpersonal and the macrointerventions to be planned and worked out together.

R. M. Andersen (1995, adapted by Burge, Lawson, Johnston, & Grunfeld, 2008) produced a useful model of factors that affected people's take-up of health-care services that would benefit them, which I have further adapted in box 3.3 to apply to social care services. In this model, we think about factors in the environment, characteristics of the population, and social behaviors that might lead to the use of services, and we divide individual factors from contextual and community factors. The importance of this model is that it makes clear that environmental and population characteristics as well as social behavior all have an impact on the extent to which people are willing to use social care services, and we have to take community factors into account rather than assume that only individual factors lead to the use of services.

Box 3.3 Access to Social Care Services

Environment ▮▮⬜⬜⟹		Population characteristics ▮▮⬜⬜⟹			Social behaviors
	Social care system	*Predisposing characteristics*	*Enabling resources*	*Need*	*Use of care services*
Individual factors	Links to service Registration with or referral to service	Demographics: ■ Age ■ Sex ■ Sexuality ■ Ethnicity Social background, expectations, and experiences	Family support Community involvement	Individual need, motivation Family need and resilience	Length/ frequency of involvement Range/ numbers of services used
Contextual, community factors	Distance to service Community knowledge or support of service	Social structure: ■ Social class ■ Education ■ Ethnic makeup of community	Community resources: ■ Income ■ Social class	Community need and resilience	Community demands for social care services Social attitudes to services

Case Study: People with Mental Illnesses in Three Different Communities

A town has a shopping and business center, with three areas of housing, each with different characteristics. The southern area is mainly good-quality, private-sector, owner-occupied housing; in the far south, there also is a mental health drop-in center in a former church hall that is organized by a specialized charity. The northeastern part of the town has good-quality rental housing mixed with small-scale light-industrial units; the mental health facility comprises a ward and outpatient facilities in the local general hospital. The northwestern part of town has lower-quality rental housing with some warehousing and large retail sites; there are no mental health facilities. Most people in the town who come from minority ethnic groups live in this area. In the south, mental illness manifests mainly as anxiety and depression, family support is good, and usage of the drop-in center and local hospital is high. The level of long-term mental illness and psychotic illnesses is high in the northwest, but usage of the drop-in center is low; it is difficult and expensive to travel to. Usage of the outpatient facilities at the local hospital is high, and some residents have been admitted to a fairly distant out-of-town specialist psychiatric hospital. The northeast falls between these two extremes.

In this example, we can see that, although need for mental health services is high in the northwest, geographical and social difficulties in access mean that residents do not use the drop-in service, which instead focuses its resources on the "worried well" of the south. They also get a lot of family support. Stigmatized groups are more likely to be living the areas where there are few community resources, of employment and support, and where incomes and the environment are not as good as in other areas. Practitioners need to develop an awareness of this kind of issue in their services; it enables them to adjust their practice and advocate for appropriate change through planning mechanisms in the community.

ADVOCACY AND DUE PROCESS

Advocacy means speaking on behalf of someone in favor of his or her interests. Social work incorporates two types of advocacy:

- Cause advocacy, or macro social work, focused on social agency. This practice identifies and works to remove or modify political and social issues that form barriers to achieving users' and caregivers' aspirations.
- Case advocacy, the process of representing the interests of individuals, groups, families, or communities in agencies or service systems. This focuses more on psychological efficacy.

Four types of advocacy are relevant to social care. First, practitioners have an everyday role in case advocacy for the needs of the users and caregivers. Social workers routinely do this by referring users to other agencies. They also, through assessment and other processes, present the case for particular users and caregivers to receive services.

We noted in all the human rights perspectives reviewed in chapter 1 the importance of ensuring that people have due process. This means that people are entitled to have an advocate for their service needs. Relationships with service should not interfere with this. Is this counsel of perfection? No. Most agencies will accept a negotiation of advocacy responsibilities and accept that these are clearly separate from responsibilities for service liaison and organization. J. R. Graham and Barter (1999), in reviewing social work literature on collaboration, suggest that the following principles may be helpful:

- A nonpersonalized approach, separating people and personalities from the issue being raised.

- A focus on the interests of different people involved and how they can be met, rather than establishing and disputing a position.

- Negotiations that take into account that stakeholders' interests always include some shared and some opposing interests, and that changes may be made on both sides, thus building on shared interests as much as possible.

- Options that ensure that gains for both sides need to be identified or developed.

- Objective criteria for whether outcomes have been achieved and realistic goals should be negotiated; setting stages to move toward goals may be helpful.

Case Example: Negotiating to Accept Advocacy Responsibilities in a Case

Mr. Graham, an elderly man with severe disabilities, had been receiving a variety of health and social care services, with mainly female care workers, for a number of years. The amount of help and their cost had been slowly rising. Two female care workers separately complained about his requests for sexual touching, and this led to a case conference of the various care organizations involved. His care manager, a social worker, discussed the allegations with him; he did not admit or deny them and instead complained about roughness and aspects of his care that he was not satisfied with. His daughter found it hard to believe the allegations. Although she wanted to attend the case conference, staff from some organizations involved felt this was not appropriate, to protect confidentiality of the man's personal information. However, as an informal caregiver, she clearly had a role in making decisions and her view needed to be heard.

The care manager talked to her colleagues and agreed that she would attend the case conference with the daughter and assist in presenting the client's point of view and the daughter's opinions and concerns. This was felt to be helpful in assuring the client and daughter that their concerns had been taken seriously. In the meeting, the care manager first put forward, separately, her employer's concerns about staff willingness to continue working with the client. It was agreed that care was needed, and two paid caregivers were identified who were self-confident in dealing with any inappropriate behavior. Those caregivers received additional training in the different organizations' processes for dealing with any problems.

> The care manager then accompanied the daughter as she joined the meeting to present the concerns and the arrangements made. This included spelling out what behavior had raised concerns and explaining why it was unacceptable to the caregivers. In this way, the client and his daughter were able to feel that their concerns had been properly addressed, and future plans were made clear to them. Moreover, the daughter, in her anxieties about her father, was helped to feel supported.

The second form of advocacy is an everyday form of cause advocacy: practitioners have a less clearly defined cause advocacy role in their services in making clear to service providers when resources or management arrangements are not adequate to meet the needs of users.

This is unenforceable in reality, because finances may not permit a reasonable level of service provision, and practitioners nevertheless have responsibility to provide the best service they can. However, involvement in professional and political activity, using social work expertise and experience, and in service development over the long term can help practitioners contribute stepwise to improvements. Also, it is important to be clear when resources are so inadequate that risk to users and caregivers arises, and at least record this, to protect the practitioner and others involved if there are future difficulties.

The third aspect of advocacy practices is that they may empower people to make their own cases for resources and services.

Case Example: An Advocacy Service for Young People With Intellectual Disabilities

> A private operator of residential care and education for young people with intellectual disabilities contracted with a youth advocacy service. It sought to ensure that independent advocates represented residents at case conferences. The advocacy service employed social workers, psychologists, and teachers for sessions of three hours to meet the young people both in groups and individually, so that general and specific points could be made on their behalf at case conferences. The advocacy service also made regular reports in writing to the young people's parents about their representations.

The fourth aspect of advocacy services is that practitioners and service providers have a responsibility to develop a "culture of advocacy" (Dalrymple, Payne, Tomlinson, & Ward, 1995, p. 118) in which providing advocacy services is accepted and integrated into the arrangements for services provision.

Brandon and Brandon (2001) analyze stages of advocacy, which I have adapted to offer practical guidance useful in any advocacy situation, set out in box 3.4. This draws attention to an important aspect of advocacy: it comes from the point of view of the client and not from the agency. Giving instructions can seem inappropriate to practitioners accustomed to responding to the needs of people as they assess them rather than working with their wishes and feelings. This is a good example of how active use of informed consent can help practitioners.

Box 3.4 Advocacy Practice

Brandon & Brandon's (2001) stages of advocacy	*Practice issues*
Explain the advocacy process.	Clients and others cannot participate before they understand what is involved.
Listen to narratives about the situation; dialogue about perceptions.	Receptiveness to and connectedness with clients' views.
Explain the relevant systems.	Clients, not practitioners, should choose among different available procedures.
Take instructions, generating informed consent.	In advocacy, clients control decisions.
Seek additional information.	From clients, family, community members, and other agencies, identify issues for other interests that may affect the advocacy process.
Give feedback concerning this information, exploring the consequences.	Information may reveal the limits of what is possible or other options.
Take revised instructions.	Even though the course of action may be unwise, clients direct the process.
With informed consent, negotiate with influential people.	Consent may involve limiting practitioners' freedom to negotiate.
Give further feedback, exploring the consequences.	
Prepare formal appeal, complaint, or legal actions.	Decide whether to instruct lawyers or other specialist advocates; if not, collect evidence carefully, constructing arguments, including answers to points against the client's case.
Evaluate the whole process to learn lessons.	Going through what happened may help clients understand their position more clearly; it may also help later cases.

Source: Adapted from Payne (2009c), developed by Brandon and Brandon (2001).

Case Example: Differentiating Advocacy and Decision-Making Roles in a Case Conference

A young person used a professional child advocacy scheme to represent her view to a case conference that she would like to return home to her parents, even though her father had been sexually abusing her. In the case conference, the very experienced social worker responsible for the child's care was publicly critical of the advocate for putting forward this point of view, when clearly it was impossible to do this in the child's best interests. The advocate was forced to point out the requirement to consider the child's wishes and feelings and that it was her role to present those effectively, whereas it was the role of conference participants, not the advocate, to make the decision balancing the two elements.

This is an example of what Dalrymple et al. (1995) mean when they refer to a culture of advocacy. For professional advocacy to be effective, the agency and its staff need to accept the validity of this approach to representation of views. It is another way clients participate in decision making, but it does not negate the responsibility to make appropriate decisions.

An essential method for achieving equality in humanistic social work is advocacy practice. Many practitioners fear that attempting advocacy on behalf of individual clients will damage collaboration with services because it will cause conflict between them and colleagues in related services. Alternatively, they feel that because they have a major role in service provision, they cannot advocate adequately on behalf of clients.

Case Example: Arrangements for a Child in Public Care

The social workers responsible for a seven-year-old child in care arranged for placement in a residential care center. After a visit, the child said she disliked some of the staff and the environment of the center, and the social worker promised to report that to the case conference that would finalize the plans. However, the child asked a residential care worker to put forward her point of view at the case conference. The social worker was angry that the child did not trust her to put forward both views. On the child's behalf, the care worker suggested that, although it was possible for the social worker to put forward both points of view, it would be hard for her to argue the case on the child's behalf. Both workers met with the child later to reassure her that the social worker accepted this distinction and valued the independence of the child in asking for support.

Another case example makes a similar point in another setting.

Case Example: Discharge From the Hospital of a Potentially Violent Mentally Ill Person

A social worker developed a good relationship with a mentally ill man with a record of violence and his family as the hospital where he was a patient moved to discharge him to accommodation in the community. An extensive program of care and supervision was set up for him, and the social worker wanted to present the arrangements at the review panel. She was angered when the medical director arranged for a psychiatric nurse to carry out an independent review of the arrangements. However, the social worker's supervisor looked at it in a different way: an independent risk assessment from a different point of view was a security both for the social worker and for the client and his family. In fact, the close personal knowledge of the social worker and the more distanced view of the nurse were both helpful to the review panel in making a decision. In one example of this, the social worker emphasized how the family wanted to support and provide care for the patient, and the nurse pointed to risks to them if his medication and the care arrangements were not properly maintained. This led to additional arrangements for security for the family.

I was involved in a survey of mental health advocacy in a British town (Emerson, Taylor, & Payne, 1996). One of our findings was that social workers had the responsibility for managing care packages of services to their clients, and they felt that they could not then advocate on behalf of their clients. Mallick and Ashley (1981) have pointed out that multiprofessional practice may inhibit advocacy because practitioners give greater priority to maintaining cooperation with colleagues than to achieving outcomes for their clients.

EMPOWERMENT

Empowerment has sometimes meant antidiscrimination or antioppressive practice (Dalrymple & Burke, 2007; Solomon, 1976), removing barriers to equal treatment or better access to services. This is because the starting point is concern about discrimination against particular groups or oppression of communities, minority cultures, or populations. However, humanistic practice focuses on broader empowerment practice because it is a more positive approach to dealing with inequalities. Present-day social care services are increasingly fragmented and contested, such that people's rights are unclear. Their rights may also be disputed and conditional. For example, communitarians say that receiving services in any society should depend on making or having made a contribution to the community (Etzioni, 1993), whereas human rights approaches say that some social services should be a right that comes with being a human being or a citizen.

A useful concept in J. A. B. Lee's (2001) account of empowerment is the idea of looking at all practice through a lens concerned with inequality and with developing empowering practice. She suggests that practitioners need to be prepared to pick up on a wide range of factors leading to inequalities that may affect people, in particular cultural factors. Awareness of those concerns allows practitioners to adjust their practice and incorporate an awareness of the aspects of their lives and social environment that may have caused inequalities and should be responded to in practice.

Adams (2008) suggests that the aim should be to move people from low-level involvement in decisions about their lives toward an empowerment process in which people have rights as citizens. Such rights are different from the rights of consumers to have efficiently delivered, appropriate services. Empowerment confers rights to participate both in decisions as they directly affect people and in the decision-making structures that create the patterns in which those decisions are made. This should involve participation in the following:

- Initiating the decision-making process: what is the basis for participation, including values, principles, and legal requirements?
- Preparation for the decision: setting aims, strategy, and proposed actions.
- Implementation: involvement in doing what is required.
- Continuation: reviewing what has been done and making sure it is sustained for as long as it is required. (Adams, 2008, p. 74)

In a focus group study of empowerment methods, Boehm and Staples (2002) identified several different factors that affected practitioners' and clients' views of how a social worker could be empowering:

- Whether clients and workers saw the role of the social worker as being directive or nondirective. Clients such as teenagers who were able to be active in meeting their own needs preferred nondirective practice. Clients who were less able, for example, older people, favored a more directive approach.
- On the duration and intensity of empowerment activities, more dependent clients preferred continuing and intense relationships with practitioners. Less dependent clients preferred practitioners to be committed to temporary and decreasing involvements.
- On the balance between the practitioner being expert or mainly a provider of support, many clients preferred a combination of those approaches; however, teenagers preferred a focus on offering expertise.

A study by David (2007) examined the factors that created cultural competence in services and practice, according to the views of families and practitioners from different ethnic groups. Family members from different ethnic and cultural communities did not only look at the effectiveness and outcomes of services, although these were important to them; they also evaluated whether the services were provided in a respectful and responsive way (I would say a human way) and whether the agency operated in a way that demonstrated commitment to culturally appropriate services and engagement in a range of ethnic and cultural communities. The analysis draws attention to how practitioner competences interlock with the organization of the service and its policy and with the agency's engagement with local communities. Therefore, the way a practitioner interacted with a family, respectfully responding to their preferences and evidently being accountable to their requirements, was only one set of factors. The practitioner would find it hard to operate in this way unless the services had a policy and organization that focused on being culturally appropriate and were set up to emphasize accountability to different ethnic cultures. In turn, recognition of this in different communities required active involvement in different communities.

EQUALITY OF ACCESS

This chapter has mainly focused on the interpersonal aspects of achieving equality through interpersonal practice, advocacy, and empowerment. However, I want to bring this concern to a close by emphasizing that making these techniques available in helping organizations is an essential part of ensuring equality of access to services. Due process, effective assessment, and advocacy for clients' choices all enable the needs of people in the community, clients, and family caregivers to be drawn into decisions about what services should be provided and how.

CONCLUSION

I have argued in this chapter that equality is not a theoretical, high-level concern for social policy. Equality in society can be achieved only if every human interaction aims for equality. Equality, advocacy, and empowerment need to be part of the skill set of every practitioner in every practice interaction. In humanistic practice, they are integral to the strategy for helping people to develop toward self-fulfillment. They are also an essential part of the policy and culture of an effective organization working in helping and caring services.

FURTHER READING

Jaworski, A., & Coupland, N. (Eds.). (2000). *The discourse reader.* London: Routledge.

A good collection of articles to enable you to follow up on ideas of discourse in general.

Payne, M. (2009). *Social care practice in context.* Basingstoke, UK: Palgrave Macmillan.

This book is concerned with the detail of social work practice in care management or managed care, exploring the social work task in assessment, care planning, and service provision.

Baker, J., Lynch, K., Cantillon, S., & Walsh, J. (2009). *Equality: From theory to action* (2nd ed.). Basingstoke, UK: Palgrave Macmillan.

A good account of equality issues with wide application in social work and other professions.

Lynch, K., Baker, J., & Lyons, M. (2009). *Affective equality: Love, care and injustice.* Basingstoke, UK: Palgrave Macmillan.

An innovative text that explores the importance of rights to love and support others and to be loved and supported.

Flexibility in Human Life and Professional Practice

CHAPTER AIMS

The main aim of this chapter is to demonstrate that because of the inherent variability of human life, humanistic practice requires flexibility. This is achieved by incorporating professional evidence into a human interpersonal interaction in the process of practice interventions.

After working through this chapter, readers should be able to

- Understand congruence, empathy, and unconditional positive regard as important techniques
- Understand the importance of incorporating different practice knowledges and skills in an improvised performance of a wise person in an eclectic form of practice developed through professional and agency validation

PRACTITIONERS: MORE AND LESS THAN HUMAN

In previous chapters, we have been examining some of the basic values and practices that underlie humanistic social work while building up a practice repertoire for dealing with these issues. In the following three chapters, we begin to put these values and practice techniques together to form a more comprehensive practice. In this chapter, we look at techniques for incorporating into a complete practitioner the range of knowledge and skills that we need to use.

How can a practitioner be a whole, complete, human being while practicing? Because they are whole, complete human beings, is it enough just to be themselves? No—they also have to be that special thing, a social work practitioner, integrating the professional with the personal, so they are more than themselves. However, does this make them more than human? Again, no. Superpractitioners do not exist; their humanity contains both the professional and the human being, and the professional is an aspect of the human being. I argue in this chapter that a social worker practicing is both less than and more than a whole person or human being. Social workers are less than a person, because they bring a particular professional self to the intervention; this is not the whole of their self. I see this as putting on a performance of professional intervening. Practitioners are also more than a person, because they bring the whole profession and its knowledge into themselves as human beings as part of the intervention.

Humanistic psychotherapies have developed various ideas about how to do this. They are called the core concepts or core conditions of helping practice, because unless clients can see, feel, and perceive that you meet these conditions, they are unlikely to want to engage with you. It is these conditions that enable practitioners operating to help people to be more than ordinary human beings. The core concepts are based particularly on the idea of congruence connected with similar ideas that have slightly different meanings, such as genuineness, realness, or authenticity (Mearns & Thorne, 2007). We met this idea in chapter 3 as part of developing an equal relationship with clients. This is because, if we want clients to be open with us, then we have to be just as open with them. Such ways of behaving show the people you are dealing with how you are responding to what they are saying and doing. One aspect of this is that you show them your weaknesses, so that you do not appear to be an all-seeing, all-successful practitioner-being but someone like them who can connect with them. In turn, you become more congruent with yourself, so your professional behaviors really do represent how you are as a human being. This is the "more than" aspect of the practitioner.

EMPATHY IN A THERAPEUTIC ALLIANCE

Hoffman (2000) identifies two ways of looking at empathy:

- A cognitive awareness of another person's internal states, for example, thoughts, feelings, perceptions, and intentions
- A vicarious affective response to another person—developing feelings about that person that are appropriate to how the person feels about him- or herself

A cognitive awareness of someone's internal states means that we know about how that person is feeling and can affirm our acceptance of those states. We say things like, "I can see you are upset about that." This may be helpful in interpersonal relationships, but helping empathy involves building an affective empathy, as well: you have to feel empathy to be helpful. It will be obvious that an affective empathic response is not necessarily our own response to the other person; we manufacture or, I would say, perform a response that we think or feel is appropriate to the person rather than one that is appropriate to us. It is like choosing a greeting card to send to someone; you think of what the person will appreciate, but you also take into account what you think represents your attitudes and cultural judgment.

Chandler (2009) discussed authenticity by comparing the "intimate personal services" (p. 16) provided by counselors with those provided by prostitutes. He suggested that most people expect to give and receive sexual stimulation and satisfaction as well as attentive and caring listening, empathic understanding, and encouragement freely in a close personal relationship. We saw in chapter 3 that affective equality means having the opportunities to build love, support, and solidarity with other human beings in just such relationships. A paid service providing such help raises problems of authenticity. Does the paid counselor fake empathy for the same reason that a prostitute fakes attraction and orgasm? However, although the therapeutic relationship is an artifice, in that it does not arise naturally, it is created by human skill and is built up in place of something else: it is real for the purpose for which it is constructed. Chandler describes practitioners as "on temporary loan" (p. 17) to enable people to offer and receive help. To allow them to work, people "suspend disbelief" (p. 16) in the same way that they do when reading a novel. Clients accept that a practitioner is a caring and helpful person, provided that he or she acts out that role sufficiently well. They regain their disbelief if the practitioner fails to perform empathy adequately.

A useful concept to start from is the therapeutic alliance, a concept drawn originally from psychoanalysis but strongly associated with humanistic psychotherapies (Barrett-Lennard, 1985). This concept suggests that the practitioner and client should develop a relationship in which they work side by side, on the same side rather than in opposition, on the issues that the client faces. Therapeutic alliance is another aspect of equality and implies that clients and practitioners can and must find ways to rely on and trust each other to make progress together. This concept is made more complex in social work, because social workers often work with more than one person in the social situation; there may be a focal client, but the practitioner has responsibilities to other members of the family or, more broadly, to achieve results on behalf of the community or the state. I return to this element of the complexity of social work in chapter 5.

Empathy is part of achieving a therapeutic alliance, connected to the practitioner's congruence. Watson (2001) has reviewed research on empathy, which has been measured by rating scales and has been found to be associated with positive outcomes in counseling and psychotherapeutic help. A variety of nonverbal and verbal behaviors are associated with clients' perceptions of the practitioner's empathy, such as the practitioner having a similar style of speech and maintaining interest in the client's problems rather than appearing bored. The practitioner's use of a variety of speech styles rather than monotony also helps.

It is most helpful to look out for and try to be empathic in particular situations:

■ When clients actively express present emotions, such as by crying or going silent
■ When clients try to analyze what happened and how they reacted
■ When clients talk about strong emotions, reactions, or repeat aspects of what happened
■ When clients make their values and assumptions explicit
■ When clients talk about positive or negative feelings about the practitioner

The main aim of empathy is to reflect clients' communication in ways that demonstrate that you have understood and have incorporated into yourself what they are saying (Carkhuff & Berenson, 1967). This is two sided: it involves the incorporation into you of your client's communication, whether verbal or nonverbal, and their experience of the fact that you have incorporated their perspective (Corcoran, 1981). In talking with clients, Watson (2001) suggests that responses seen as empathic are the following:

- Understanding—trying to validate clients' experiences and emotions: "You must be tired if your daughter has been keeping you awake . . ."
- Evocation—trying to rephrase clients' ideas in rich, imaginative, metaphorical, language: "By doing that, your husband seemed to want you to mother him . . ."
- Exploration—facilitating clients' unfolding of their experiences and emotions in more detail: "I imagine you must have thought a lot about what the housing office said . . ."
- Conjecture—trying to unlock things that clients have left implicit: "Your reaction there seemed to be worried rather than angry . . ."

In humanistic psychotherapy, such interjections are normally explicitly provisional: "I wonder if I'm right in thinking that . . ." This is because humanistic psychotherapy is generally nondirective in style. However, we saw in chapter 2 that social work has broader accountabilities than the client's own perceptions of his or her self-actualization. Therefore, social work practice may require a more assertive style: "I am worried that what you did there may have left your child unsafe for a while. Did you do something to make sure she was all right? How do you see it? " This is still provisional and open but more clearly testing in its content and style. Moreover, it focuses on the important issue of the security of the child; both emotional and physical security is an important issue for accountability in social work. Another factor in this more assertive response is that it permits due process to take place around an issue that may become a matter of professional judgment or even compulsory intervention.

UNCONDITIONAL POSITIVE REGARD AS PART OF POSITIVE PRACTICE

Unconditional positive regard means "prizing" the client, as Rogers (1982/2007) puts it, valuing what they are and what they become. It connects to the social work idea of acceptance (Biestek, 1957). Of course, we know that a client may have problems or challenges to face or that others might see the client as problematic. This may lead others to stigmatize the client, to see him or her as bad or mad. But if we are going to be equal with the client, we have to put that aside. We may see a positive side to the client or elements of the self that are valuable. However, because humanistic social work focuses on people's personal growth, the main basis of unconditional positive regard is the possible futures in which they may achieve that growth and attain a different identity from the stigmatized one we see now. So, we don't have to focus on the things that are wrong; rather, we should aim to set them right.

Ways to achieve this in the process mean focusing on positives in practice. A number of helping techniques have developed in the late twentieth century and early twenty-first century that emphasize this approach to practice, including positive psychology, possibility work, strengths-based practice, and solution-focused practice. The aims of these practices are to find out about, accept, value, and celebrate people's existing capacities to deal with their lives and to build up new ones. Many approaches to positive practice use social construction ideas; these suggest we can reconstruct a situation to create future change, in the same way that, as we saw in Chapter 3, we can re-story a narrative to understand the past differently.

The crucial point about social construction is that it is a social process; that is, we share our reconstructions with other people in our social environment so that they support each other. Some writers criticize social construction ideas because they view them as leading to a relativist position; that is, nothing is certain because a different experience will lead to a different construction. This is an oversimplification. Berger and Luckmann's (1971) original analysis of social construction sought to explain why people develop strongly held ideas about appropriate social behavior. Why are those ideas so strongly held when they are different in different cultures? Their research makes clear that we develop constructions of our world through experiencing social interactions with others, initially perhaps with parents or other caregivers, but eventually with many other people. Archer (1995) has shown that later experiences either confirm or deny these. So confirmed constructions are reinforced, whereas constructions that do not seem to be right are altered or rejected. This connects with the psychological research discussed in chapter 2, on intuition and reasoning. Children start with some intuitions about the world and adjust them according to the evidence and their own reasoning. Social construction ideas tell us that our ideas about the world can be very strong building blocks because of the wide social agreement that they are useful and appropriate. However, social construction also holds out possibilities for us. Instead of just having to adapt to or fit in with how things are, it is possible to rebuild the constructions we have developed. It may not be easy, and it will certainly require interactions with everyone who is important to us, but it must be possible because all social behavior has been jointly constructed within the culture of our society.

PAUSE AND REFLECT: The Positive Futures in People

Examine the listing of typical client groups in social work services in box 4.1; they broadly follow a life course. The group is listed in column 1, and column 2 lists for the first three groups some of the issues that people in these groups face. Perhaps you have experienced some these issues in your life yourself, or perhaps you have worked with clients facing these issues. In the third column, I have listed some possible futures for people facing this issue. The table is incomplete, and you are invited to reflect on client

Box 4.1 Common Social Work Client Groups and the Issues They Face

Client group	Issues faced	Possible futures
Fertility	Inability to have children	To be able to achieve fertility or accept alternates such as adoption, foster care, or childlessness
	Being unable to cope with a large family	To be able to accept a greater degree of family disorganization, to manage behavior and family systems more successfully
Children	Developmental delay or problems Behavioral problems	
Families	Marital or family relationships Low income, unemployment, housing problems affecting family life	
Physically disabled people		
People with learning disabilities		
Mentally ill people		
Older people		
Dying people		

groups that you are familiar with, build up issues that you have come across, and think about alternative futures. Perhaps you could identify positive futures that did not seem to be possible at the time you experienced these issues.

Some Suggestions

Thinking through a range of alternative futures indicates that there are always possible ways forward for every issue that can be positive. You may also think that not all the possibilities are positive. For example, you might feel strongly that childlessness is not a positive outcome for people who are unable to have children. However, for some people it may be, and for some people it may not start as an option, but they may come to prefer it to further fertility treatment or adoption.

One of the difficulties of focusing on positive practice is that some people may find it impossible to develop positives in their lives. However, there are always positive and less positive opportunities in any situation. The starting point has to be to identify the limits of the choices. For people who are unable to have children, a choice may not be available; that sets the limits of the situation within which positives need to be established.

Case Study: A Violent, Mentally Ill Offender

Jacko had a disrupted and violent childhood and later committed a series of violent, sexually motivated murders. He was incarcerated for life in a secure mental hospital, and it was agreed that he could never be released. Initially depressed and feeling that his life was at an end, a wide range of practitioners helped him to develop positive activities in the gardens of the hospital and begin educating himself. The social work contribution to this was to assist him to rebuild relationships with brothers and sisters and to arrange a regular program of visits from them. An important proviso of helping someone who is a security risk is that we must avoid being fooled or tempted into the view that the person's developing self makes him or her safe. Development and being safe are different things.

SOCIAL WORK PRACTICE AS IMPROVISED PERFORMANCE

I suggested in the previous section that the humanistic psychology core conditions enabled practitioners to be more than an ordinary human being, to be the special person who is able to be helping and caring. In this section, I examine how the core conditions allow practitioners to overcome the "less than" aspect of the intervention—that social work practice is an improvised performance because we cannot be in a permanent personal relationship with the client.

The first area to think about is performance. In chapter 1, looking at microsociology, we met Goffman's (1968, 1972a, 1972b, 1972c) dramaturgical role theory and interaction framework analysis. It suggests that we respond to human situations by acting out roles that are appropriate to the situation and the others involved. To understand our own and other people's responses, we have to understand something about the roles that they are trying to enact and the framework within which we are interacting. We present ourselves in ways that are relevant to the situation, and we exclude or downplay elements of ourselves that are less relevant to our intervention. Social work can be seen as a performance in which we do things that represent something of ourselves as individuals and something of our role as social worker. This performance interacts with those of other people acting out their roles as troubled or sick people, parents, spouses, or members of a community. The troubled role is not the whole of them, as the helping role is not the whole of us. They take from the set of roles that connect with parts of their lives those that are relevant to the moment and use them in the interaction with us. So in each performance interaction, we are less than the whole, because we are using only part of our being.

The second area I want to discuss is the improvisation that humanity and social context in all their variety demand of us. Many social work techniques have a basic underlying idea, such as task or crisis, but to elaborate on these, social work textbooks produce complicated lists or diagrams. We cannot readily hold these in our head, and even so, they are still too generalized to apply to all the situations we have to deal with. This conflict between the apparent solidity of our elaborated theories and the variety of the real world is one of the major features of the conflict that many students and practitioners see between the real world and the theory world.

How can we understand this? I understand it by saying that the value of the theories lies in their fundamental creative idea, not in the elaborated model of practice. Social work practitioners mostly need only to grasp the idea and apply it as they think about what they are doing. I argue that the elaboration is useful only in teaching and learning to help students grasp the idea in all its complexity so that they can use it well. After they have grasped it, they have little need of the elaboration.

I think of it as like an improvised jazz performance. Jazz performers are, often as part of a group, presented with a theme. They have finely honed and developed skills in playing their instrument, as well as experience of various ways to respond to themes with their instrument. Moreover, they build up a relationship with the group so that they can respond to one another in ways that they understand and can respond to. If you know a performer and a group, you can understand where their apparently improvised performance comes from; you can see the patterns in the way it develops. Applying this analogy to social work, you have a repertoire of responses to the themes that you can identify in the situations you commonly deal with. The way you respond to themes and the aspects that you identify to work on partly come from your training and understanding and partly from what people present to you. You develop relationships so that you can perform together with the people you work with. The result is one shared experience, in which each person contributes something to the accumulation of shared experiences that you have. The practitioner gains as someone who tries to understand, explain, and do social work, as part of the organization.

EMBODYING PROFESSIONAL KNOWLEDGE AND PRACTICE

An apparently flexible performance is, therefore, if you understand it fully, created by a well-established and professional process. To achieve the improvisation that flexibility requires, social work performances cannot use knowledge formally or in structured ways. Workers therefore embody or incorporate knowledge and understanding to become the wise person. I use the term *embody* here to refer mainly to the way we see this knowledge as valuable because it is part of the person, the practitioner, who is valued in the use of it; it is perceived as the wisdom of this person. Again referring to microsociology, we can see the personal, physical presentation of the worker to the outside world as a factor in the perception of him or her as a wise person.

Case Example: The Formality of the Group Worker and the Volunteer

A male group worker with a caregivers project facilitated a series of eight sessions with caregivers bereaved of their spouses, working together with a female volunteer who was especially trained for the task. Two to three months after the series of support groups, there was a reunion at which group members were asked to complete an evaluation form; discuss the group experience; and less formally, catch up with one another. After completing the form, they had a discussion about the value of the whole service they received from various hospitals and from the caregivers project.

Part of the discussion was about the professional behavior of doctors and nurses, with their white coats and uniforms, compared with the practitioners at the caregivers project. The group worker, a young white male, was always informally dressed and the volunteer was a middle-class Jewish woman who wore a lot of jewelry and was always dressed smartly but casually. The discussion was about how the junior doctors often wore their white coats and stethoscopes to demonstrate their profession, whereas grades of nurse were identifiable by their uniforms. Did the informal clothes of the group worker mean that he was not professional? He used a facilitation technique that involved guiding rather than directing the group's discussion. Was this because he was particularly open? The volunteer was closer to participants in age. For some people she was more sympathetic, because she engaged more warmly, but some group members saw that the group worker was using a professional technique. Several group members saw his relaxed style as cool, a positive judgment, whereas others saw it as cool, or distant, a less positive judgment. This meant that they were kept to task but felt less personal than their experience of the volunteer. Several people also agreed that the volunteer was sometimes tenser and intervening rather than letting things go along naturally.

This discussion made explicit some of the perceptions and issues that arose for clients because of the embodiment. How practitioners dress, where they sit, how they hold themselves, and how they communicate all demonstrate both their profession and something of their nonprofessional person.

Cameron and McDermott (2007) demonstrate how important being body cognizant is in social work. Many aspects of social work—health care, providing care services to adults with disabilities or in old age, child protection, and mental health—are concerned with risk to and problems with clients' bodies. Moreover, our life experience is represented in our bodies: smokers may have cancer or heart disease because of this addiction, which may in turn come from lack of concern about healthy behavior which perhaps arose from living in poverty in childhood. Environmental and social factors may lead to illness or concern about body shape, as in people who are anorexic. As our body image changes, for example in middle age or old age, our personal identity may change (Cunningham-Burley & Backett-Milburn, 1998). How we experience our bodies and other people's bodies affects our view of ourselves and of other people. Therefore, how practitioners hold themselves, how they look, is an important aspect of the interaction they take part in with clients. We therefore need to be aware of our bodies, other people's bodies, and how other people react to their own and our bodies.

Social work theory, knowledge, and practice skills interact. Social work practice is a performance between individuals in which social workers embody or incorporate theory, knowledge, and skill as elements in the interaction. We saw in chapter 2 that evidence-based practice is integral to all humanistic practice because it tries to promote certainty and order in interpersonal practice, which is inherently uncertain and flexible. In pursuit of this, it produces ever more complex accounts and models of practice (Payne, 2005), or it demands rigorous empirical research to support particular actions or organizational and social structures that cannot be consistently reproduced in the real world (Gibbs &

Gambrill, 2002; Webb, 2001). Moreover, different kinds of knowledge from different sources have been identified as relevant to social work practice (Pawson, Boaz, Grayson, Long, & Barnes, 2003; Walter, Nutley, Percy-Smith, McNeish, & Frost, 2004), and therefore different aspects of knowledge produced and used in different ways are relevant.

There are many ways research can examine how practitioners do this. Sheppard and his colleagues (Sheppard, Newstead, di Caccavo, & Ryan, 2000; Sheppard & Ryan, 2003) explored social workers' thinking processes. Texts and debate concerned with reflective practice (Gould & Taylor, 1996), reasoning processes (Taylor & White, 2006), and reflexivity (Taylor & White, 2000) in social work practice all seek in various ways to develop structured ways of thinking critically to guide practice. Such work connects with an approach to education in practice professions that are not always amenable to the application of technical knowledge. This approach, reflective practice, associated with Schön (1983) and his associates requires practitioners to reflect in an organized way on their action as it happens and afterward to reconstruct practice guidance. It is also important to pick up recent cognitive research, discussed in chapter 2, which suggests that organized knowledge and professional reflection and reflexivity adapt and manage an intuitive response to situations that guides many human reactions to social situations. We saw in chapter 2 that there are widely shared, inborn, intuitive features of "mind design" (Hood, 2009, p. 23), which guide initial reactions and that evidence and rational thinking adapt and rationalize.

In the following section, an account and analysis of a case experience inform these issues. The written account of this practice experience has been disguised to make anonymous the practitioner and clients involved. It is presented as an illustration of Pawson et al.'s (2003) analysis of social work knowledge, which is based on an extensive review of sources of knowledge in social work, and Trevithick's (2005) analysis of social work skills, also fairly exhaustive. I develop the analysis of the case experience as a starting point for showing how we can examine social workers enacting their role in practice. I classify and comment on the case account after the practice events described to illustrate the important points; the practitioner was not trying out the model. It is important to say this because I want to suggest that this model may be applied to any practice event, however complex or prosaic, or to parts of it.

PRACTICING KNOWLEDGEABLY AND SKILLFULLY

Box 4.2, column 1, presents a practice experience. Column 2 provides some analysis and commentary on knowledge use in this experience. First, the kind of knowledge used is classified according to Pawson et al.'s (2003) analysis. Pawson et al.'s (2003) work refers to the following:

- Organizational knowledge, about government and agency organization and regulation
- Practitioner knowledge, drawn from experience of practice, which tends to be tacit, personal, and context specific

Box 4.2 A Practice Experience Analyzed

Experience	Knowledge for understanding	Skills for doing
I was standing in for a social work colleague in our hospice who was ill; a nurse asked me to see a patient in an inpatient ward urgently who was concerned about her mother's reaction to her admission for terminal care.	*Organizational, practitioner.* An emergency situation in an institutional setting.	*Partnership.* With colleague and multi-professional team.
The patient, Julie, was 39 years old. She was affected by brain metastases of her cancer and consequently experiencing expressive dysphasia.	*Practitioner.* Knowledge about the client. Technical knowledge from shared understanding of the illness.	*Assessment.* Collects relevant beginning information from referral.
Having read her file, I arrived in her room just as her nurse was completing some work on medication; she was sitting in a recliner by her bed.	*Organizational, practitioner.* Situation defined by procedures of the agency and existing setting of the client.	*Assessment, observation.* Prepares for encounter; observes others' interactions as the encounter begins.
I introduced myself and she invited me to sit down. I said I could be with them for an hour, as I had another engagement.	*Practitioner.* Limitations to flexibility of contact are made clear. A normal courtesy, probably drawn from experience in interview technique.	*Communication, interviewing, direction.* Communicates clearly; engages, basic interviewing, directs the engagement.
Although she could not always find the right words, Julie explained that her mother was not accepting that she wanted to stay in the hospice until her death, which was expected soon. I suggested various possibilities: I could see her mother at the hospice, visit her, or we could see her together. It turned out that her mother was in the visitor's lounge a few doors away; Julie asked a nurse to go and get her.	*Client, practitioner.* The basic pattern of the intervention is defined by the client and the availability of the mother.	*Listening, interviewing, direction, empowerment.* After listening to the basic issue, offers suggestions about the direction of the intervention and allows client to decide and take control of calling mother.

Box 4.2 Continued

Experience	Knowledge for understanding	Skills for doing
The mother came to join us, rather uncertainly, and I explained that Julie was concerned about how she had reacted to her admission to the hospice. Julie could not find all the words that she wanted to say, and our conversation proceeded with both her mother and me trying to interpret the unfinished sentences until Julie said we had guessed correctly.	*Practitioner.* Communication problems dealt with in a practical way that reflects the worker's self-confidence in communication.	*Observation, listening, communication.* The mother's uncertainty perceived, and communication updates her on discussion with her daughter.
The mother started out by saying that she and her other daughter had worked hard to make sure that Julie could be cared for at home and had made a lot of adaptations to make this possible.	*Practitioner.* The mother is facilitated to present her view—a courtesy and a basic interview technique.	*Listening, empowerment.* Listening empowers the mother to say what she wants, even though she may disagree with client and practitioner.
Then, Julie became angry about her mother not accepting her wishes, and not being prepared to discuss what she wanted. Her mother responded to this by saying that she did not want to talk all the time about Julie's death.	*Practitioner, client.* Different points of view are made explicit to enable better understanding by the people involved.	*Observation, listening, empowerment.* Clients are empowered to bring out the disagreement.
God would make the decision when she should die, and we should not give up. Julie was still angry and I asked her mother to talk more about her views.	*Practitioner, client.* Expression of spiritual and religious views is facilitated.	*Observation, listening.* The conflict expressed.
As she talked about this, several things became clear. First, she wanted to maintain a positive hope for whatever life Julie had left. Julie wanted her mother to accept that she would die soon, and she knew that this might be true, but her mother would handle that when it happened. It was important to maintaining her support for Julie that she did not discuss this possibility all the time. She connected this to wanting to make provision for Julie to go home, even if this never happened.	*Client.* Expression and clarification of more complex feelings about the situation is encouraged.	*Observation, assessment, help, direction, guidance.* The practitioner develops a hypothesis about what is going on in this situation.

Box 4.2 Continued

Experience	Knowledge for understanding	Skills for doing
Her mother was quite angry, which is common in family members of dying people. Here, her anger was centered on Julie's wish to stay in the hospice.	*Practitioner, research.* Knowledge of common behavioral characteristics of relatives of dying people.	*Observation, assessment.* Hypothesis about the observed behavior, connected with stage theory of grief.
Second, her mother feared that remaining in the hospice would accelerate Julie's death. This is also a common fear, and I responded by making clear the palliative care policy of the hospice, that we helped to make people comfortable so that they could make the best for their life for as long as possible, but we never made the death quicker.	*Client, practitioner, organizational, research.* Understanding of common reactions to the institution and explanation of policy drawn from worker's understanding of agency policy and practice.	*Assessment, communication, direction, guidance, accountability.* Assessing the emotional reaction, guidance, help, and explanation of policy and practice. Accountability through expressing agency policy.
I pointed out that Julie's involvement in the hospice program when she was a day patient had been very active and had led to several achievements.	*Practitioner, organizational.* Explanation and argument drawn from the worker's knowledge of previous events in the institution.	*Direction.* Takes control of the interview.
Further discussion, with my interpretations in between: Julie wanted to make clear to her mother that she should not contest her choice to stay in the hospice; her mother wanted to make clear that she accepted this, but to maintain her hope, she did not want constantly to be involved in discussing the death. When it came, she would accept it.	*Client, practitioner.* Expression of views by the client is facilitated.	*Interviewing, listening, communication, help, guidance.* Repetition so clients feel empowered by expressing their feelings; practitioner guides discussion by clarifying their positions.

Box 4.2 Continued

Experience	Knowledge for understanding	Skills for doing
I pointed out to them both that what had been happening was a circle of communication in which each was trying to deal with something that was important to her, but when they did so, they made it more difficult for what the other person was trying to do. Julie's attempts to get her mother to accept her choice meant that her mother's attempts to maintain her own hope were being constantly attacked. Her mother's attempts to maintain her hope by making arrangements for care at home and by avoiding discussing death increased Julie's feeling that her mother was not accepting her choices.	*Practitioner, research.* The worker's explanation, clarification, and rationalization of what has taken place, relying partly on an understanding of the importance of hope drawn from literature on emotional reactions to death.	*Communication, help, direction.* By expressing explanations that both clients could accept, practitioner gives direction and meaning to the interaction.
I suggested that we make an agreement. I would make clear to the multiprofessional team that they would discuss things with Julie's mother only when doing so was essential for Julie's care. Then decisions would be Julie's, and her mother would not receive a constant reminder of Julie's impending death.	*Practitioner, research.* Worker's proposal for an informal contract, drawn out in a practical way.	*Negotiation, partnership empowerment.* Proposes and negotiates agreements to help move the situation on.
I checked with Julie that she was clear that her mother did understand and accept her decisions and that her arrangements at home and putting aside the likelihood of death in the near future were her mother's choices.	*Practitioner, research.* Clarification and reinforcement of the informal contract.	*Negotiation, partnership.* Negotiation confirmed.

Box 4.2 Continued

Experience	Knowledge for understanding	Skills for doing
In turn, I checked that her mother would not seek to press Julie to change her mind about her choices. I pointed out that God would make the decision about Julie's progress and her death. There might be improvement, and she might want to change her decision. If she did so, she knew her mother and sister were ready to help.	*Practitioner, research.* Clarification and reinforcement of the informal contract.	*Negotiation, partnership.* Negotiation confirmed.
At this point, the chaplain's assistant came to take Julie and her mother to the chapel for the Christmas carol service.	*Organizational.* Events in the situation intervene.	*Interviewing.* Practitioner manages the interruption.
My next engagement was to play the piano at the service, so we met again, with Julie's family, over the drinks and mince pies after the service, having joined in it together.	*Organizational.* The organizational provision and the situation as it arises are used to reinforce relationships.	*Partnership, professional competence.* Further involvement reinforces the partnership.
I met them again in passing some days later in the day center; things were going well between them. Julie died shortly after Christmas.	*Organizational.* Postintervention contacts, developed through organizational knowledge, used to check and reinforce the intervention.	*Partnership.* Continues to be reinforced.

- Client knowledge, drawn from clients' knowledge of their lives, situation and use of services (the original terminology used was *service user*, U.K. jargon for *client*, and in this discussion, I reverted to the usual international usage)
- Research knowledge, drawn from systematic investigation disseminated in reports
- Policy community knowledge, drawn from administrators, official documentation, and analysis of policy research

Column 3 takes this further, because practitioners are not limited to knowledge use; they also do things. Column 3, therefore, analyzes what the practitioner does by looking at the skills used. This relies on the analysis by Trevithick (2005). She goes into skills in great detail, but I have used here the five main groups of skills that she identifies:

- Communication, listening, and assessment skills
- Basic interviewing skills
- Providing help, direction, and guidance
- Empowerment, negotiation, and partnership skills
- Professional competence and accountability

PAUSE AND REFLECT

To start with, glance through the account of the case situation in box 4.1. I have purposely chosen a rather prosaic and routine event, because I want to show how you can make this kind of analysis in the most banal of interventions that we all make. Then take a look at the analysis I have made drawing on the two listings of social work knowledge and social work skills. Would you identify other areas of knowledge and skills that you would put alongside the ones chosen? Would you identify different areas of knowledge and skills that come out from the case situation?

Some Suggestions

You probably found that the analysis was only partial, that each part of the intervention drew on areas of knowledge that the analysis does not identify. In particular, you could probably identify a more refined and detailed analysis of skills. This is almost certainly the case, because I have used only Trevithick's (2005) broadest categories of skills, not her detailed description and categorization.

Examining this example and the commentary might raise a variety of issues; I want to look at five areas. First, different kinds of knowledge and skills are used at different times in the interaction. At the outset, practitioner and organizational knowledge is most important, alongside communication and basic interviewing skills, as the practitioner is given the task and develops enough preliminary understanding to begin working in the situation. Then client and practitioner knowledge becomes important, alongside empowerment, help, and guidance skills, in particular with the practitioner taking responsibility for guiding the progress of the interview. The clients bring their concerns and perceptions into the situation, facilitated by the practitioner's observation, interviewing, and communication skills. The way the practitioner works probably derives from a researched knowledge base about appropriate professional behavior and communication in a helping situation. Toward the end, the practitioner uses practice theory and knowledge, as well as skills shifting toward negotiation and partnership with clients and the agency's multiprofessional team. These derive originally from research but, again, applied in a fairly commonsense way to help resolve the situation. This humanizes them. Finally, through participation in the organizational context in various ways, the practitioner checks on progress and reinforces the intervention.

To sum up these points, although there is some degree of progression in the use of knowledge and skills as the interview moves forward, this relatively brief and routine intervention contains the whole gamut of knowledge and skills. The sophisticated and well-researched formulations of knowledge and skills from which I have drawn the categorization used in the analysis are all employed in a brief and routine social work intervention. If you look in detail at any social work intervention, therefore, you will usually see quite a range of social work knowledge and skills routinely deployed. We can understand this only by accepting that practitioners bring together all at once a complex world of knowledge and skills.

Second, in setting out to assess the situation and make a specific intervention, the practitioner relies on researched professional knowledge, a specific professional role, and professional skills. However, as we saw in the discussion on informed consent in chapter 2, practitioners do not say that they are doing this—it would all be too complicated. The practitioner to some degree negotiates the approach with clients, but clients accept the practitioner's professional competence and accountability, because both practitioner and clients are part of the agency that they accept as helping them. They might become more questioning in other situations, in which case more negotiation about role and action would take place.

Third, on the contrary, most of the knowledge used derives from the practitioner's experience in the agency of the sort of problems encountered and from generalized skills and ways of dealing with people. For example, specialized experience of a hospice promotes engagement in discussion about death and faith experience, which might be unusual in other settings. The general skills of interviewing, communicating, and negotiating are employed with this additional, rather specialized content.

Fourth, it is striking that by routine referral and by self-introduction, the practitioner rapidly engages in important interpersonal interactions between a mother and her daughter who is close to death. The mother and daughter feel the need to have these interactions, so they accept the human being who is presented to them by the agency as a helping person. The practitioner confirms this by being a human being who is acceptable and by helping; being unacceptable in some way or failing to help might lead to more questioning.

Fifth, the organizational context of a hospice, a residential institution in which people and their families are cared for as a family member is dying, influences how participants, both clients and practitioners operating in the setting, carry out the interaction. Knowledge of the organization and shared past events within it, as well as sharing in present and future events, is crucial to clients' understanding and acceptance of the intervention by the practitioner—so, too, are the professionals' professional skills and knowledge and human helping. But these are not differentiated into some analytical process; they take place all together and in one event with people engaged in one interaction. It is one human helping event.

BEING PRACTICAL, KNOWING THEORY

As soon as we begin to generalize from these particular situations, consistency and coherence begin to take over. Thus, Julie presented herself, and so was referred, as extremely troubled to the point of needing emergency action. Attempting careful assessment and a planned therapeutic treatment (seen in chapter 2 as an empowerment or self-actualization intervention) or simply organizing some practical services (seen in chapter 2 as a problem-solving or social order intervention) would not deal with the present situation, which was apparently creating anxiety and difficulty for Julie and her mother. It is a fair guess that the social roles of being a sick and dying person and the need to be admitted to a specialist health and social care institution were contributing to her distress. Because it was an issue between mother and daughter, the impact of gender relations will almost always be a factor, but it was too early and might never be appropriate in this particular engagement to deal with those wider issues. It is necessary to deal with the present situation in the role that social workers have been given by their colleagues and organizations and in the role that the people they are trying to help perceive and accept. So the practitioner acted out the part of the social worker responding in a hurry to a situation that colleagues claimed and participants felt to be urgent. In turn, they acted out their concerns. They must have been acted out before with nurses and doctors, and Julie and her mother had also acted them out in interaction with each other. They did so again, and the practitioner acted out a specifically social response. They reacted by accepting again that, for the time being, their social performance as loving and mutually valued mother and daughter could continue. This joint performance of roles represented only part of the complexities of their lives and the practitioner's profession.

For Julie, it may have been a crucial experience allowing her to continue on her dying path with a further step in reordering and reclaiming her relationship with her mother in this situation, so that she could know when she died that work had been done to secure her position in relation to her mother. For her mother, it secured something for the future about her relationship with her daughter, to go alongside all the other experiences of her daughter; she will always know that they might have had an unpleasant conflict at the time of her death but had resolved it. It may have been particularly important for her future recollection and use in her further relationships because her daughter's path toward death was a time of crisis in their lives. I have used the word *secured* here to emphasize that achieving stability and security is an important objective of many small- and large-scale interventions in social work; I look at this more extensively in chapter 8.

Even the performance on this occasion illustrates the importance of establishing communication, the courtesies of entering in a helping and caring, if temporary, relationship within a wider institution and a wider set of helping services. This single incident illustrates many of the principles of social work as a practice and the practitioner's personal self and life experience as elements in it (Payne, 2006). It also begins to establish social work as other things: it incorporates a formal role, the use of knowledge and research, and the social values that social workers seek to achieve. The practitioner was called on and acted as a professional person, part of the machinery of health and social care, carrying out a crucial value objective of social work. The work focused on the social factors that created the apparent urgency, and maintained a stance that they could be resolved. The authority of the agency, the expectations of professional knowledge, and self-confidence derived from knowledge and experience were part of the practitioner's knowledge. Later, organizational roles and knowledge and participation in the organizational situation, as a volunteer pianist and as a practitioner around the hospice taking an interest in patients, contributed to reinforcing the work. This included assessing some of the underlying factors in their relationship and starting out on a process dealing with the social issues that they faced in a more complex way.

Where were the professional theory, knowledge, and skills in this situation, and where are they in most of the situations that social workers deal with? The first point to make is that social work theory, knowledge, and skills were integral to all that was done with Julie and her mother, and we have seen that it is possible to identify them. It was knowledge about how to approach a situation, understanding about issues and emotions that were likely to arise between mother and daughter as the daughter was dying at a young age, and understanding about communication processes. All these were evident and could be sourced back to original research. However, the practitioner primarily operated as a professional in a human, and humane, way in the particular situation of a hospice.

The second point, therefore, is that, as is usually the case, practice was part of an agency with its own history, systems, and ways of working. The practitioner was called on by nursing and medical colleagues in the ward according to an agreed-on convention about when they call on social workers, and the practitioner responded because of the agency's system for dealing with urgent matters when a staff member, the ward social worker, is sick. From the point of view of social work, this situation was probably not urgent. But nursing and physician colleagues have to provide care in a ward of people dying alongside their families, friends, and members of their community. Distress and difficulty in a family need resolution to give them and other people in the ward and the visitors' lounge peace of mind. Reacting to a disruption helps in managing the care environment. Also, people who do not have much time left in their life do not want relationship issues getting in the way of the living that they need to do. So the needs of the family invoked the requirements of the organization and thus set practical requirements, which overrode a social work professional judgment that this did not require an urgent response.

Also, again as in many situations, the nurse, doctor, patient, and family members accepted unquestioningly when they were referred to a social worker, that someone would arrive who was able to deal with the particular things that the organization, professional convention, and social expectations consider the role of social workers. I refer to this as the wise-person expectation (Payne, 2007, 2009a, 2009b). Social workers are not necessarily wise about everything in their lives. But when called on in their profession, people expect them to be an appropriate kind of person for the role and to have the knowledge, values, and understanding that allow them to do the work well.

This wisdom often appears to be practical rather than theoretical, and it is practitioner knowledge. Even though it can be traced back to more theoretical and structured understanding, it goes with the person who seems to have this capacity and so comes to be regarded as a wise person. A good agency employs successful wise people, and agency clients take for granted that the organization will have such wise people available when required; they will also have other wise people available to fill different kinds of roles. Moreover, that practicality and flexible responsiveness has personal value and content, because although organized knowledge informs it, people experience it as a personal response to their personal reality. It is also organized by its relevance to the agency role; knowledge is developed, managed, and negotiated in the agency to be particularly useful to it.

USING KNOWLEDGE ECLECTICALLY

You might see the foregoing as eclectic. Thompson (2000) is one of a long line of social work writers who comments that being eclectic in our use of knowledge often means juxtaposing disparate knowledges that are inconsistent with one another. Another writer called, less politely, what social workers sometimes do in adapting specific knowledge from different sources a "process of violent bodging" (Jordan, 1978), that is, squashing together weak and inadequate material to fill holes in our practice. Epstein (1992), a wise and experienced practitioner, argued that eclecticism may offer flexibility but should be carefully developed in consultation with professional colleagues so that knowledge is used appropriately and consistently across an agency and so that practitioners can test out their judgments about using knowledge with other colleagues. We saw this happening in the case analysis, when specialist knowledge and experience in the agency adjusted the practitioner's response based on generalized theory and personal capacity. In this way, participation in an agency strengthens the evidence base of practitioners' work by ensuring that their flexible adaptations are consistently tested.

Therefore, saying that practitioners should stick to evidence and well-developed, tested models of practice is only partially helpful in practice, because they have to discover and ease themselves into a situation, as in the early interactions around Julie, and embody their knowledge in their personality in an interpersonal relationship as they become the wise person in that situation. However, practitioners may be able to apply evidenced interventions in highly structured treatment situations, and it is possible for them, in concert with their agency and colleagues, to be more explicit about the basis for the decisions they are making about whether and how to intervene. The practitioner in Julie's case might develop a more evidence-aware approach by doing this. However, it would also be useful to think again about and to research how knowledge is incorporated into social work practice and embodied holistically in the practitioner.

SOCIAL WORK AS A PRACTICE

The third point I want to make about practice is that two aspects of practice are in tension. It is, first, a practice, a convention, standard, or approach to the things that social workers do; we say "it is our practice to . . ." This conveys that social work has continuity, certainty, evidence, accepted standards. However, practice, as we have seen, is also provisional (Payne et al., 2009); it is a jazz player improvising or a musician rehearsing. No prior prescription of intervention was available, so improvisation was required. If working through their present concerns had descended into virulent dispute or reticence and nonengagement, something else would have been tried. One of the ways social work and its relationships with the people it serves come to be valued is by sticking with it and trying again. This is also a good model for people in difficulties. It is hard to try again when things do not work out in adversity, but the social worker sticking with it is likely to be more valued than someone who tries once or twice and then washes their hands of the situation.

To offer both the certainty of accepted practice and the flexibility of being provisional seems inconsistent, and this inconsistency is another thing that concerns students and practitioners about social work. It would seem better to be clear what social work does. Managers would like to be able to prescribe procedures to be followed on all occasions; academics would like to see evidence that social work techniques are effective in particular situations; social workers themselves would like to be clear about what to do next and seek guidelines or practice models that will help them. This attempt to deal with the flexibility by promoting certainty is another of the difficulties that practitioners face in the connection between the real world and the theoretical world.

SUPPORTING FLEXIBILITY IN CLIENTS' LIVES

Guillemard (2005) suggests that the life course is divided into three phases by major changes in the way people are supported financially, yet most people's life courses are increasingly flexible. The three major phases are as follows:

- Childhood, during which we are maintained by our parents and state support for education, leisure, and personal development
- Adulthood, in which salaried employment allows us to maintain ourselves; if we cannot work, social security provides some compensation
- Postretirement, when financial transfers from our adult period and from the rest of the population through various pension and medical supports allow us to retire from employment

Increasingly, the shifts between the three phases are changing. For example, enterprising children with physical skills for sport or in contact with modern technology and popular culture can see ways to make millions of dollars from early business or sporting success. Adults take sabbaticals on which they travel and concentrate on personal development. Older people continue working, either because of lack of financial support or to maintain a more interesting and better-financed lifestyle. Increasingly, too, people want a better work-life balance in the adult phase. So they work part-time, with reduced income, so that they can enjoy being with their children or pursuing leisure and personal development interests.

Such flexibility is more accepted in modern societies and provides opportunities for people to achieve personal development goals. However, our societies apply pressures. For example, in developing countries or underdeveloped areas of rich countries, there may be few opportunities for successful educational development in childhood; money may be so tight that children have to contribute to the family income. Alternatively, family difficulties may mean that children have to take on adult responsibilities. In adult life, illness or learning disability may mean that pursuing success at work is not a viable option for many people. Using positive practice, we must help them identify useful things that they can achieve. In later life, people may lose in retirement many of the things that created a structure and forward-looking commitment in their lives. One of the ways life can deal you a poor hand of cards is by having to become a caregiver for a disabled relative when you are a child.

Case Example: Young Caregivers

Kandy is a forty-three-year-old mother who has suffered from depression for many years; it led to the breakup of her marriage. She was left caring for her two children, Samantha (now twelve) and Kain (now nine). Kandy has become morbidly obese and is also agoraphobic—she is almost unable to leave her house unless her sister takes her out. But her sister lives a long drive away and has her own family. She is irritated by the direction Kandy's life has taken and is not a sympathetic helper.

Kandy is able to do some housework and cooking when she is feeling well, but Samantha, with Kain's help, does all the shopping. They spend a lot of time with Kandy, and being with them does lift her mood. But their childhood is all about caring for their mother and the house, not about doing the things they might prefer. They were supported in doing what they did in their home and given a chance to do young people's things by a group run by social workers working for a charity for young caregivers.

An important reason for practice flexibility is the opportunity to make something positive of experiences like these. As people's lives become more flexible, they often need more support to achieve their own personal growth in caring roles. This is true of adults caring for older parents or for friends or relatives with disabilities or mental illness. We saw in chapter 2 that offering support for caregivers, family, and community members around people we are helping is an important way to promote equality, because doing so reduces the losses that arise from having to be flexible in life.

DISCRETION AS FLEXIBILITY

An aspect of flexibility is the use of discretion. Social work agencies have become more managerial. That is, they have responded, like much of government, to financial pressures on state finances by setting targets and schedules for work based on numerical data and scales rather than interpersonal managerial processes such as supervision. This has led to the development of managed care, care management, and programmed services. These are humanistic in that they focus on fairness and equality and derive from evidence, but they do not allow for judgments to be varied to take into account human variation. Murdach (2009) identifies several ways to organize discretion:

- A social choice perspective, in which interventions are developed from the particular circumstances of each practice context. Practitioners use a combination of methods to strengthen social bonds, thus empowering individuals and groups in joint decision making and trying to increase communication and exchange of resources between groups.
- Planning or policy approaches seek to identify the main policy drivers for intervention, shifting between a macro perspective on policy and a micro perspective on interpersonal relations. This enables practitioners to connect the aims of the agency and other services to clients' needs, interpreting one as they respond to the drive and needs of the other.
- Mediational approaches use knowledge of services to guide people through complex negotiations, forging consensus between different parts of the system and clients and their families. This is typical of practice in health-care settings, where social workers are particularly involved in interceding with a range of professionals and clients and families.

Case Example: Personal Assistance for a Young Disabled Man

Jacob, a railway worker, had a serious motorcycle accident. After extensive surgery and a great deal of inpatient physical rehabilitation, the question arose of where and how he was to live. The social worker in the rehabilitation unit had meetings with Jacob, his parents, and his girlfriend; eventually they also had meetings with a care management agency that negotiated packages of care in people's own homes. Jacob's mother wanted him to continue to live at home. There was also discussion about his moving in with his girlfriend, which had been his plan before the accident. However, the girlfriend, though she had been supportive emotionally and remained in contact with him, confided to the social worker that she was not sure she could handle a lifetime of caring responsibility for a severely disabled man. Thus, part of the practice involved an exploration among the social worker, Jacob, and the girlfriend about where their relationship was going. Jacob's mother, feeling some of this tension, rejected the girlfriend and asserted very strongly that Jacob could return to the parental home. However, he felt he had made considerable progress in life and did not want to move back in with his parents. Eventually, it was resolved that Jacob would try to live alone. A care agency was contracted to help Jacob appoint two personal assistants, who would rotate to provide daily care for him. Jacob's mother also rejected this option because she felt it was a waste of money; care by her (in the absence of care by the girlfriend) was the best choice for the family, she felt.

The starting point of this set of care decisions was a social approach: could relationships be built that would provide care without a service being required? Yes, but Jacob felt that his mother's care would limit his long-term life plan for independence and inhibit later possibilities of work or personal development, which care in the parental home might hamper if it created greater dependency. The policy approach of the agency was for independence and family involvement, so all the options were appropriate. But professional policy in this field seeks to build independence; again, this led to a preference for a more expensive but potentially self-actualizing option. Finally, the social worker needed to mediate the various interests while keeping open the possibility of a change of mind. Even though the mother rejected her, the girlfriend might decide to become reinvolved. Although independence was preferred, Jacob might need to return home if he could not manage on his own and with personal assistants.

CONCLUSION

Weick (1999) has argued that an important characteristic of social work is that "it is formed from the humble stuff of lived experience and values" (p. 327). She presents the image of an adult offering a lap for a distressed child to argue that this is an important role of much of social work and allied roles in caring settings, such as hospitals and care homes. Such roles emerge from the interaction of experience and formal knowledge. We may debate whether such tacit knowledge can be formalized, but the primary focus has to be on how it is used.

To see certainty and flexibility as inconsistent with each other is to misunderstand the nature of social work and of humanity. What social workers do and how they interact with others are flexible and variable, because their work reflects human and social variability, and the people involved, both practitioners and clients, will not accept anything else.

However, their instruments of practice—knowledge, skills, understanding, and value objectives—need clarification, coherence, and consistency if they are to be used well and to develop. My conceptualization of practice is to say that it is always provisional. We improvise a performance with and alongside the people we serve and our colleagues. We incorporate and embody knowledge and understanding that we have achieved as our persona as a wise person. We restructure and incorporate knowledge and evidence in accordance with the needs of the situation and the people in it; that is our wisdom. If we chose to, we could identify where it came from, and we should be able to do so if the accountability to clients and agencies discussed in chapter 2 requires it. We can take up ideas from our theory and use them to incorporate knowledge into our practice. So I argue that expanding our understanding of theory gives us as practitioners and gives the students we help to learn ways to incorporate and structure knowledge and evidence so that we may embody and perform flexibility. Elaborated models and the detail of evidence underpin that flexible performance, but they cannot be an everyday part of it. The way particular theory struggles with social work's overriding and ambitious claim to connect the interpersonal and the social is a way of understanding the structure of our thinking about the people that we work with.

FURTHER READING

Cameron, N., & McDermott, F. (2007). *Social work and the body*. Basingstoke, UK: Palgrave Macmillan.

A thoughtful and comprehensive discussion of the body as an element of assessment and practice in social work.

Borden, B. (Ed.). (2009). *Reshaping theory in contemporary social work: Toward a critical pluralism in clinical practice*. New York: Columbia University Press.

An imaginative collection that offers many ideas for flexible practice.

Complexity in Human Life and Professional Practice

CHAPTER AIMS

The main aim of this chapter is to understand how to deal with complexity in social work practice. After working through this chapter, readers should be able to

- Understand different kinds of complexity in the social work task
- Use the ideas of chaos theory to build nonlinear explanations of the social situations that practitioners work with and manage complex situations
- Develop complexity rather than dichotomous thinking in assessing and responding to whole situations, and identify resources to deal with complexities rather than using oversimplifying explanations required by very structured social work practice theories, which may only appropriately be used for partial situations
- Work through complexities in applying social work values

WHAT IS COMPLEXITY?

We often talk about how complex human beings are, and how difficult and complex that fact makes any kind of professional practice that deals with them. Social work adds to this human and professional complexity because it aims to deal with the social as well as the personal, so it adds the complexity of trying to respond to families, informal caregivers, communities, and broader social issues that might affect a client. Humanistic social work ideas have to deal with complexity because they propose treating as a whole human beings working with other human beings on human social issues. That is complex; other practice theories try to simplify and divide up the complex whole.

Case Study: Patient and Family in Health Care

Jocasta was admitted to a hospital renal unit with kidney problems; she had two adult children, now independent, by her first marriage to a Muslim man, and two children (one of whom was eight years old) by her second marriage to a Roman Catholic man. Her husband worked in another part of the country, and when he was away, his mother often cared for the child. Doctors and nurses battled ceaselessly to deal with her illness; complex drug interactions and physical treatments were a difficult burden. Nurses managing the ward found it very stressful to deal with conflict between different members of the families who wanted to visit; in particular, her present husband's mother found it very difficult to meet the children of the first marriage, but she wanted to spend as much time as possible with the eight-year-old at the hospital. A social worker was asked to see members of the family and help manage the situation; she discovered that behind the difficulties was Jocasta's decision that, when she died, her property and savings would be used to support her youngest child through to adulthood, and the daughters of the first marriage, one of whom was struggling financially, would get nothing from Jocasta's estate. A nurse had a big argument with one of the daughters, who was trying to broach this with her mother. The nurse felt that Jocasta should not be worried by these matters while she was so ill. The daughters from the first marriage felt that it needed to be sorted out.

In this case, the doctors and nurses could focus on one aspect of the situation—Jocasta's illness—and the family's relationships were an irritating interruption to their main responsibilities. For the social worker, however, the main focus of her work were the complexities of a mixed family and the consequences of the illness for the different relationships that involved more people and a broader range of activities.

Complexity can mean two different but connected aspects of a situation:

- It can be a point at which different factors we are concerned with come together.
- It can be a situation in which different factors come together in a way that confuses and challenges our ability to understand.

Case Example: Different Forms of Complexity in a Hospice

The hospice where I work helps people who are dying. Public and professional policy is that, as a specialized agency, the hospice should deal with the more complex cases instead of general services. A working group reviewed what this meant and came up with three possible definitions:

- Additive complexity, in which there were more issues to deal with than usual and having to work on many different matters at once
- Progression complexity, in which problems were getting worse, and they were difficult to deal with and becoming more so
- Interactive complexity, in which the problems interacted with and affected one another, thus making the whole situation more complex

Many cases exhibited more than one of these forms of complexity. We dealt with these issues by having very experienced and highly trained staff who could unravel the progression complexities of very difficult situations. Also, we are a multiprofessional service, so several different types of expertise and skills were brought together to deal with additive complexity. However, this sometimes increased the interactive complexity of cases, because integrating the different staff and their expertise became part of the complexity.

One of the issues that came up was that complexity sometimes emerges as family problems arise and come to the notice of agencies. Then, the involvement of more agencies in a situation raises the level of complexity. Box 5.1 presents this emerging complexity model.

Not all complexity develops in our awareness in this way. Complexity may vary as various agencies get to work. This leads us to think about a varying complexity model, presented in box 5.2.

Complexity and chaos theory are types of systems theory that try to explain how complexity comes about (Halmi, 2003). There are problems in doing this, because the theories were devised as mathematically based and scientific, to deal with the complexities of the real world (Gleick, 1998). It is therefore important to realize that we are not applying a scientific theory here but using ideas from it in an analogy to help us think through human complexities in a quite different context. Chaos and complexity theory thus give us ideas about how to think through issues.

Box 5.1 Emerging Complexity Model

Increasing complexity

Family manages social situation	Referral point to services	Referral to further services	As services interact, complexity increases
The family manages its problems itself. Needs may remain hidden from services. As the problem trajectory rises, involvement of other family or community resources may also increase. Services working with informal caregivers may become aware of concerns.	Referral to an agency takes place ■ To support family actions ■ Because increasing concern leads to a search for more services ■ Because an agency already involved proposes referral	This occurs because ■ Service responsibilities are met, but other issues are identified ■ Assessment by other agencies and/or professionals is needed to make use of their services ■ Existing engagements with other agencies are identified	New issues and challenges emerge from interaction between services: ■ Each service identifies problems in its specialty ■ Interaction discloses that known problems are more complex ■ Interactions between problems that increase complexity are uncovered

Box 5.2 Varying Complexity Model

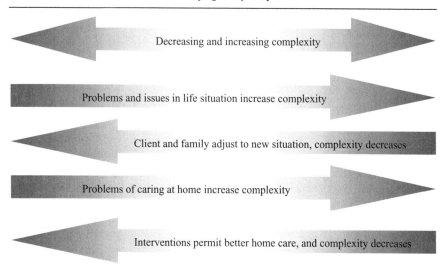

In this context, they fit well with humanistic practice because they are nonlinear kinds of explanation. That is, according to these theories, in complex situations, so many different events have an impact on the situation that one thing does not lead to another; instead, a wide variety of factors interacting in many different ways, many of the factors not obvious, may need to be taken into account. A linear explanation looks like this: "Events A and B happened, and because they happened together, event C was the result. If we intervene by doing D, it will change how A and B came together, and instead of event C, event E will happen." Nonlinear explanations say: "Events A, B, C and D all seem to have an effect on how event E occurs, and we need to understand how they affect each other and how their interaction influences event E." Nonlinear explanation makes understanding seem so complicated that describing and explaining how anything happens seems impossible; and if description and explanation are impossible, we cannot begin to decide how to intervene. In science, chaos theory proposes that there are patterns even in very complex events, if we look behind surface turbulence; in fact, an early use was trying to predict the movement of water flows when they were disturbed (Gleick, 1998).

Humanistic practice starts from the position that dealing with human beings as a whole has to respond to the complexity of humanity and its relationship with the social environment. It is impossible to set laws and standardized ways of understanding the interaction of complex beings. Halmi (2003) reviews several different ways of modeling the complex real world so that we can understand it. Simple explanations of human behavior used in theories like cognitive behavioral therapy make predictions on the basis of recognized laws of behavior or social interaction. Alternatively, and slightly more complex, we can make a good guess at probable outcomes through statistical analysis of the usual variation and the likely outcome. But this is often useless in complex situations.

Instead, we can try iconological modeling, in which we compare different possible overall pictures of the situation with what seems to be happening to decide which picture best fits what we are seeing. Structural modeling similarly seeks to identify possible structures in social situations and to examine logically which structure works best to explain a particular case. Ideal typical strategies look at different cultural explanations and other pictures of the world that exist and test them out against events. Finally, historical modeling looks at the story of a particular event and compares it with other similar events to see how this particular instance is different.

Case Example: Romantic Love or Arranged Marriage?

A case example, picking up a case being discussed in the press at the time of writing, may make this clearer. A young Islamic woman, of Pakistani origin, in a Western city has formed a relationship at school with a Christian young man. Her family members said that this is not acceptable, removed her from school, and imprisoned her in her room at home under the constant supervision of her mother and married sisters. They told her that a marriage had been arranged in Pakistan, and that tickets had been booked for the family to fly there. Her brothers tell the young Christian man on his way home from school that if he sees their sister again, they will beat him up. She is ambivalent—she values the relationship with the young man but also her loyalty to her family. Simple explanations might be about the social impact of intermarriage between different religions, bullying, concern about loss of opportunity to complete her education, or illiberal attitudes in a traditional family that has not acclimated to a new social situation. All of these have some relevance but do not give a full explanation. Official intervention by a school social worker or counselor, the police, ministers of religion, or other social services all seem inadequate, at least partly because they might not deal with all the factors in the situation.

Thinking humanistically, we might think that human growth should involve these young people learning to make their own decisions and accept the consequences for themselves. But this is the view of a Western society in which the main objective of personal growth is people's development of autonomy from their families. In an Eastern society, the objective of personal growth is more about developing interdependence among family members, and a different set of values might be the main focus of our thinking.

Iconological modeling offers us a picture of a migrant family isolated from its roots and in a Western society with a focus on cultural expression of individualized love as more important than family loyalties and interdependence, with a view that young people should be free to experiment with relationships, and in a society in conflict with Islamic states. Structural modeling identifies religious conflict, gender and power relations, and ethnic conflict as potential issues. Ideal typical explanations focus on what ideal family relations in different cultures should be like, on what freedom to express love and establish relationships might be. Historical modeling looks at the sequence of events and might include a history of doubts about sending the young woman to a coeducational school. There might be guilt because the family could not pay for a private single-sex school or because they feel they gave too much freedom to the young woman at too young an age or failed to supervise her relationships. There may also be a history of social

expectations from the particular place the family comes from in Pakistan and provoca-
tive behavior of the young couple. Looking at a range of narratives of the whole situation
might uncover many other factors.

In summary, dealing with complexity involves looking at a range of explanations
and issues, not trying to limit the issues simply by referring to agency mandate, the presenting issues, or the issues demanded by a research or practice model. So we should look
not just at the school's responsibility to ensure continuance in education or the social
services and police responsibility to prevent a forced marriage. Our more complex ways
of looking at the situation identify the ambivalence and a history of ambivalence in the
family that are real and relevant to what we should do next. Different people in the family dispute may represent different sides of a complex social debate. To take one side of
it, for example by supporting young people's rights to make an individual decision, fails
to recognize and work with human uncertainties. The most appropriate help would be
to work with those ambivalences while recognizing that the family has to deal with these
alternates.

Stevens and Cox (2008), looking at child protection, usefully identify several ways
to look at situations drawn from chaos and complexity theory that can help us in a wider
context. First, they remind us that complexity theory relates to systems theory, which is
familiar to most social workers. Systems theory tells us that all the aspects of a system
interact and affect one another. At the micro level or the individual, our psychological,
physical, and spiritual feelings or body, mind, and spirit interact and affect one another.
For example, if we are feeling physically fit, we have the energy to take on emotional
stresses and the changes they create in our lives; we can be more resilient (I look more at
resilience in chapter 8). At the meso level, our family and community, for example, a new
baby, a child leaving home to go to college, or the death of an older member of the family has an impact on everyone in the family. These are stresses that each person also has
to deal with at the micro level, as individuals. In communities, a new neighbor, a new
youth leader, or a new teacher will have an impact on the street, the youth club, or the
school, which in turn will affect the families in that community and the individuals in
those families. Again, the knowledge and cohesiveness of the family and community will
mean that they deal with such difficulties in different ways. At the macro level, a social
change such as a newly elected government or a new policy direction will have an effect
on many groups and individuals, all of whom will react.

A commonplace idea of systems theory is that systems use energy to maintain
themselves, and this keeps the system in balance and coping with the events that affect it.
Closed systems, typical of machinery, need energy fed into them to function at all: to
make the computer work, you have to switch on the power. Open systems, like human
beings, can create their own energy through imagination and reflection; this means that
openness to new experiences and working together to do things can give us new ideas to
move forward with. If an individual, family, community, or society seems lifeless,
immovable, this will have an impact on all its members and make it difficult for many
different members. One of the things that can stimulate progress is awareness, reflection,
and analysis: our mental energy can get us moving.

Case Example: Groups in a Community Agency

I once worked as chief executive of a community development agency in a major U.K. city. The agency had two elements: one that found and disseminated funding for community organizations, and one that served as liaison with community groups and supported new developments in the community. When I joined the organization, there had been a period of instability; my predecessor had been ill for some time and had then retired, and people had been waiting for the replacement for some time. Two managers had applied for the job that I had; one indicated his intention, not having been appointed, to move on in his career, and another did not have such an opportunity, so he would stay until his own retirement. More junior staff were anxious to progress to a more open, democratic style of management and develop their own roles. However, the trustees of the organization remained the same, and there were divisions between those concerned with financing community organizations, who needed to maintain organizational stability and traditions to sustain support from their constituency, and those concerned with community development and liaison roles, who were focused on more rapid social change and involving organizations working with excluded minority ethnic groups.

Internal reforms and organizational development were fairly easy to achieve, and liaison and development work with new community groups made good progress. The remaining manager, however, focused on the financing side of the organization, increasingly felt that the changes were alienating financial supporters, and some groups of trustees agreed. They sought to prevent some of the more innovative engagements on the community development side, because they saw them as interfering with their fund-raising responsibilities. This came to a head over a conflict among groups representing minority ethnic group residents and local businesses. It made the situation seem immovable, stuck in a field of mud; it seemed impossible to make further changes in the organization.

Looking at this conflict, we can see the internal workings of the organization as a partly closed system: it needs the energy of its funding and traditional support to maintain itself. The community development side of the organization was a more open system, because engagement with local groups enabled staff to be more creative and see new things that they could do without the need to achieve traditional support and funding. A power analysis might suggest that the energy brought into the organization from the new groups and the creativity generated internally threatened the power of the manager and his supporters among the trustees: their control over funding no longer gave them the influence over the work of the organization that they previously had, because creativity and new energy was pushing the organization in a new direction.

Several actions resolved the situation, including work on new ideas on the funding side, which provided new opportunities for development among the group of trustees and staff, and some open negotiation to work out principles for managing the possible downsides of work with new community groups of minority ethnic groups. Thinking humanistically, again, this is an example of the way all sides of an individual and organization need to achieve development; personal and organizational growth need to be balanced among different interests. It is also an example of the importance of openness in dealing with issues and maintaining equality of condition between different elements of an individual or organization.

Complexity and chaos theory take us beyond systems ideas, in part because of an emphasis on dissipative systems. One of the features of systems is entropy, the tendency of the system to run down unless constantly fed with energy, either imported or created. In the case study, the financial side of the organization was experiencing entropy because the energy of creativity and external connections that were helping the community side to develop did not stimulate it. Complex systems are often dissipative systems, which run down very quickly (Halmi, 2003); this is because dealing with complexity dissipates energy.

In very complex social situations, keeping a balance is difficult, and people feel on the edge all the time, so they make tremendous demands of the environment around them and export a great deal of chaos to other systems. Because everything in a system is affected by everything else that happens, and the interactions are complex, sometimes only a small event is required to push the whole system off balance. This feels like chaos for the following reasons:

- We are all the time at risk of being off balance, so we feel uneasy and insecure.
- Minor events seem to have a disproportionate impact, and we can never guess what the impact might be: sometimes it is a big impact, but sometimes nothing happens at all, so everything feels out of control.
- When this happens, normal feedback mechanisms, such as giving support to people or giving them helpful advice do not always work; as a result, sometimes a vast amount of energy is required to get back in balance, and even then, we still feel on edge.

Many social work situations seem like this, and box 5.3 lists typical client groups that social workers often help, giving examples of apparently minor events that can disrupt carefully planned support and lead to the feeling of insecurity in the arrangements we have made.

Case Example: Helping With Parkinson's Disease Symptoms

This is a more concrete example of a situation of chronic illness. Mr. Hernandez had severe Parkinson's disease and was supported by a home nursing service and his wife; he took extensive medication. This stable arrangement continued for some years, but his condition worsened, and he experienced a sudden freezing up of his body movements, with severe pain. His inability to move meant that his wife could not administer pain and symptom relief medication. In great distress, he was admitted to the emergency room of the hospital several times. His wife felt that he was no longer safe at home and that she could not manage such very distressing events. A social worker was asked to arrange admission to a care home, but Mr. Hernandez understandably resisted this. The practitioner asked, "What do the emergency nurses do when he goes there?" His wife didn't see, and the nurse did not know, but Mr. Hernandez's reply gave them the answer to the disruption in care. The hospital nurses used an eyedropper to administer small doses of medication to his mouth, which trickled down his throat and eventually took effect. With some training by the home care nurse, Mrs. Hernandez learned to do this, and stable care at home was restored—until a different symptom disrupted the arrangement.

Box 5.3 Examples of Complexity in Common Social Work Client Groups

Client group	Service	Example
Children	Child protection and safeguarding	Minor family problems suddenly escalate into abuse
Young people	Young offenders	They agree to commit to avoiding situations in which they are at risk of offending, but minor events push this aside, such as an argument with their parents that leads them to go out drinking.
Families	Support with poverty and family disorganization	Failure to make small regular payments to meet a debt leads to legal action, which then destroys the family's coping
People with intellectual disabilities	Support in daily living	Minor conflicts with social contacts, bullying at the local bar, or sudden illness disrupts routines
People with physical disabilities	Support in managing life in special adapted housing	Minor physical change disrupts normal support
People with chronic illnesses	Support in avoiding admission to care home	Changes in symptoms make it hard to cope
Older people	Planned package of care delivered by visiting carers working with family members	Family event or carer illness disrupts normal caring supports and means hospital and care home admission is inevitable
Dying people	Symptom control and stable social support	Rapid change in symptoms or family capacity can lead to hospital admission or inability to maintain medication

Complexity theory, according to Stevens and Cox (2008), suggests a number of things that happen in complex social situations:

■ The system becomes self-organizing; that is, so many internal interactions take place that there is no certainty that external observations will be accurate or interventions will work as expected.

■ Because explanation is nonlinear, trying to understand complex situations by looking for a few factors by way of explanation and understanding is unlikely to work.

■ Reactions emerge from a variety of factors in the situations that cannot be predicted from knowledge of the individual participants of factors. We may think that a mother is very protective of her child, but in a chaotic family with many different individuals in the household all affected by matters that may be difficult for them to deal with, the mother's protective behavior may not protect the child from abuse by other family members.

■ Dissipative structures mean that there are many positive factors, but they never quite become secure systems of support or help; again, there is the impression of being on edge all the time. We cannot evaluate the situation by counting the many positive factors and assuming they will overwhelm the few negative factors.

■ There are bifurcation points, in which a system seems to oscillate between two alternatives; the range of alternatives and interacting factors resolve themselves down to these alternatives, but it is never clear which will win out in a particular circumstance. However, we can identify the two reactions that the family or individual typically oscillates between. These are the patterns of chaos theory that are hidden in apparent disorganization.

■ Attractors are factors at the bifurcation point that pull it toward one alternative or the other.

These ideas suggest that it is possible to help even in very chaotic and complex situations. However, in doing so, we need to recognize some of the accountability issues discussed in chapter 2. A self-organizing complex system cannot be accountable to a practitioner, who is an external intervener. For example, people are unable to describe what is going on or to tell a story that accounts for what happened; it all appears out of control. Nor can they comply with genuinely meant agreements about the action they will take if a particular event happens. However, it is often possible to limit the number of alternatives. It may also be possible to identify attractors that can operate when there is a bifurcation point, so that positive alternatives emerge.

Case Example: Mr. Hernandez Again

Let us return to Mr. Hernandez and try to understand what happened in terms of complexity theory. His illness was very difficult to manage, and support at home was possible only while his medication was effective, his wife felt able to cope, and occasional nursing support reduced their level of anxiety. All these factors were destroyed by the sudden freezing episodes: these were self-organizing, and the couple dealt with them alone, reacting with fear, anxiety, and distress. Although such episodes do happen with Parkinson's disease, the severe distress they caused in the Hernandezes' marriage and their domestic arrangements could not have been predicted.

Some of the relevant factors might have been the fact that their children lived a long way away and could not provide practical support, the way in which the new symptom was viewed as a feared deterioration on his condition, the limited availability of their home care nurse after hours, and the experience of the emergency room. The pattern of behavior that emerged was either stability or distress because of fear of another episode; this made the couple feel on edge all the time, as if they were waiting for the next episode when they would be unable to cope. The positives in the situation seemed dissipated, and

the only possible resolution seemed to be admission to full-time care; it was either instability at home or stability in care. The social worker's question led to a practical way to
reassert the previous stability. Learning to use the eyedropper was a successful attractor
for various reasons. For example, it had the authority of "this is what the hospital does,"
it reaffirmed Mrs. Hernandez's control, it was something she could learn, and it reduced
fear and distress when a freezing episode took place.

Looking at this example, we might say that this is describing an average intervention in new language. The point to emphasize is that this approach helps us think
through very complex, apparently intractable situations; it makes us feel less helpless. It
reasserts our human capacity to deal with situations that have too many factors in them
to understand. The practitioner (without knowing this terminology) went looking for an
attractor, some additional factor in the situation that might begin to shift it back to a new
stability. We know this stability will be only for the time being until the next difficult
symptom; the practitioner will not be able to handle that new situation in the same way.
Thinking, "I need an attractor here," that is, a potentially positive factor, she might again
be encouraged to cast around for another possibility to use in the renewed chaos.

COMPLEXITY IS A MAJOR ROLE FOR SOCIAL WORK

Most social workers, wherever they work, deal with complex life situations like this in
their practice. If situations were not difficult in various ways or complex in their ramifications, people would manage them without calling on help from a social worker. Realizing this and focusing on the implications of complexity also have implications for the
way social workers use theory and skills in their practice. Some social work theory tries
to simplify situations so that they can select elements of them to work on in isolation.
However, humanistic ideas argue that whole human practitioners need to think about
the whole human beings in their social relationships and in their social environment;
selecting parts of the situation to work on can be done only within that holistic view.
Therefore, much social work theory and skills analysis does not adequately guide social
workers' practice in complex situations. They need to incorporate a range of additional
knowledge and skills to make good use of practice theory.

This is one reason social workers often comment that the theory that they are taught
in their courses is unhelpful when they reach full-scale practice. In education, in writing
essays about the application of theory to practice and in practice placements, it is possible to limit the range of factors that a practitioner deals with. There are no such luxuries
in full-time professional practice.

Practice theory is an aspect of social work theory concerned with how to do social
work, in which ideas are developed to prescribe particular models of practice or ways of
practicing (Payne, 2005). Practice theory tries to make sense of the work social workers
actually do, and it includes formal and informal sets of ideas. Formal practice theory is
written, usually published, evidence and analysis worked out in a rational structured
form, which offers general ideas that may be applied deductively to particular practice

situations; that is, the ideas are applied to the situation rather than the situation itself generating ideas. Informal practice theory draws on ideas and experience gained in life and practice. It is applied inductively; that is, the theory derives from particular situations and is generalized to other relevant practice situations. This requires decisions about similarities and differences between situations to decide whether a generalization is relevant. Practice theory is not the only form of social work theory: there are also theories about what social work is and of psychological and social knowledge about the client's world (Sibeon, 1990).

The assumption of evidence-based or research-aware practice is that fairly clear prescriptions for action can be identified from research, but this does not consider how official or legal responsibilities or agency function mediate these (Webb, 2001). Practice theory generally prescribes actions that take place with one client or family. Many practice theories such as task-centered practice, solution-focused work, and cognitive-behavioral practice presume precise targeting of specific behaviors (Payne, 2005). These systems of thought may give us ideas about a situation and organize a response that people can understand and accept. For example, task-centered practice helps practitioners and clients identify a series of tasks to be shared. Solution-focused work generalizes successes in clients' lives to other issues with which they are having difficulty. In both sets of ideas, this helps practitioners and clients understand what they are doing and identify progress.

Although such theories may be helpful as part of practice, the situations practitioners work with are not the main focus of much social work practice theory. Because theory defines the ideas that should be applied to a situation, it does not make provisions for ideas to emerge from the particular situation that practitioners are dealing with. Therefore, theory does not allow clients or others in the family system to develop and act on ideas about how they might deal with situations. Complex relationships between different family groups all require some aspects of social welfare provision, and the provision of packages of caring services lie outside most practice theory prescriptions. Practice theory also does not deal with working across several organizations with different roles and legal and administrative mandates.

Case Example: Yvonne's and John's Care Needs

Sixteen-year-old Yvonne and eleven-year-old John, the children of Catherine and Sean, are an example of the kind of complexity that many social workers face in their practice. There were several breakups between Catherine and Sean after Yvonne was born, partly caused by Sean's violence; the final breakup came just after Catherine's pregnancy with John was confirmed. Sean eventually went to live with another woman, whose children were considered at risk and removed from the home because of his violence. Catherine brought up Yvonne and John largely on her own, but about three years ago, she was first diagnosed with cervical cancer. The local child protection team had been involved, partly because of continuing contact with Sean, who was considered a risk. More recently, it became clear that Catherine had only a few months to live, and arrangements for the children after Catherine's death needed to be planned, because by law Sean would be entitled to resume parental responsibilities after Catherine's death, and he was not considered a safe parent. As Catherine became frailer, Yvonne remained at home with her mother, but John increasingly stayed with Catherine's sister, Louise, and his cousins. The family's plan was that he would move there permanently when Catherine died, whereas Yvonne would stay in Catherine's home. During the last few weeks of Catherine's life, Sean, who had sporadic contact with the children, took to turning up at Catherine's home and asking to see the children. On two occasions, he was drunk and contact was refused, but his attitude became more demanding as the weeks went on. On the weekend of Catherine's death, he appeared, drunk again, at Louise's house in another town to try to see John, sat outside in the car, was threatening, and had to be asked to leave by the police. Louise had no rights as a parent, but she and her husband were concerned about Sean visiting. The child protection responsibility for John would transfer to the authorities in Louise's hometown, and a meeting was set up to transfer the case; however, Yvonne also explained to the social worker that she felt the need for protection if Sean visits the original family home.

The various strands of this situation highlight different aspects of social work practice. Among those strands are the following:

- The children's direct experience of marriage breakup and domestic violence in their lives from a young age
- John's experience of impending and actual separation from his sister and incorporation into another family, which is itself re-forming to include him
- John's integration into a new school at a time of bereavement and the consequences of that for his school and other pupils
- The children's recent experience of the death of a parent, probably the first major death of someone close to them in their lives
- The children's experience of threat from their father's behavior and their perceptions and understanding of those family dynamics
- Sean's issues with alcohol and his emotional and social responses to parenthood in his two families
- The legal complexities of parental rights and responsibilities by which children are protected by removal from or separation from their parents and family members take on parental responsibilities
- The responsibility of the social workers involved to assess and respond to the need and risk affecting various participants on behalf of the state
- The social work principle of engaging family members and finding respectful, open ways to do so, especially in the face of hostility or violence
- The complexity of trying to create safe contact between children and their noncustodial parent or parents to maintain family relationships, identity, and belonging
- The delicate balance of a strengths-based practice approach in child protection work while considering risks, needs, rights, and wishes of all parties
- Yvonne's taking on of independent responsibility for her own living arrangements and a house at the age of sixteen upon her mother's death

- The administrative complexities of transferring responsibility for children at risk from one public authority to another
- The professional and administrative responsibilities for liaison about a complex family situation involving different public authorities and responsibilities

This list of issues is not exhaustive, but it reminds us that social workers deal both with making practical arrangements and with the emotional and behavioral content of situations. In addition to their interpersonal practice, they are part of official and administrative systems and have to make them work, taking into account the legal rights and duties that they have as professionals and officials and those that their clients have as parents and citizens. For example, there is an informal arrangement between Catherine and her sister for John's care after her death, which might be fine in many families, although it would usually be better to confirm that arrangement through legal processes, an example of social workers ensuring that people's security is protected through due process. In this case, informality is inadequate in dealing with the complicated parental rights and behavioral difficulties. As with Jocasta's case, where we started this chapter, Catherine's doctors and nurses mainly focused on her treatment and comfort as she approached death. However, the focus of social work is on the social systems of which individuals are a part, so social workers were involved with important social issues for several members of the family and were responsible for making a variety of social systems work properly. For example, a thoughtful social worker would realize that John's bereavement of his mother at a young age might well have an emotional impact on his classmates at school that would need to be managed.

The complexity is of different kinds. Some of it arises because there are several individuals and family groups involved, some because a variety of social and behavioral issues are present, and some because of a mixture of agencies and legal and official responsibilities. These are additive complexities, which often generate interactive complexities. Social workers have to deal simultaneously with each of these different aspects of complexity; as we saw in boxes 2.2 and 2.3, complexity may develop as we understand the situation better or engage more agencies in the situation, or it may vary as we deal with some aspects of the situation or as others arise.

BRINGING KNOWLEDGE AND UNDERSTANDING TOGETHER THROUGH COMPLEXITY THINKING

As we saw in chapter 4, social workers need more than practice theory to deal with complex situations. They need to bring the ideas and techniques that come from practice theory together with other aspects of social work knowledge and understanding to incorporate a range of knowledge about the services and social environments in which they work. Payne, Adams, and Dominelli (2009) describe doing this through a process called complexity thinking, which starts by moving away from thinking about alternatives as dichotomies, either-or decisions. Practitioners are often accused of doing too much or too little, intervening too readily in people's lives, or not intervening enough. They are criticized for making the wrong decision or for being indecisive. We have seen that Mr.

Hernandez's case was viewed as an either-or situation—either manageable at home or requiring admission to a care home—but not as requiring creative learning that would enable a different way of managing to develop. Casting situations in dichotomous terms means missing the opportunities to help people progress their aims for a better quality of life contained within every piece of practice.

Complexity thinking moves away from the oversimplification of dichotomous thinking. Instead of saying, "If we do this, we cannot do that, and if we think this, we cannot think that," complexity thinking is inclusive, in the same way that humanistic thinking aims for equality by focusing on people's rights to be included in, to participate in, their social environment. Humanistic practice looks for alternatives and different sides of the situation; it tries to grasp and integrate them into discourses. Because the meanings that a social group gives to events or actions are always constructed in a discourse, social meanings always include complex and competing elements that reflect competing and shared interests in the situation; they are never one thing or the other. How we react to them and interact with others as they react to them provides opportunities for moving in different directions and opening up new possibilities.

Social workers also bring this knowledge together to practice in ways that respond to their personal style of relating to people and forms of response determined by their agency and colleagues as appropriate to their roles (Payne, 2009d). Practice frameworks provide further opportunities to collate theory, research, and knowledge types into conceptual guides for practice (Connolly, 2006; Healy, 2005). Social work supervision also provides an important mechanism for the exploration of these issues so that practice is informed in ways that strengthen good outcomes for children and their families. This is because humanistic practice means more than doing. Because complexity develops alongside our understanding and engagement with family situations and varies as we act to deal with some aspects of those situations, we need to revisit and reflect critically on our understanding and assumptions about the situation. We need to listen repeatedly to the narrative that we started from and rethink it to reevaluate it in light of our developing understanding. Our ideas about it become deeper and refined, and we may be able to test and change ideas about the situation that faces us.

Looking again at Yvonne and John's situation, the various social workers involved would need a great deal of organizational and practitioner knowledge about how the agencies and organizations needed to be contacted, followed up with, and supported to deal with the various problems the children face. Intervening in this situation required active pursuit of the links to ensure that John and Yvonne were safe. The responsibility was splintered so much that practitioners could not assume that the cases would transfer between authorities cleanly, that Yvonne would be helped to deal with her bereavement in her new fairly isolated position, that the police would intervene effectively to protect Yvonne in her mother's home, or that the school would be able to understand and deal with John's emotional difficulties arising from his bereavement and change of placement. The family situation was so complex that practitioners relied on family members to interpret behavior and understand what would work in the various relationships. They could not solely rely on oversimplified assumptions about family or human development, although, of course, this knowledge helped them know what kinds of issues to raise questions about.

Understanding the process of what was happening for Yvonne and John in their bereavement and various losses was also important. Loss often destroys people's identity as coping people, because it reduces their sense of hope that things will be all right, and hence their security and resilience (Flaskas, McCarthy, & Sheehan, 2007). When things are going well, people are able to tell a narrative about how they are managing, and they become hopeful of the future; their self and their family identity becomes a coping, hopeful identity. Loss trips this into despair; it becomes a bifurcation point, and they oscillate between despair at the loss and hope that things will work out. The dual process theory of bereavement (Stroebe & Schut, 1999) describes this oscillation in families and individuals who have experienced the death of a loved one, but it also affects many people in loss situations.

In this way, practitioners could work out how concerns would mount at the time of loss and when extra effort to help was required. It was important to be prepared to listen to the different concerns of the participants: John's and Yvonne's losses and fears; Louise's anxieties about the impact of the bereavement and taking John into her family; and also Sean, as his behavior might have been reflecting increased stresses and providing opportunity to facilitate some intervention to help him and secure relationships for Yvonne and John. Being prepared to act to help resolve particular issues as they arise is supportive because it means standing alongside people at a difficult time.

I have argued that dealing with complexity requires more of social workers than following prescriptions of practice theory that may be too oversimplified to be useful in complex situations. Practice theory may be applicable to particular aspects of situations within the complexity of people's lives. It may offer ideas about how to see the situation that clients are dealing with. However, social workers also need to call on a range of sources of knowledge and respond to the complexity in many of the situations that they deal with by analyzing and understanding the process and trajectory of issues as they have arisen in clients' lives. They need to use that knowledge and theory in a caring, emotionally intelligent, and supportive way with the aim of disentangling the various elements of a complex system and enhancing the resilience both of the people involved and of the social and organizational systems that they are entwined with.

COMPLEXITY THINKING AND SOCIAL WORK VALUES

A useful way to focus on complexity thinking is to re-form our ideas about social work values. Many of our social work values are framed in codes of practice or ethics as rules for practice. However, we rarely face situations in which a rule applies clearly. More often, a rule alerts us to a situation in which a particular issue will present difficulties, and we need to be careful to look at all the ramifications of the situation. Codes of ethics in the form of sets of rules present us with dichotomies in which we either comply with a value or fail to do so. Instead of seeing things as either-or situations, it is helpful to think about "and also": we want to keep that rule, but also we want to achieve this outcome. As a useful way of thinking about this, I previously presented values as complexities (Payne, 2006), and I reproduce in box 5.4 the value complexities identified there.

Box 5.4 Value Complexities

Value	Duality	Complexity
Individualization	Collectivization	When do we individualize clients' needs or deal collectively with shared interests? For example, people on a housing estate who want to change their environment and how repairs to their houses are carried out.
Acceptance	Antidependency	How do we balance acceptance of need for help with the process of helping people to become independent? For example, parents who make their child with learning disabilities too dependent on their care.
Being nonjudgmental	Critical evaluation, confrontation	How do we balance being nonjudgmental, with the need to critically evaluate behavior, and confront unsatisfactory behavior and social realities? For example, when protecting children from abuse.
Antidiscriminatory approach	Avoid labeling and victimizing	How do we balance breaking down barriers caused by inappropriate discrimination with avoiding people in minority or oppressed groups from feeling picked on, avoiding pressing them to take on battles that they cannot afford or cope with, and avoiding treating them as always the victims instead of having influence and freedom of action? Taking an antidiscriminatory approach sometimes involves focusing on aspects of life that label and victimize. Clients and workers often differ on the value of expressing or avoiding difference as part of antidiscriminatory practice.
Self-determination	Rule following or interdependent	How do we help people to be more autonomous when often they should be interdependent? Everyone follows rules and conventions of behavior: to be self-determining implies partly that one can choose whether or how to be rule following.
Respect for persons	Respect for community	How do we respect individuals' needs but also heed the value of community support and involvement? At times, wider social networks take priority over individuals.
Confidentiality	Openness	How do we promote confidentiality and openness at the same time? Confidentiality is a decision to limit openness; openness is a decision to forgo confidentiality in favor of openness for some reason.

Source: Payne (2006).

Case Example: Karina's Self-Determination

A more detailed case example may help explain practice with value complexities more fully. Karina was the twenty-two-year-old daughter of a single parent and had intellectual disabilities. Her progress at a special center for development and employment deteriorated. Lois, a social worker, was helping Karina and her mother, who was concerned that Karina was becoming involved with a group of other center members, perhaps misusing drugs and being sexually promiscuous with young men in the group. Karina said that her mother was overcontrolling and that she should be free to go out with her friends; she denied taking illegal drugs and thought going out with her boyfriend and his friends was reasonable. In a negotiation between mother and daughter, the temptation for Lois was to side with the mother, perhaps emphasizing all that her mother had done for her, the struggle to provide for the family as a single parent, and the lack of wisdom in Karina's current behavior. As a representative of the agency, she also had to bear in mind the need to manage behavior in the whole group of members.

However, in discussing informed consent in chapter 2, we noted that lack of wisdom was not a reason for enforcing a particular intervention. Also, using authority to enforce a course of action with people who have the ability to make their own decisions is often counterproductive because it focuses on the social order role of social work, thus setting social workers against their clients rather than helping social workers make decisions that incorporate all relevant aspects of the situation. The fact that this was a self-determination issue for a client who had not had much control over her life alerted Lois to a value complexity. She tried to hold in her mind the dichotomy between rule following and self-determination as she worked through the argument between Karina and her mother. To achieve personal development, everyone needs to have growing self-determination and maintain rule-following behavior, because this integrates into our behavior the needs of everyone in the social network around us.

Lois therefore tried to prevent the mother from using simple parental authority, both for the practical reason that it would be oppressive to enforce and because experiencing self-determination with helpful support would enable Karina to make progress in managing her own life in the long term. Lois's approach was to start from thinking through the best way to help Karina achieve the things she wanted to do, *and also* to help her mother feel secure about where Karina was and what she was doing, *and also* help Karina think through rules for herself that would enable her to be in control, *and also* help Karina think through what she wanted her time with the group of friends to be like and how she could influence the group's activities and behavior.

This was not achieved in one meeting, because people with intellectual disabilities often need to repeat information they have received and review, renew, and reinforce decisions they have made. Lois also felt, after discussing this with her supervisor, that in the early stages she had been unhelpful because she had focused too much on making the mother feel secure, so as to reduce conflict between mother and daughter. On reflection, Lois felt that she should have focused more on what Karina wanted to achieve, and she could probably have managed this if she had done more preparation with the mother about how the discussions would proceed, thus developing informed consent for the processes that they would move through.

This case sums up an important point about dealing with complexity. Lois was responsible for helping both Karina and her mother in a social environment with anxiety about young people's behavior, a sense of the need to protect people with intellectual disabilities that extended perhaps to overprotection. Lois also had responsibilities to her agency, the center, and less clearly to the local community. Local people might have wanted this situation managed in a way that maintained an orderly community, maintained supportiveness for the young members of the center, and disciplined social behavior among them. A general rule of self-determination for the client is inappropriate because the client cannot be limited to Karina; the client is also the mother and any other family, the community, and the center. Neither can the rule be to follow conventional behavior, because there would be disagreement about what that should be and what was appropriate in this particular situation. The appropriate humanistic practice approach indicates that there is a range of human freedoms and needs, so how can participants in this complex situation best achieve personal fulfillment.

CONCLUSION

This chapter has taken up the issue of the complexity of whole human beings in their social environment being helped by whole human beings with wide accountabilities to people, communities, organizations, and agencies involved.

Complexity can emerge from our engagement in a social situation, as we become aware of the many elements that it contains. Moreover, complexity may come not only from the number of human beings and social factors involved in a situation but also from the many ways they can interact. It often seems to increase, but equally often we may find that some aspects of situations we deal with become more complex, whereas other aspects are resolved and reduce the complexity of what we have to deal with. In this way, the complexity of a case may vary over time. Chaos theory tells us that we can only hope to understand such situations in a nonlinear way. Trying to look for simple causal steps in the situation to guide our practice is usually inadequate. Most human beings are too complex for us to be able to move from the antecedents of an event to the behavior or event that needs to be resolved, so that we can intervene and achieve change. Instead, we need to model the situation in different ways so that we can identify different approaches to understanding participants' situations.

We cannot avoid this complexity, because complexity is social work's role. Social workers are asked to deal with matters that go beyond the people involved. Social work practice engages not just with one social welfare objective but also with incorporating them together, with the flexibility we discussed in chapter 4. That flexibility also brings a wide variety of knowledge and skills to bear. In this chapter, we have also noted that values presented as simple rules of behavior alert us to value complexities in the situations we deal with. Humanistic practice addresses value complexities by seeing potential alternatives not as either-or decisions but as and-also decisions. Our practice can be most helpful to clients if it considers the interests and aims of all participants, including interests in social orders and behavioral requirements. Practitioners may need to achieve a range of self-actualizations for several people and social interests engaged with a complex social and human situation.

FURTHER READING

Halmi, A. (2003). Chaos and non-linear dynamics: New methodological approaches in the social sciences and social work practice. *International Social Work*, *46*, 83–101.

Stevens, I., & Cox, P. (2008). Complexity theory: Developing new understandings of child protection in field settings and in residential child care. *British Journal of Social Work*, *38*, 1320–1336.

The two preceding articles helpfully explore complexity and chaos theory.

Taylor, C., & White, S. (2000). *Practising reflexivity in health and welfare: Making knowledge*. Buckingham, UK: Open University Press.

This book builds on research that shows how practitioners can develop more complex understandings of the situations they deal with through exploring the interaction of people's thinking and social expectations.

Achieving Caring and Creativity in Practice

CHAPTER AIMS

The main aim of this chapter is to explore the role of caring and creativity in humanistic social work. It argues that humanistic social work emphasizes caring rather than helping, because caring practice requires a focus on personal development toward self-actualization. Creativity is the positive active aspect of caring, offering a vehicle for developing a self-actualizing practice.

After working through this chapter, readers should be able to

- Evaluate the role of helping and caring as part of everyday life and as part of social work and similar professions
- Understand a model of caring that arises from human connectedness, thus allowing us to look at the environment and elements of caring people, behaviors, relationships, risks, and outcomes
- Understand the importance of developing in people's lives creativity as the positive, active part of caring
- Consider opportunities for creativity to extend empowerment beyond pragmatic adaptation to limitations in the environment toward becoming productively creative
- Understand the use of life review and reminiscence in practice

CARING AND HELPING

In this section, I want to discuss humanistic practice in those aspects of social work that are caring and helping. This is because humanistic social work sees caring and helping others as fundamental aspects of being human. Therefore, they are also important in the tasks of practitioners in social work and similar professions. Similarly, they are an important part of what informal caregivers do for members of their families and their community. How people think about and see caring in families informs their view of what paid professional helpers and caregivers do. Sometimes, we think of these aspects as defining such professions.

PAUSE AND REFLECT: What Kind of Profession Is Social Work?

List and think about some professions that you know about. Can you think of one or two words that describe each? You might think about accountants, architects, counselors, doctors, journalists, librarians, nurses, police officers, psychotherapists, teachers, university professors. Are they caregivers or helpers?

Some Suggestions

We often describe practitioners of social work, counseling, and psychotherapies as part of the helping professions. I think we might not call counselors and psychotherapists part of the caring professions, but we perhaps would say that about medicine, nursing, and social work. We would not talk about accountants, architects, journalists, teachers, police officers, or university professors as either helping or caring. As individual personalities, they might be. Their roles might involve helping, being careful in their practice, and being concerned about responding to human needs. But we would think in terms of communication professions, learned professions, or criminal justice professions.

I was recently teaching about professionalization in a discussion with doctors, nurses, ministers of religion, and social workers. I asked them to compare their professions with other professions, such as accountancy, architecture, or civil engineering. One of the doctors said, "I don't see those as professions." I asked why, and he said it was because their responsibilities do not involve caring for people. Another member of the audience said that the decisions of those professionals were not as personally significant as those taken in health care. When I asked why again, many people in the room agreed that it was because their decisions did not have the personal impact of health-care decisions.

Just about then, we were experiencing a major economic downturn, and I pointed out how bankers and other financial professionals had been accused of causing personal disaster for many people who had lost their savings and homes. One group member said that this was because such people had behaved unethically, without consideration for the people who might personally suffer from their decisions. Discussing this point, the audience agreed that this meant that such professions had ethical requirements and that their decisions would have personal consequences. I asked them whether they would like to be in a multistory building or crossing a big bridge that I, a social worker, had designed. They agreed not, and that architects and civil engineers had demanding knowledge requirements and that their work could have important personal consequences, just as much as health-care professionals. This discussion illustrated for me how committed practitioners in the professions I work with every day are to the idea of being helping and caring in their work. Indeed, they often talk about health *care* or social *care*.

So to understand social work and other similar practices, we might ask what caring and helping imply. Caring and helping must involve a personal response by practitioners to other people and their worlds. Individualized, atomlike behavior is not credible caring or helping (Sherwin, 1992); we are not just pieces of the universe following our own paths set by natural forces. Humanistic social work is about connection with others because it is an interpersonal practice to work with people's own experiences of their self and their situation. Practitioners therefore need to make and demonstrate their connection with those experiences; they must experience another's experience. To do so, they have to make a connection. Therefore, humanistic social work can never be individualistic because it always involves the practitioner and another or others. Also, the social work task is concerned with how social relationships affect people and groups. Caring for and about people and helping them must be relational; that is, it must be about relationships among practitioners, clients, families, caregivers, communities, and societies.

Helping implies assistance that is offered or given, but in an astute and classic social work text, Keith-Lucas (1972) points to the oppressive paternalism of viewing social work as a helping activity. An implication of offering help is that people who are helped must accept it on the giver's own terms; the relationship is one of "I give, and you receive." If it is helpful, why would you reject it? Yet people resist being given help: doing so might place them under an obligation to the helper, or it might not be the kind of help they wanted. We saw in chapter 2 that practitioners have accountabilities to a wide range of interests, not merely the person being helped, so their accountabilities elsewhere may mean that their accountability to the person helped is less important than their other connections. There is a long history of help, and particularly of social work help, being associated with requirements to comply with the social order or the moral views of the help giver. The poor law, a source of social work in many European countries and influential in the United States, or the charity organization societies that influenced the early development of social work in the same countries, both had clear moral and social control purposes integrated in their practice. This continues to be true of many public social and helping services, and we have seen that many services are at least partially involuntary: people have to accept them. If we offer help and the receiver says, "I don't want to do it like that," then we feel entitled to be aggrieved and rejected. With helping, therefore, the society and the helper are a focus for concern, as is the person being helped; we give help to meet all these needs.

Another problem with the idea of helping as the basis for social work is that it is something of an outsider activity; a helper stands away from the client, does not get involved. The principle is that the client is the actor, whereas the helper enables and facilitates the client in acting, but does not do anything. There is good reason for this therapeutically, because it means that the practitioner does not make the client dependent on his or her doing things for the client. Heron's (2001) book on helping, for example, identifies six types of helping interventions, divided into two categories, which are set out in box 6.1. These all focus on working with the client, not family or community members

Box 6.1 Heron's Helping Behaviors

Authoritative	*Facilitative*
Prescriptive—directs client's behavior, usually in matters outside the relationship	Cathartic—enables client to discharge painful emotion, mainly grief, fear, and anger
Informative—improves client's knowledge, information, and meaning	Catalytic—elicits client's self-discovery, self-directed living, learning, and problem solving
Confronting—raises client's awareness of limiting attitudes or behavior	Supportive—affirms worth and value of client's person, qualities, attitudes, and actions

Source: Heron (2001).

or other services that may be part of the helping process. Another example is Carkhuff's (2000) book. I have developed a diagram to describe his model of helping in box 6.2. The helper involves the helped person in the helping process, and then facilitates the communication between them and the thinking through of what actions might be taken. However, it is the helped person who does the thinking through and is left to take the action.

Various social work models of practice recognize the weaknesses of this standing-back approach. For example, task-centered practice proposes that the practitioner and client should both undertake a share of the tasks selected for action (Reid, 1978).

Montgomery (1993) explores some of the problems with viewing helping as caring. In her discussion of caring, there are always opposites within people that are combined in ways that lead to internal debates and conflicts. Helping processes enable people to work on issues in their lives by uncovering the internal debate and helping resolve or manage such internal conflicts. Relationships, attachments, and connectedness are an essential element of caring, but personal growth views of development minimize them

Box 6.2 Carkhuff's Model of Helping

Helpee's contribution: internal processing

Action

Initiating—facilitating acting

Personalizing—facilitating understanding

Responding—facilitating exploring

Attending—involving the helpee

Helper's contribution: interpersonal processing

Source: Carkhuff (2000).

because of their focus on how people change in a linear way; they do not examine the trails of relationships that provide continuity and community for people. Shared humanity and vulnerability enable practitioners and clients to develop relationships that go beyond the tasks and events they are involved with (Montgomery, 1993).

Humanistic social work focuses more than many models of social work practice on holistic caring processes rather than helping for two reasons. One is that many social work and similar services are involved in helping people with long-term-care needs; children whose parents cannot care for them; people with mental illnesses, intellectual, and physical disabilities; and older people (Payne, 2009a). Therefore, social work requires more than a quick problem-solving intervention or social change and then standing aside; it requires developing the client's personal capacities to resolve difficulties and live an improved quality of life over a long-term involvement. Second, as we saw in chapter 2, social work aims at psychological efficacy, as humanistic psychotherapies envisage, but it also involves a focus on empowering the social agency of social networks in the client's environment.

The second reason for focusing on caring is that many people see it as a moral prerequisite of providing services for other people, alongside ideas such as dignity and responsiveness. Caring for other people in society has been considered a moral responsibility in Western societies since the Enlightenment. Virtuous citizens care about others and about things of importance in society because it is part of their duty to maintain that society. Caring for others in society, we saw in chapter 1, is both a responsibility and a right that binds us together in social relationships in society. This moral responsibility has become associated with public and professional services because they are an organized and collective form of that moral responsibility (McBeath & Webb, 1997). They are particularly said to be caring if they operate within the domain of personal or intimate matters. It is clear, perhaps, that medicine and nursing are such domains; it is less clear that social work is a caring domain. This is because, first, it has a history of association with involuntary and perhaps oppressive helping. Second, its caring is not bodily or intimate caring, as in medicine and nursing.

Nevertheless, social workers spend much of their time concerned with caring in various ways. For example, social work plays a major role in ensuring that parents' care of their children is as good as possible to maximize children's personal development when there are questions of abuse or quality of parental care. They are also involved with organizing care for adults who are unable to be completely self-caring. Holden (2004) draws attention to the reality that the role of caring in women's lives incurs both personal costs and personal pleasures. Problem-solving approaches to social work emphasize the costs, whereas a humanistic approach incorporates pleasures. Moreover, many services emphasize the responsibilities or burden of caring rather than the positives. This reflects social attitudes: Holden's example is unmarried mothers during the period when sex before marriage was stigmatized and any resulting children were evidence of parents' misbehavior. Another example is the way the freedoms that go with adulthood are often seen as limited by the pressure of caring for and rearing children, and responsibility for elderly and dependent parents blights later adulthood.

CARING AND CONNECTEDNESS

It is important, therefore, that practitioners think through the nature of caring so that they can build it into their practice. An important distinction is between caring about and caring for. Caring about something or someone means thinking that they are important in your world, taking an interest in, and giving priority to them. Caring for something or someone, for example, a valuable vase or your child, means actively taking steps to make sure they are safe and carrying out tasks to look after them. In social work, we are talking about both, because congruence means that we have to care about people to provide them with services; otherwise, our efforts will not be genuine. It also means carrying out tasks that would look after them. But what would caring tasks be?

PAUSE AND REFLECT: What Is It Like When You Care?

If you were to imagine just one image of caring, what would it be?

Some Suggestions

I have asked this question in various training courses, and people usually mention two images. One is a mother and her child; the other is a nurse caring for someone who is very ill (one person called it "mopping the fevered brow"). The mother and child is an exceptional caring situation; there is usually a close physical and emotional bond between them, because the mother has carried the child in her body. Both images are exceptional in another way because there is a significant inequality between the two people involved: both cared-for people are very dependent on the caregiver, in the mother-child relationship particularly so.

Thinking more broadly about caring situations, we still call it caring when a parent cares for or about a child who is an adult or when a visiting caregiver provides practical care for an older or disabled person who is not able to manage aspects of his or her everyday life. This may be personal physical care or helping manage the finances; it is all considered caring if it is associated with a sense of commitment. However, caring has a special meaning for many people. Pembroke (2004), for example, discusses charm in human service. We can connect this idea with the bedside manner of doctors. It is pleasing if we are pleasant to one another and if our clients and the people around them view us as attractive. It may enable connections to be made more easily and/or the achieving of influence through relationships. But charm is a superficial quality; charm alone is not useful. It must be congruent with what we are trying to achieve as a practitioner with our clients and with our understanding and use of ourselves in relationship to them. In turn, we cannot achieve this only by ourselves: it connects with whether clients trust the agency and caregivers, whether it is reliable, and whether they see us as belonging to it or as separate from or competing with it.

In exploring what caring means, philosophers and psychologists have established two points of view. Mayeroff (1971), starting from the historical position coming from Enlightenment thinking, analyzes caring from the view that it is a natural response in cooperative, social animals such as human beings, which has led to it becoming a moral responsibility in society. He proposes, in a humanistic way, that caring is defined by the emotional requirement of caregivers to seek the personal growth of the cared-for person. Caregivers must pay attention to and be directed in their caring by what the cared-for person wants to achieve.

The second point of view, a feminist one, is associated with the psychologist Gilligan (1993), the ethics-of-care view. She compared male and female moral development, arguing that it was characteristic of a male view of caring to think about caring in terms of concepts such as justice, equality, and moral responsibility. She suggests that writers like Mayeroff focus on the caregiver, and possibly a principled caregiver, when the crucial aspect of caring is that it is a relationship and depends on both the people engaged in it. In a study of young women's moral development, she identified their caring as depending on personal connectedness with the cared-for person. Thus, their caring emerged directly from their relationship with the other, not from general moral principles. Noddings (1984) extended this view to say that caring deriving from relatedness is essential to all ethical behavior, for both men and women. To go further, Roach (1992) argued that caring is a crucial aspect of being human. Caring, Noddings (1984) pointed out, cannot always come from universal love or universal justice; it must arise from a personal mental "engrossment" in concrete situations (p. 90). That is, if we care for someone or something, our responses to that person or thing burden us; we worry about it; it matters to us. To understand caring, we must explore memories, feelings, and our personal capacity to care in particular situations because such internal responses lead to being engrossed with another person's needs. This idea also extends caring from something that takes place in natural relationships, such as mother-child or husband-wife relationships, to professional relationships that come about because the professional caregiver is engrossed in caring for a patient or client.

Among the important ideas in Mayeroff's (1971) analysis and that of Noddings (1984) is the importance of such personal and interpersonal reactions as commitment, guilt at our inadequacy in caring, reciprocation between the caregiver and cared-for person, and the reality that all caring has limits. If caring is a relationship rather than an ethical response to social responsibility and rights, the cared-for person has an effect on the caregiver. If the cared-for person recognizes caring presence and attitudes, he or she will be responsive to and confirm the caregiver's feelings. People may have a caring presence even if they are physically absent, as their potential responsiveness to the cared-for person's needs may be apparent. For example, the cared-for person may be certain that the caregiver is prepared to turn out in difficult circumstances if required.

But what does a caregiver actually do? Although I have suggested that we should be careful about seeing a mother-child relationship as the model of all caring, we can learn from it. Gilbert (2005) used parental care to propose that caring actions are protection, provisioning, mediating the child's exposure to the world, and teaching and socializing the child to enable it to manage its relationships with the world on its own. He suggested that all forms of caring develop through relationships in which there is positive social reward for caring, and that this provides the motivation to continue and develop caring. This can lead people to strive to obtain care or to provide care to others. Striving to care and to be cared for is different from contentment, because we may switch off our need for care or to give it when we are satisfied and happy.

Similarly, Benner and Wrubel (1989), in discussing nursing, see professional caring as concerned with "persons, events, projects, and things that matter to people" (p. 1). If caring is about things that matter, those things must also establish what options are available for dealing with what matters: caring creates possibilities. The possibilities must be specific to the person being cared for. Caring emerges from the particular relationship between that person and the caregiver; there cannot be lists of tasks or ways of coping, only a response to the care needs in a particular situation. Therefore, a caregiver must be connected to the person to enable the concerns of that person and the possibilities available to be precisely identified. If the relationship is caring, there must be the possibility of giving and receiving help.

Attempts to make professional provision scientific may easily lead to the application of controlling techniques. In a study of teenage mothers' transition to mothering, Smithbattle (1994) showed how a technical approach to dealing with social problems often replaces a moral view of behavior. Thus, an issue is no longer a moral problem, as with premarital pregnancy condemned as "bad" behavior. Instead, it is defined as a social problem: teenage parenting is a failure in psychosocial development or socialization, which may be prevented through technical interventions such as education or counseling. Such approaches conceal the moral element by focusing on technical actions to control disapproved behavior. Smithbattle argued that the appropriate professional approach was to focus on understanding the narrative of the teenage mother herself. In this way, we may join with the lived experience of the young person and respond to it rather than impose distanced explanations.

If caring is seen as wholly personal, can caring be a professional responsibility with an evidence base drawn from science? The distance engendered by scientific explanation stands in the way of understanding of personal relationships and experience that will enable a direct caring response in a relationship. Fjelland and Gjengedal (1994), in exploring nursing, suggested that many current ideas about professional caring derive from humanistic and phenomenological ideas that distinguish understanding human experience from scientific knowledge that seeks to explain human beings. We may describe caring, explain its part in society, or develop principles that confirm its role in life, but we do not understand it except from experience. This fundamental distinction is the contribution of phenomenology and hence humanistic and existential ideas to the understanding of our practice.

It is important, therefore, not to neglect the moral principles that underlie the role of caring and of caregivers in society, but to see caring as a mixture of both this and the ethics-of-care positions. Noddings (1984) pointed out that caring that is natural, for example, the caring response of a parent whose child cries out in the night, may be a burden if the parent is tired. However, it is different in kind from caring that comes from an ethical position. For example, I might dislike a violent client or disapprove of violence, but I might still believe in rights to due process in deciding how that person should be treated. Here, I am acting as a moral person, concerned about people's rights rather than responding to my natural emotions; the burden of caring still exists, but it is different in kind. There is also evidence that caring within families, at least in Western societies, is a negotiation. It responds first to the relationships among family members and to well-established social rules, which have moral elements. For example, in Finch and Mason's (1993) study in the United Kingdom, people expected that parents would care for children but that adults had less responsibility to care for older parents, though it was morally valued if they did so. Such research helps us understand how caring works and contributes to how we may use it as part of our practice.

We can also understand caring actions by looking at their opposites. Gilbert (2005) counterposed cooperative and competitive behaviors as well as caring and exploitative and hostile behaviors. Caring and prosocial behavior, that is, behavior that seeks to develop social relationships, is counterposed with cruelty, where people are indifferent to or gratified by others' suffering. In this discussion, caring is about a positive rather than a negative connectedness. Caring cannot be indifferent or cruel; on the contrary, it must be engaged.

To provide a caring response, then, Benner and Wrubel (1989) have suggested that practitioners need to understand the relationships among the concepts they are working with. Their example, nursing, led them to talk about health, illness, and disease. That is, what does it mean to a person to be healthy, what does it mean to be ill, and what is it about a particular disease that makes a person not healthy and ill?

Extending this analysis more widely, in social work, we need to know how continuities in people's lives have been disrupted. How was this marriage and family life positive for the people in it? How and by what social issues among people involved has it been disrupted? How has this disruption led them to see those issues as problems that need to be dealt with or as opportunities? What is it, then, that is getting in the way of dealing with the problems or taking advantage of the opportunities? Practitioners need to listen to and understand the story of these issues so that the explanations contained in the stories are clear. It is important that they engage with clients, present with them as they experience the story, and are able to develop relationships with them as they come to appreciate the client's understanding and share in the client's feelings. Narayanaswamy (2006) has argued that caring may have important spiritual dimensions, for example, demonstrating to people that they are significant to others in their lives, worth someone taking trouble over. It also includes being nonjudgmental and sensitive about cultural values, physical preferences, and social needs. All these issues connect to the dialogue, narrative, participation, and empowerment skills discussed in chapter 3.

CARING PRACTICE

If we see social work as caring as well as helping, what do social workers actually do in their caring profession? First, we have seen throughout this book that all social work involves establishing a relationship with clients and people around them, and that social workers do this as whole persons, incorporating their professional knowledge and skills into their human identity. Second, we have seen, particularly in chapters 3 and 4, that most social work develops its relationship through interpersonal interaction and that an important aspect of that interaction is dialogue and communication.

Thinking about caring as a form of communication between people is therefore a useful starting point. Montgomery (1993) has argued that humanistic psychology has

developed unhelpful ideas about communication between professionals and the people
they serve, because it emphasizes formal counseling settings rather than settings in which
health and social care services are provided or settings in which communications are
brief and focused on service provision rather than personal growth. Learning interviewing and counseling techniques does not always help in developing a relationship that
enables caring to take place. It often leads us to focus unhelpfully on the nature of the
relationship and how we conduct it rather than on the client's needs. Also, many clients
do not like to talk in a "therapeutic style" (Montgomery, 1993, p. 15) and rarely have time
to use a reflective style of thinking to try to elaborate feelings and experiences. Montgomery argues, then, that caring requires other and different skills from helping.

Box 6.3 presents Montgomery's (1993) model of caring; there are several useful features about this model. First, it does not assume that caring is necessarily a wonderful
thing: there are problems and risks associated with it. This warns us against care as a
cheerleader, something that seems so self-evidently right that we do not think critically
about it. Second, the model does not assume that caring is something that is solely about
the nature of the caregiver or the relationship between the caregiver and the cared-for
person. It suggests that it is built up, created in an environment that is propitious for caring. Montgomery takes this view even though she describes caring as "a way of being. A
state of natural responsiveness to others. Because caring requires personal involvement,
it is the antithesis of alienation, detachment, or apathy . . . caring is a natural condition
of being human" (Montgomery, 1993, p. 13) The third advantage of this approach to caring is the suggestion that it emerges from practice; people do caring things and this
becomes a caring relationship. This connects with some of the social construction ideas
we have looked at in previous chapters, in which we saw that behavior is not just there—
it comes out of what goes before and develops over time. It also connects with Mayeroff's
(1971) analysis, which suggests that the commitment to the cared-for person's personal
development results from undertaking tasks with and for that person.

Seeing caring as developing from initial caring tasks is also important for professional caregivers. Following the ethics-of-care view, caring requires practitioners to

Box 6.3 Montgomery's Caring Process

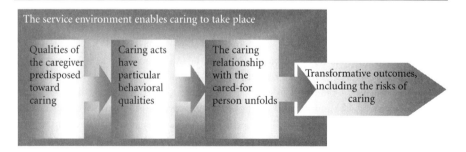

Source: Developed from Montgomery (1993).

develop connectedness with a client; this emerges as the caregiver undertakes practical tasks that begin to demonstrate concern for and responsiveness to the client. Paid professional responsibilities such as being efficient and responsive to a client's request for assessment and careful listening are the beginning of developing the connectedness that provides the security of being cared for. Organizing practical services such as financial help or help with maintaining the house are also valid starting points for connected caring.

Another important point to note about many of these aspects of care is the importance of physical and practical tasks, which often connect with the bodily needs of the client. A simple touch on greeting, when leaving, when helping someone, and as part of games or dancing can facilitate communication by improving eye contact and attention; it can also make people feel more connected, spontaneous, and socially aware. Caring involves a relationship with the cared-for person's body. For example, people with intellectual disabilities may need education with personal care, for example, developing healthy eating habits and hygiene routines or managing sexual needs appropriately (Carnaby & Cambridge, 2006). Pratt and Mason (1981) pointed to evidence in nursing that touch can be a prime means of reducing both physical responses caused by brain conditions and social withdrawal. Help with physical and practical tasks forms the context in which emotional caring is offered. Caring also involves physical presence (Engebretson, 2000), the feeling of security that someone is there or prepared to be there.

Case Study: The Porn Viewer

Jerry was a disabled man with a serious progressive neurological disability who received extensive care services from a home care agency to maintain him at home, despite his increasing disability. His marriage had broken up, and his active social life had become increasingly limited. He used the Internet as a substitute for social contact but also took to downloading and viewing pornographic films. One of the female caregivers who provided regular physical care for him found out about this and was worried that it might lead to a risk of sexual abuse against her during her home visits. The agency decided to send only male caregivers in the future. The social worker was asked to discuss this with Jerry; he was disappointed with the agency's decision, because it further reduced his social contacts, and he had enjoyed having social contact with women visiting to provide care for him. The social worker formed the assessment that violence or abuse was unlikely.

In this case, the social and personal relationships that had developed for Jerry with his female caregivers were disrupted by what he felt was a "politically correct" concern for agency staff. Who was present in his home was important to him. The caring relationship had developed and met some of his broader human and social needs. The social worker was able to negotiate a renewed arrangement by supporting the original female caregiver and talking through with Jerry how he could reduce his caregiver's awareness of his viewing habits. This situation also makes the point that, to care for someone, you also have to be cared for. The social worker offered this to the informal caregiver in a personal way, whereas the agency took the formal organizational route for a rather risk-averse form of safety. The practitioners' connectedness with Jerry increases his connectedness with the world outside his home and his experience outside his disability.

We have seen in chapter 3 that empathy is a crucial part of humanistic psychologies and an important basis of equality through dialogue. Empathy implies an active, imaginative understanding of another's feelings and reactions to the world, a high degree of immersion in their view of the world. However, many helping relationships involved maintaining a degree of distance and boundaries between the other person, which is inconsistent with empathy (Montgomery, 1993). Confirmation is the process of recognizing, acknowledging, and endorsing the other person. Recognition involves acting in ways that deal with the other person as a subject, acting for him- or herself in relationship with a caring person. Acknowledgment involves responding to communications from the cared-for person relevantly. Endorsement involves accepting the value of the other person's experience and demonstrating that you are willing to become involved with that person. Montgomery (1993) has argued that these things are related to but different from caring.

Connectedness is a form of social exchange. In this view, a group member contributes to a group and receives something from it in exchange. The connectedness continues as long as it is beneficial to both the individual and the group. People develop patterns of connectedness, and some connections are socially approved, for example, connectedness with a family or with groups in a workplace, such as work teams. Some connectedness continues because, although there are personal disadvantages, people value the pattern that has been established. This comes from attributions that people make about the value that they and the people around them place on family life, from particular ways they have learned that families "should" operate, or from teamwork in their employment. They have an idealized view of what a family or workplace should be like, and they try to behave in accordance with their attribution.

MAKING CREATIVITY THE POSITIVE PART OF CARING

We have seen so far that caring involves ensuring that people can achieve personal development, but helping often creates a more distant relationship. But we have also seen that connected caring develops from practical helping tasks—by being present, caregivers affirm the human value of the cared-for person. However, this seems a weak basis for personal development; it seems to be merely about maintaining the cared-for person or developing relationships. There is one further ingredient in humanistic caring practice: creativity as a factor in producing development.

In looking at humanistic psychologies in chapter 1, we identified the importance of creative experiences as part of the personal growth that caring aims for. Part of that importance is the value of peak experiences, something beyond the ordinary. We have seen that caring goes beyond helping because it involves direct interpersonal connectedness, a presence with someone together, and it aims at personal development, certainly of the cared-for person but also of the caregiver. I argue in this part of the chapter that creativity is an important part of humanistic practice because the peak experiences of creativity can, in the same way, be an important instrument of personal growth. How can we incorporate creativity into humanistic practice?

PAUSE AND REFLECT: When and How Are You Creative?

Do you think of yourself as a creative person? Do you find your clients creative? Think about yourself for a moment: can you identify occasions in the past few months when you were creative? If so, note down what they were and what you did that you would define as creative. Then, think about your clients or people you know: do you remember moments when you thought they were creative? Again, what happened and precisely what was creative? How would you tie all these experiences of creativity together?

Some Suggestions

Here are three occasions when I thought I was creative:

- Helping my granddaughter with needlework—she was completing a kit but needed reassurance about whether the stitching she had used looked appropriate and in choosing extra colors.
- Helping a colleague think about how to present her work in a presentation for a lecture—I suggested presenting her work with a series of photos of her doing it, which I would take; she liked the idea but had not previously had to handle the practicalities.
- Helping the son of a patient at my hospice think positively about his father's death—I got him to remember and write briefly about occasions when he had experienced good times with a father whom he had experienced as distant and not involved with him.

One point that ties these experiences together is "doing" something practical rather than being someone or something or thinking about something. As we have seen, doing things with and for people is an important aspect of caring. Our idea may be creative, but creativity always has a practical, doing outcome. So my granddaughter had thought about extra colors, but it did not become an issue about creativity until she was trying it out. My colleague had ideas about how she wanted to teach but was daunted by the practicalities. The patient's son was thinking about his father, but the creativity came in making that thinking concrete, representative of actual experiences that he could test his thinking against.

Another important point is that, in various ways, the practical outcomes must be new and connected to the person creating them; the person must produce them alone. Creativity is always personal to the people involved in the creation, sometimes a group. The result may be a group production but with personal elements.

The doing that is the main aspect of being creative is not something exceptional that we do in a vacuum. We often think about creativity as something special, unusual, something only some kind of genius does. But being involved in creativity is usually part of a structure, a kit to be completed, a lecture in a teaching program, or part of the work of a social agency. Being creative does not have to be something extraordinary, because the structure sets us up to do creativity. However, creativity usually involves stepping beyond the structure to do something exceptional: adding something to the kit, making the teaching a bit out of the ordinary, finding a way to make our feelings concrete.

In summary, being creative requires a number of important steps in practice:

- Structures and organizations that facilitate creativity
- Stepping beyond the limits of the structure and organization into something new, perhaps something risky
- Showing something that is personal, connected to an individual or group, to his or her personality, or to the things or social structures he or she is part of
- Practical actions that lead to an outcome that can be new or different to the people involved

Case Study: Photo Sessions

Every summer at our hospice, we have a joint creativity project. One summer, we set up a photo studio and obtained a number of costumes from a theater costumer. Patients, family members, visitors, and staff could try on a costume and someone else would take a photo of them. There is a montage of the results in our entrance hall. The chief executive (a social worker) tried on the Supergirl costume. In doing so, she ran the risk of people thinking she was arrogant. Several other people also became Superman or Supergirl for a few moments. Others dressed as a monarch or in the sweeping costumes of nineteenth-century men and women. Each looks different because each is different: frail, confident, large, or incongruous. All ran the risk of looking silly or inappropriate. But none of the pictures, seen among the others, looks wrong. Also, the person who took the photo made each one different, a different angle, a different aspect of each person and the costume.

We can see in this example an organized structure to support a creative activity among people who would not have seen themselves as creative but were facilitated to become creative. People were helped to take risk, to expose themselves a bit, and they produced a creative outcome whose quality was enhanced when put alongside a cooperative outcome.

To take these points further and generalize, creativity involves turbulence in the expected. This is why it can be so useful as part of humanistic practice. Used as an intervention, practitioners have to devise a structure that helps people feel safe to go beyond the everyday and produce something that is clearly them but also new and different.

Practitioners can use three different aspects of creativity:

- Trying to stretch our practice by incorporating new ideas and possibilities into our work with clients
- Trying to generate connections beyond ordinary living in social relationships and thinking processes among clients and their social networks
- Using clients' creativity in artistic and other activities to empower them, particularly in gaining a stronger consciousness of what is happening to them in their lives

CREATIVE ACTIVITY CAN BE EMPOWERING

I pointed to evidence and experience in chapter 1 that significant, developmental experiences in people's lives can often be achieved around music; this extends to many forms of artistic activities. E. R. Smith (2001) has suggested that it may help people to awaken empowering consciousness about their world through taking a narrative approach. Constructing the narrative of important events in their lives allows people to perceive and incorporate into their identity the importance in a sequence of events of suffering and exclusion. Neimeyer's (2001) analysis of meaning reconstruction during bereavement is another example of such processes taking place.

Enabling people to adapt to their present lives merely accepts the limitations imposed on them by their environment; creativity allows people to develop a greater quality of life within whatever limitations exist. Child (1973) has reviewed some of the early psychological research on creativity, connecting it with other analyses of different forms of creativity:

- Some people are adaptable in a pragmatic way to their environment, giving up their personal inclinations and freedoms in favor of adjustment to the social pressures on them. This is a shallow form of adjustment because it means that they just fit in with everybody else.
- Conflicted or thwarted people (Child, 1973) try to achieve some creativity in the way they live their lives but come up against barriers because of social expectations; they could be creative but their creativity is obstructed.
- Productive people are enabled by their social environment to use their creativity.

I find this helpful in understanding how we approach creativity with people, and it connects with my experience in using the arts to work with older people in hospice and care home practice, described more fully in Hartley and Payne (2008). Many people have been told at school or in their early years that they are not artistic. They have accepted this, and it becomes a barrier to them, such that they do not become productive. If they are freed to become adaptable, they can become productive and often produce imaginative work. The approach we take to this is, first, to teach them simple but adaptable techniques so that they can rapidly produce good results. They can then expand these to achieve greater flexibility in artistic activities. It helps them to become more productive if they have or if we can identify with them a particular message that they want to offer to the world. In work with older and dying people, this is often about conveying life experience and family history to other people. With children and young people and with people with disabilities, it may be about conveying something about their lifestyle and priorities.

Related research on architects showed that children whose parents granted them unusual freedom to explore their world responsibly were most likely to become productively creative, whereas less creative people emphasized meeting professional expectations and standards rather than exploring their own ideas independently. More creative people also valued and looked for complexity and richness of ideas; we saw in chapters 2 and 5 that being able to deal with complexity is an important aspect of effective helping practice. Other research reviewed by Child (1973) tended to show the value of oppositional thinking; focusing on two ideas that seemed to be in conflict helped people rise above the conflict and develop further ideas. Again, we saw in chapter 5 that complexity thinking is important to developing effective practice.

Case Example: Norman

Norman was an African Caribbean man, quadriplegic because of a progressive or gradually worsening neurological disease. As this developed, he was unable to move any of his limbs, needed comprehensive care, and lived in residential care for people with disabilities. Because of his origins from a family of low socioeconomic status, he had mainly blue-collar jobs and had not developed any long-term relationships outside his large family; in particular, he had no wife and few regular visitors. Lying unable to move in bed, he reviewed his life. A community artist visiting him from a disability project found that, as he thought about his life experiences, he was formulating them into musings about particular episodes and events. She defined this as poetry. He did not understand himself as a poet, but she filmed him speaking these musings, and they were of great interest to others as description of his experience. In his life, he had mainly been adaptable, but his ability to develop original thinking, usually thwarted by the social requirements of his life, was enabled to emerge by his disability and with the artist's help and encouragement.

Practitioners often meet people like Norman, who have creative capacities but have not been enabled to be productive with their creativity. This does not have to be artistic creativity. In this case, it happened to be a community artist who did the enabling, and it came out as an artistic product. It is easy to imagine a care worker or practitioner from a range of professions bringing out Norman's thoughts.

BEING CREATIVE IN ROUTINE PRACTICE

Creativity involves helping people move from adaptability and thwarted creativity toward being productively creative people. Health and social care professionals need this just as much as their clients and patients do. At times, our life routines make us all feel hemmed in. How can we find the time and space in busy lives to be creative? Where do we get the ideas from? A lot of social work practice seems routine. Caring involves repeated supportive actions; organizational requirements can make repetitive paperwork seem more important in practice than responding to the possibilities in people's lives.

PAUSE AND REFLECT: How Can We Be Creative?

Review your practice, or, if you are a student, another activity that has been important to you recently. Think about occasions over the past six months when you did something new. What was the idea that lay behind it? When did it happen? What were the circumstances?

Some Suggestions

We can learn to be creative in anything in our lives if we put ourselves in situations that require new actions from us. For example:

- When it seems impossible to do something, but we have to act, this forces us to think about new possibilities.
- When we are very familiar with a situation and often repeat our actions, we can have the confidence to try something new.
- Most important, ideas can come from listening to the people we work with; we can look for ideas in their stories.

One of the important ideas in Rogers's work is the focus on the individual "person" rather than practitioners' generalized theories that prescribe their practice (Child, 1973). I would extend this idea to the generalized requirements of the service that practitioners are part of. In his work, Rogers is thinking mainly of people practicing independently as counselors or psychotherapists, whereas many social workers and other practitioners are part of agencies that provide particular services or objectives. If these cause practitioners to lose focus on the needs and wishes of the person they are dealing with, they cannot provide the services or meet the objectives of their agency.

Metaphor is a valuable aspect of working creatively with people as a "language of discovery" (Appel, 1980, p. 47); it allows people to confront their experiences, clarifying them by juxtaposing a different idea with it.

Case Example: Metaphor of a Family Path Through Life

I often use a diagram of a family path through life for explaining palliative care social work (box 6.4). I am involved in palliative care, a multiprofessional practice that includes social workers and doctors, nurses, and other professionals working with people who are dying and their families, who are bereaved as their family members die. Most practitioners in this field are health-care professionals with a tradition of focusing on the patient. One of the roles of social work in this setting is to maintain a focus on the family of the patient, because family members also need help in managing the consequences of a serious illness and a family member approaching death. To explain how this is a different practice, I draw attention to how, as individuals progress through life, they start out with a family that they are born into and travel along the road of their life with that birth family. At various stages, people join and leave the family. For example, when someone marries, the birth family may move away from the main path of the family when a spouse joins them in their journey. People know of the reality of death, the second tree, which will come to them, but for much of our lives, this is not actively in our minds.

When individuals die, their family goes on without them and will face many challenges, which mean that their path continues around the corner. Most people toward the end of life want to finalize their relationships so that, in turning future corners, the family is strengthened in facing life challenges. In palliative care, people become aware that their death is imminent; the tree is not so far. Palliative care aims to allow individuals to speed up their journey so that they can spend some time sitting under the tree, completing the

Box 6.4 Metaphor: The Family Road of Life

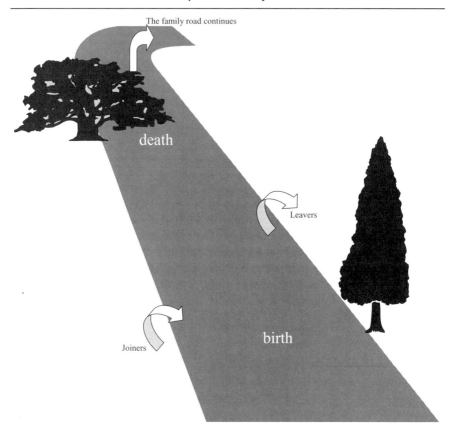

final tasks that will help their family prepare for stronger resilience in managing their future road. The idea of sitting under the tree comes from an African idea in which people tell stories and reminisce in ways that help their family and community learn about and deal with life.

I find that this metaphor of the journey and sitting under the tree helps colleagues see the brief period of palliative care in the context of a patient's whole life. It helps position the importance of their role (ensuring that patients are pain and symptom free) so that they can sit under the tree in comfort and manage their final life tasks better. Similarly, some patients and family members find it helpful to see that their weakness and incapacity, caused by the illness, facilitates important tasks; they are not useless because they are dying, and in some ways, their family role is enhanced.

Other uses for the family path are for different members of a family or students to compare the path of a previous generation with their own or to begin to create a narrative of their life.

In her book on using art to achieve greater self-understanding and spiritual fulfill-ment, Allen (1995) has proposed that we might travel through a number of steps in using creativity. I have adapted, developed, and presented these in box 6.5. As with other tech-niques explored in this book, Allen's idea starts from thinking about some basic objec-tives for using creative approaches. Then, it focuses on finding out what skills a person possesses and would like to develop. Finally, it identifies some issues that may come up when working on a creative project.

LIFE REVIEW AND REMINISCENCE

Life review and reminiscence are important creative techniques that build on narrative approaches to practice. They are particularly powerful because they are natural acts that everyone does in their lives.

Reminiscence is often undertaken as a group technique. It is a verbal interaction between two people who elicit memories; they recall or tell each other about events or memorable early experiences. Recent events and experiences are excluded: this is not a therapeutic technique looking at the here and now. The aim is generally to increase inter-actions with peers, to focus conversations between them and find commonalities. It can thus be an equalities technique. It may help reduce isolation, increase self-esteem, and improve communication skills. It may also provide a basis for story writing, poetry, or music activities (Burnside & Haight, 1992).

Box 6.5 Steps in Using Creativity

Knowing . . .	*Basic steps . . .*	*Personal content*
Imagination Memory How to begin	Drawing Painting Sculpture Writing Storytelling Music	Obstacles Background Work Soul Story
Thinking through what you're trying to do	Skills in and facilities for the art of your choice	Identifying and working through issues in your life

Source: Adapted and developed from Allen (1995).

Case Study: War Reminiscences Among Older People

A group of older people in a day care center in London agreed that they would spend two weeks talking about their experience of the war. They brought official documents from that period; for example, many of them had retained ration books, magazines, and family photographs. Several had lost their homes in bombing, and they talked about being rehoused in unfamiliar parts of the city. Another rather younger person had been evacuated as a child to a rural area to avoid bombing. They discussed music from the period, and the following week, some people brought music to perform, and others brought old records to share.

Life review is a one-on-one experience, performed between a client as the reviewer and a therapeutic listener (Burnside & Haight, 1992). The aim is to recall, examine, and evaluate the entire life span as a basis for making plans for the future. The process often examines the client's conscience and responsibility for what took place; it may therefore contain spiritual elements. It involves recalling both remote and recent events, and addressing both sad and happy times. Planning for the future, for example, death or an important decision, or dealing with a crisis may lead to identifying elements of the self; what has continued and what has changed; and evaluation of the events reviewed, what the client contributed and lost as a result of what happened.

Case Study: Fatima Reviews Her Arranged Marriage

Fatima had left an abusive arranged marriage in which domestic violence had led to injury to herself and her two children. The police, a women's refuge, and a specialist agency for people affected by forced marriages had helped them. Members of her own family had criticized her and excluded her because she had complained about her husband to the police, which others felt was disloyal to the cultural expectations of women in her minority ethnic community.

As she prepared to move with her children in another part of the city, her social worker suggested a life review. This started by using a brief, open-ended questionnaire that asked about her childhood and family of origin, adulthood and work life, the here and now—particularly her marriage and the impending changes in her life. The discussion focused on the positives of her religious and cultural background, which in many ways gave her strength in living her life, and on how she could separate these from those elements of her background that had led to her oppression in marriage. She was also able to identify allies within her family and cultural background, and to make plans to retain contacts with those allies. So she was putting away the old difficult times and planning to look forward to a new life.

Life review can be used to reevaluate shared experiences in people's lives. For example, McDougall, Blixen, and Suen (1997) studied older homeless people with mental illnesses in six-week life review groups who were identifying shared themes in their reviews. Many of the following connect with the sorts of aims explored in this book about how humanistic practice can help people:

- Anxiety—a state of being uneasy, apprehensive, or worried about what may happen about a possible future event. With people with mental illness, this may be intensified, and there may be emotional disturbance and psychic tension.

- Denial—a statement opposing another point or identifying a contradiction and leading the reviewer to disown or repudiate something that has happened to him or her.

- Despair—a feeling of being overcome by a sense of futility or defeat or of having no hope.

- Helplessness—a feeling of being incompetent, ineffective, and powerless or of feeling weak in the face of what needed to be done.

- Isolation—a feeling of separation from a group or whole or, perhaps more positively, free of external influence or insulated.

- Loneliness—a heightened sense of solitude and gloom about being alone; unhappiness at being alone and longing for family, friends, or company.

- Loss—a feeling of being harmed by losing, being lost, or being deprived of something.

- Connection—a feeling that people have had relations between themselves and other humans in which they depended on, involved, or followed one another.

- Coping—a feeling that people had the ability to contend or strive especially on even terms or had success with difficulties and acted to overcome them.

- Efficacy—a feeling that people had the power or capacity to produce a desired effect.

- Hope—a feeling that what one wants will happen; a desire accompanied by expectation.

- Trust—a belief or confidence in, for example, honesty, integrity, reliability, and justice of another person or thing, also faith and reliance.

These feelings show how, even for quite seriously disabled and excluded individuals, people can identify and share important feelings by reviewing their life experiences. The research also defined and demonstrated the emotional themes that often emerge from and are the focus of humanistic practice.

We saw in chapter 5 when looking at systems and complexity theory that an open system is able to create its own energy to maintain itself and keep going; this process is called synergy. This points to the importance of creativity as a way to energize ourselves. We can specify some of the aspects of this by exploring D. K. Andersen, Furman, and Langer's (2006) account of a poet-practitioner:

- Dedication or commitment to improving the craft of practicing poetry
- A concern for the aesthetic value of the product, the poem

- A concern for the content and message of the poem—content may include subject matter and how it is dealt with, whereas the message is the shift in perception that the poet seeks to achieve in a reader
- A capacity to turn the everyday into the extraordinary
- Use of linguistic devices to highlight the significance of the everyday
- A sensitivity to the possibilities within the everyday
- A sensitivity to the impact of experiences, both everyday and extraordinary, on the individual and on social relationships
- A belief in the value of understanding the order and beauty of events, experiences, and sights

WHY SHOULD SOCIAL CARE SERVICES DEVELOP ARTS WORK?

Artistic and creative approaches to practice are often not at the center of social agencies, and they often seem to be a peripheral part of dealing with social and psychological problems. However, if we take a humanistic view of positive practice and see our role as human growth building beyond problem solving, artistic and creative practice has several advantages:

- It is a vital human activity in human life, and everyone has the right to try out their creative side. Agencies have a responsibility to think about artistic development and other forms of development for children or people with intellectual disabilities. People with mental illnesses or physical disabilities and older people all gain social and personal benefit from engaging in creative activities.
- It enhances emotional stability, personal enrichment, and self-fulfillment.
- It is a diversion from depression and anxiety.
- It can be interesting and engaging in an otherwise oppressed or boring life.
- It may be developed, as in life review and reminiscence as a therapy.
- As a therapeutic activity, engagement in creative activities may enable people to get at feelings and thoughts that are not otherwise available to them.

As an aspect of social care services, creative practice allows agencies and practitioners to emphasize the positives of their work and promote positive achievements of their clients. This may, in turn, help destigmatize clients' positions in society by showing what they can develop. Creative projects can be a useful activity as part of groupwork and can help develop communities by enabling people to take part in stimulating shared activities. Where agencies and practitioners provide residential or day care services, artistic achievements among participants can lighten the mood and provide a more stimulating environment. Residents of care homes and attenders at day care centers are happier, and the residential or care environment can seem a happier one to outside visitors and may be more motivating to potential clients.

Some useful principles in carrying out arts work are as follows:

- Make sure that it is offered in all aspects of an agency's work, for example, in people's homes, at hospital bedsides, in residential and day settings, and at all times of the day. Creative activities can help a service be very flexible.
- Use creative activities to engage members of a family in communication with one another by doing something positive and practical together. Doing so may enable them to discuss difficult relationship issues away from conflictual patterns of behavior that have become a habit or to do something together that distances them from conflict and difficulty that they may be experiencing.
- Offer a range of different arts so that people can choose; for example, some men may see painting or music as "women's" activities and prefer artistic work using computers or gardening.
- Encourage people to vary work the work that they do, so that they do not always repeat the same kind of activity.
- Enable people to develop creative work, so that they go on to more difficult activities and their skills and confidence grow.
- Give them a choice in media. Rather than always drawing, use watercolors or oil paints.
- Use the skills and creativity of practitioners to provide a variety of activities and personalities to engage with clients.
- Avoid a set program so that creativity does not become uncreativity (Hartley & Payne, 2008).

An important aspect of being a poet-practitioner, according to Anderson et al. (2006), is using poetry yourself to express your experiences in practice. This does not limit us to the art on which we are working. For example, Dobbs (2008), in describing her work in art therapy, conveyed some of her experience in a poem, and Tasker (2008), in describing a project in which women were working on dressmaking and fashion, shows how a woman created a poem to describe her emotional experience. Thus, we can demonstrate some of our experience using one artistic form through the opportunities offered by other artistic forms.

CONCLUSION

This chapter examined putting together the variety of skills and humanity of practitioners in complex ways. It looked at some of the problems of seeing social work and similar practices as helping, and it explored caring in some detail as an alternative model of seeing the full complexity and flexibility of practice. Caring involves connectedness with other human beings, demonstrated through practical tasks that develop into a commitment to achieving the cared-for person's personal growth. I have argued that for caring not to get stuck in merely maintaining a nondeveloping client, it is important to develop a creative approach to practice, by being imaginative and renewing our practice actions. Creative provision as part of social care services can enhance the personal growth of clients individually, in groups, and in communities, and it can provide beneficial environments for clients.

FURTHER READING

Phillips, J. (2007). *Care*. Cambridge, UK: Polity Books.

A good summary of ideas about care and caring.

Hugman, R., Peelo, M., & Soothill, K. (Eds.). (1997). *Concepts of care: Developments in health and social welfare*. London: Arnold.

An interesting conceptual and historical collection of articles about caring.

Robb, M., Barrett, S., Komaromy, C., & Rogers, A. (Eds.). (2000). *Communication, relationships and care: A reader*. London: Routledge.

A useful collection of articles focusing on the practice aspects of care provision.

Noddings, N. (1984). *Caring: A feminine approach to ethics and moral education*. Berkeley: University of California Press.

A useful analysis of feminist views on caring.

Garland, D. (2001). *Life review: The process of knowing yourself*. Hove, UK: Brunner-Routledge.

A good introductory, practical account of life review.

Haight, B. K., & Haight, B. S. (2007). *The handbook of structured life review*. Baltimore: Health Professions Press.

A comprehensive text by experienced practitioners and researchers.

Hartley, N., & Payne, M. (Eds.). (2008). *The creative arts in palliative care*. Philadelphia: Kingsley.

Although it refers to a specialist setting, this book contains useful and inspiring accounts from a range of practitioners of arts work with a range of clients.

Pritchard, J., & Sainsbury, E. E. (2004). *Can you read me? Creative writing with child and adult victims of abuse*. Philadelphia: Kingsley.

A practical book that describes practice and provides guidance for involving people who have been abused in creative writing as a way to explore and come to terms with their experiences.

Developing Self and Spirituality in Practice

7

CHAPTER AIMS

The main aim of this chapter is to enable practitioners to work to develop personal identity, a self, incorporating spiritual experience, their own and that of clients, appropriately into social work practice.

After working through this chapter, readers should be able to

- Understand the importance of self as an aspect of personal and social identity
- Appraise critically the problems of self-actualization as a practice objective
- Identify quality-of-life issues as a way to set clear objectives for personal growth
- Consider ways to help people with self issues and self-care, including developing emotional and social intelligence
- Review the role of spirituality and religion in social work agencies and social work practice
- Identify practice needs around clients' spirituality and religion
- Consider ways to assess and respond to spiritual issues

SELF-IDENTITY: THE CORPORATE AND PERSONAL

We have seen that an important aspect of humanistic practice is personal development and growth, to help move toward self-actualization. Earlier in the book, I have taken this for granted as an important objective. However, to practice, we need to understand these objectives in a more complex way.

Self-actualization presents several theoretical and practice difficulties. The first point is that, in humanistic psychologies, self-actualization or similar concepts are considered an important aim in life, and these psychologies assume that we have a psychological need or social expectation to achieve that need. The problem is this: how would we know it when we experience it? Does seeking self-actualization mean that we are always likely to be dissatisfied, always seeking but never finally achieving? Are we allowed to get to the point of being more or less satisfied, or does that mean that we are not achieving our human potential?

This issue is particularly important in social work. Many clients are not particularly ambitious for their own personal development. This may be because, as we saw in chapter 3, their starting point in life does not give them the opportunities or the strengths to achieve psychological efficacy or the social environment to achieve social agency in their social group. It seems ethically wrong to foist on them the demands of achievement; they are entitled to choose an unfulfilled state. Ethically, however, it is a concern that we may reinforce their unequal start in life by accepting their lack of motivation; then they lose the chance to achieve through whatever we are working on with them. However, again, our responsibility is often to provide services or help someone through the complexities of the various forms of help that are available. It is presumptuous to seize on this as an opportunity to work on what we think might be more fulfilling.

In answer to these ethical and practical doubts, we have to think of the social aims of humanistic practice. People should be able to attain their human rights. And this involves them in freely determining what they want in their life, so building their capacity to make decisions is also important. Taking us back to empowerment in chapter 3, this also leads us to enable people to think about various possibilities for themselves, and our discussion of equality focused on positives that people may be able to achieve. One of the answers to this question is the same as the points made in chapter 6 about being caring: the idea of helping people move toward personal growth gives us a sense of direction in what may be a long-term and slow-moving situation. Clients may not want substantial personal or social change now, but as human beings, they are entitled to the chance to decide freely how far they want to go, and they may be able to achieve steps toward greater self-fulfillment even if they cannot go as far as we might want for them.

The second point of criticism of the idea of self-actualization is that such ideas imply a deficit—our self is always capable of further actualization, so we should always be seeking to develop. Where will it ever end? A useful answer to this question is to think about quality of life. Quality of life has an everyday meaning: the extent of a feeling of well-being, enjoyment of life, and an ability to pursue and achieve desired life aims for an individual or community. A more specialized meaning would focus on measurement or indicators of the impact of social and environmental factors on the sense of well-being of an individual or community. Care-related quality of life is a measurement of the impact of need for care and provision of care services on the sense of well-being of individuals and their social networks (Payne, 2009a).

The idea of quality of life comes from health care; it is an attempt to measure the value of the outcomes of interventions. Health-related quality-of-life measures are available for many physical conditions, and they may claim to be objective or clinical and holistic (Jacobs & Rapoport, 2003). Objective measures examine issues such as mortality, rates of cure, and survival. Survival measures have led to the concept of quality-adjusted life years (QALYs), that is, the period that an individual might expect to survive at a particular level of quality of life. Holistic measures include patients' perceptions as well as objective information. The perceptions may be an overall sense of well-being; how well someone feels in relation to an identified condition; or how well someone is able to pursue some aspect of life, such as ordinary living or employment. Such ideas can easily be applied to social care services.

The third point is that self-actualization implies always being inward looking, as it aims to work on self-identity perhaps selfishly. An issue for humanistic psychotherapies is that, if practitioners focus all the time on a client identifying and strengthening a sense of self, they never get on with the practical needs of the client in family or activities of life. People call this navel gazing, always looking at some insignificant part of yourself instead of getting on with the things you have to get done. The way humanistic social work responds to this criticism is to say that our aim is to help people become self-directing, true to themselves, rather than governed by others (Geller, 1982). Thus, looking at yourself, or more accurately, your "self," is limited because self-development is needed only to be able to get on with life and relationships.

The fourth point is that an individual's values define self-actualization, so practitioners cannot impose their own views about how people should develop; they should enable people to think through their values so that they can decide for themselves.

Finally, self-actualization implies the existence of a real self as compared with some only partially realized or understood self, and it implies that understanding the real self can help people live their lives better (Daniels, 1988). What would that imply for intervention? Simply being aware of that real and now understood self is not enough; its development implies making it more complex or rich in some way. Or it might imply strengthening it, like filling the gas tank of a car or not using its energy to keep us in control of our lives, so that it becomes a guttering candle. Drawing attention to these analogies warns us that the nice idea of self-actualization involves making assumptions about what we are trying to achieve. Fortunately, social work objectives offer an important corrective to the purely psychological approach that understanding and cognitive processing will permit self-actualization. The social work focus on interaction with the social environment as a source of energy for people and the removal of barriers to participation in society as equal citizens through empowerment draws attention to possible strategies that overcome theoretical weaknesses in the idea of self-actualization.

Therefore, human interaction with the social environment allows us to identify expectations in people's social environments to see whether they are fulfilling possibilities that may be open to them or whether social agency may be empowered so that they can use more opportunities than they have at present. Actualizing our self can be achieved only by actualizing the environment in which that self operates, and that can be achieved only by actualizing for the benefit of other participants in that environment, too.

Case Study: Roberto's New Home

Roberto was a twenty-seven-year-old man with intellectual disabilities; he had lived with his parents until his early twenties, and they had helped him to set up his own apartment. But that arrangement had become very chaotic because they had not given him enough specific training in managing his money and everyday living requirements. Among other things, he was not feeding himself well, and he was drinking a lot in local bars to have social links, and people were perhaps exploiting him by getting him to give them money. His parents put him in touch with a local charity, which ran a training program and their own housing program. The social worker with the charity supported Roberto through the practical training, during which he improved his skills, and this also introduced him to the local community college. Once he was settled and functioning well in the new apartment, the social worker introduced him to a current affairs class at the college, which he had gained enough confidence to attend. She then encouraged him to take a photography class so that he could take pictures of trips arranged by the charity and friends he made in class. Eventually, he also went to a picture-framing class to frame his photographs, and his apartment was full of displays of the photos he had taken, which also gave him reminders of people and events he had been part of.

Roberto's case illustrates a steady development of self given the capability of someone with limited opportunities and skills. This redirected his interests by raising the quality and range of possibilities open to him. It also strengthened his affective equality, because he gained positive relationships with new friends and contacts who did not exploit him.

IDENTITY, SELF-IDENTITY, AND SELF-CARE

Identity is the set of characteristics that makes us similar to other people; the word has the same root meaning as *identical.* Identity is an important basis of our human equality; we all share characteristics with others, as we all share the reality that we are diverse and different from others. Looking at people's identity involves understanding what characteristics they share with others, how that sharing takes place, and how their diversity and difference emerges. Nobody, even twins who are genetically identical, is completely the same as another person; we all have social experiences that make us different from others. Our personal identity comprises a continuous sense of self, which interacts with our responses to others' perceptions of us. We interpret how they see us from how they behave. Our own characteristics develop as we differentiate ourselves from and model ourselves on other people in our social relationships. From infancy onward, we look at others and say, "I don't want to be like that," or "I should like to be more like them." Identity is thus socially constructed from our experiences of others.

Our identities make us part of collectivities of other people. Both our identity and the collective interests we engage in mold our social roles (Parker, 2000). Because we may see ourselves as like people in the collectivity, or others may see themselves as like us, our identity attaches us to them. This, of course, means that identity may exclude us from participation in other groups. Thus, we may be part of a family, a community in a neighborhood, or a faith group, or our attachments may exclude us from groups. For example, a Muslim is not usually considered part of a Christian faith group. However, such identities may be complex. For example, a Muslim may prefer her child to be cared for in a Christian children's organization that recognizes the importance of faith rather than not cared for at all or cared for in an avowedly humanist or secular organization.

Identities may be even more complex. For example, do we become a member of our spouse's family in marriage? Do we lose that identity with divorce, when families may keep in touch through any children? The family path (box 6.4) offers a way to think about and talk through such issues. The answer to these questions depends on, among other things, our culture, cultural expectations, and views of the families involved and personal preferences, and they might vary over time. Therefore, understanding people's identities involves complex social perceptions. Recent research on identity often focuses on social categories, such as social class, nationality, ethnicity, and gender (Alcoff & Mendieta, 2003). It is clear that attachment to some social identities, for example, a particular gender, faith, or nationality, may limit or help us in attachments to other identities. Transgender people often feel that their physical sexual markers do not reflect their own feelings about their gender identity.

We take parts of our identities from our attachments to social and work groups such as clubs, communities, or families and professions, organizations, or teams. Through involvement in such groups, we develop a commitment to that collectivity of people—a feeling that our membership of the group has meaning for us and that in some ways they reciprocate our feeling. However, these identities may be in conflict with one another. For example, sometimes our personal, family, or community commitments may conflict with work identities; our family or social life may get in the way of commitment to supporting the team. Work-life balance is a common issue for employed people.

Another complexity of identity is ambivalence: we may feel a part of our family or community but find parts of that group distasteful. We rebalance our identities according to personal attitudes and experience.

Case Example: Racism in the Family

I grew up in a family where expressions of racism were commonplace. My grandmother believed that black people were dirty and that the black would have worn off with washing; she cited the experience of looking at their hands, which had pink grooves in them. She was concerned that my cousin, who was felt to be rebellious, would seek a husband from a minority ethnic group merely to upset the family. Intuitively, I disliked this constant criticism of the personal characteristics of other people that we did not know. In another of the collectivities that formed my identity, my school, I learned about the factual inaccuracy of some of these views and the social inappropriateness of expressing those ideas.

There are two aspects of personal identity: one aspect is inside us, a personal consciousness of ourselves as a human being, our self. The second aspect is a social identity: how we build this up through relationships with others. Our professional identity as practitioners is a social identity, interacting with personal identities. Developing an identity requires continuity so that people may keep the same picture of the world and of themselves in relationship to it (Archer, 1995). An important point is that this therefore means that we are always separate from the world. It is a principle of Jean-Paul Sartre's existential philosophy that, because we exist, we are forced to think about and react to the world within which we exist (Craib, 1998). Jenkins (1996) describes social identity in this view as a dialectic between our internal and external views of our identities.

The process by which social identities are created has been changing. In the past, dominant organizations and interests in society had the most influence in establishing identities (Castells, 1997). They did this as part of the process of maintaining authority and control in an ordered society. The structure of society, traditionally, had a strong influence on our social roles and our identity. Identities were ascribed to people because of the social roles they occupied. A woman who married became a wife and later usually a mother, and there were common assumptions about how such female roles should be enacted. Similarly, there were established power relations between professions, and the role allocated to professions was well understood.

In recent years, social relations have changed. Identities are no longer so strongly controlled and ascribed, but they are patterned by how we understand the whole set of relationships in which people participate. So, to continue with the same examples, a woman has a much wider range of choices of gender behaviors than the traditional wife and mother models. Even if she takes those on, she has opportunities to live through a range of different kinds of wife and mother roles. She works those out for herself, participating in debates in society about the roles and in social interactions with people around her. The debates and interactions form a discourse, in which she continuously modifies her identity as she experiences her life, other people's reactions to her way of living, and the debates and discussion that she hears about. Similarly, interactions with professions close to ours may vary from traditional professional hierarchies and give us a variety of interprofessional experiences that we may learn from.

Identity politics is concerned with how many people's personal and group identity is constructed in dominant identities that are not their own. For example, women's identity is defined in relation to men's in societies that assume male dominance. This is also true of people with disabilities, whose identity is defined by the able bodied: they are disabled. Social work has often seen its identity as formed by the attitudes of other more powerful professions, especially medicine.

Illouz (2007) has argued that organizations develop an emotional style, which comes from their role in society. In capitalism, organizations maintain a tension between suffering and emotional satisfaction. We can see this in the long-standing tension in management studies between Taylorism or scientific management, which emphasize managing workload using numerical techniques such as work study, and human relations management ideas, which focus on developing human beings as part of the organization, through training, support, and teamwork. This conflict has been renewed in debates about managerialism in public services from the 1990s onward. Managerialism asserts that management is itself a discipline and practice, separable from activities such as social work that are managed and capable of general application to many different kinds of organizations. Also, managerialism applies generalist management techniques for controlling work and employee behavior in the public services. The assumption of generalist management, for example, is that you don't need to have a social work qualification and understanding of practice to manage social workers because techniques of management apply to all manager-worker relationships (Payne, 2000).

The self, personal identity, develops through experience, and that experience may be positive or difficult. Illouz (2007) has argued that experience of suffering may be particularly powerful and that helping professions derive their identity in capitalist societies from concern for the emotional field of suffering and reactions to it. Therefore, health and social care organizations and the professions associated with them develop an identity connected with suffering. This is one reason caring seems to be an important mode of practice in social work, as we saw in chapter 6.

Identity politics may also be concerned with broader issues about how identities are often constructed from difference. The issues that are most often raised in discussions of identity as difference are race, class, gender, and nationality (e.g., Alcoff & Mendieta, 2003), in particular as they represent or connect to culture (Hall, 1992). People may resist the connections that other people make or try to re-create new identities. For example, a child of migrants may work hard to establish an identity that reflects the culture and assumptions of the place that the family migrates to, but this may lead to conflict with parents, who may want to maintain a connection with their past identity. A later generation may want to reestablish understanding of their origins, resulting in conflict with parents who have tried to distance themselves from their migrant past.

All these changes mean that identities are less clear and continuous. They no longer offer the certainty and security of the traditional, socially developed forms of personal identity interacting with group and social identities, ascribed by established social roles and dominant, controlling social structures in societies. Instead, they are more like flickering images on the cinema screen. Social identities have become less substantial and clear as a cultural basis for personal identity; groups have resisted traditional ascription of identity as a form of social control, and they have begun projects to create alternative forms of identity. Identities have become attenuated, fragmented, and less central to people's lives.

PAUSE AND REFLECT: Your Identity or Self and Your Clients

Looking back through your life, try to identify the main factors that have contributed to your identity and how they made their contribution. You may find the family road in box 6.4 a useful guide. Your self is the present amalgam of the factors in your identity and how they affect your interaction with other people; see if you can define your self.

Then think about a client, family, or community you have worked with. Against every factor that affected your identity, list similar factors that you are aware of that formed the identity of that client, family, or community. Thinking about your self, how might its interaction with the identities of other people affect your self and those other people? How is your identity like and unlike theirs?

Some Suggestions

In thinking about just one factor in my identity, I focused on my experience of racism. To my family and school experience, I add my experiences of interesting and enjoyable relationships with able African people in college, learning about communities and behaviors across the world when studying anthropology, and my early experiences of social work in a city with a high proportion of Asian residents. I also remember my first experiences of employing black people when I was a manager; I was worried about the fact that they lacked some conventional skills, but I learned that their cultural and skill contributions to the workplace balanced this. This is an example of my learning through an equality-of-outcome approach, discussed in chapter 3. These colleagues did not have conventional skills, but because we had expanded our idea of what could contribute to our work, they offered other kinds of skills and knowledge that were just as important but different from our expectations. I was also involved in teaching and writing on issues concerned with inequalities and racism.

All these combine to make a fairly liberal self on the matter of racism. However, some African and Asian clients in my workplace must be anxious to be introduced to me in my jacket and tie as a fairly conventional management type, and I realize that I have to work hard to demonstrate openness. If we go back to the wise person discussed in chapter 4, those clients may take it for granted that an employee of my agency will be open on matters of race and see around them antidiscriminatory notices and policies. Nevertheless, many people from minority ethnic groups have experience of racism in their lives, which means that they are always cautious or uncertain when facing an agency like mine and an individual like me.

We also saw in chapter 3 that affective equality (Lynch et al., 2009) means that people need to be enabled to receive love and caring from people around them and are able to offer love and caring to others. This means that they have opportunities to build solidarity within families, communities, and other social groups. Love and caring, having feelings about other people, is thus an important basis of membership in social groups and, in turn, an important basis of the social identity that people gain from social groups. If people cannot or do not have loving and caring relationships, their identity is damaged and their interaction with social groups around them is also disadvantaged.

Robinson (2008) has usefully provided a model or how self issues arise for people, which I have extended from a health-care setting and from its focus on spirituality in box 7.1. Its humanistic approach focuses on the self, or personal identity, and how life experiences may disturb this; this applies complexity thinking in seeing a disturbance not only as a problem but also as an opportunity for change. He also has identified ways in which the focus of intervention may change as the issue continues to affect clients' lives. The humanistic approach also moves people forward from identifying the issues that are important toward facing and dealing with them.

How, then, can practitioners help people with issues about their identity or self? Self-care has two main meanings:

- Caring for social and other needs without accepting help from professionals or others. This view of self-care connects with self-medication, for example, buying and taking pills from a pharmacy rather than going to a physician for professional advice and a prescription. We might do this to maintain our privacy from intervention or to reduce costs that may be charged for a service.
- Thinking about and working to maintain our identity of self.

Box 7.1 Interventions with Emerging Self Issues

Emerging self issues	*Interventions*
Life issues arise	Assist with greater awareness of life issues
Client becomes aware of issues	Help deal with immediate threats
Client tries to defend the "self" in the context of the issues	
There is a period of meaninglessness and chaos	Help with exploring chaos and complexity
Understanding about the issues and opportunities for a new self emerge	Help with understanding and exploration
The new self helps clients find ways to live with or through the issues	Help with life planning, finding satisfaction and opportunities in new situation

Source: Developed from Robinson (2008).

PAUSE AND REFLECT: What Do You Do to Take Care of Your Self?

Johnson and Webster (2002), in discussing solution-focused practice, have suggested that a useful way to think about caring for our self is to ask people, "What do you do to take care of your self?" because this often elicits a wide range of examples of positive experiences that people attempt to use to maintain, protect, and restore their well-being in ordinary life. It usually means, also, that these ideas are practical, because they are already part of people's lives.

Ask yourself this question and note the answers. Then go on to ask how these contribute to caring for your self; note the difference in this formulation.

Some Suggestions

While struggling with writing, I might go for a walk, play the piano for a while, have a cool drink. When feeling lonely, I might go out for a cup of coffee at a local café or call a friend for a talk.

Going for walks contributes to my self-care because it keeps me fit, playing the piano relaxes me, and the drink makes a break that allows me to focus again. Being around people or keeping in touch with friends or family maintains connectedness with other human beings and people in relationships with me.

EMOTIONAL AND SOCIAL INTELLIGENCE

To explore the self, both social workers and clients need to improve their emotional and social intelligence, that is, the ability to observe, assess, evaluate, and then act appropriately to other people's emotions and responses in social interactions. Such ideas have a long history. Thorndike (1921) coined the term *social intelligence* to refer to acting wisely in human relationships, and Goleman (1996) identified the importance of emotional intelligence in parenting and many other social situations. Emotional intelligence comprises an interaction between self-awareness and self-management (intrapersonal intelligence) and awareness of others and capacity to manage relationships with others (interpersonal intelligence) (Morrison 2007).

People with emotional intelligence have developed skills in perceiving and identifying feelings in others. They integrate emotions with thinking in a way that facilitates effective cognition and demonstrates a preparedness to think about their own and other people's feelings and manage their own emotions and emotions collectively with others. Social workers who have developed emotional intelligence are likely to be better able to engage with others, carry out social work assessments, make decisions, and collaborate with others. As professionals, they are likely to be better able to deal with stress, build resilience to adversity, and cope better with difficulties in their practice (Morrison, 2007).

Howe (2008) has argued that emotional intelligence permits practitioners to move from observing and monitoring their own and clients' behavior toward managing the environment around them. He sees the connectedness required in caring relationships as part of intuitive human awareness of and responsiveness to other people. It is part of the development of the human self and its actualization that human beings seek and want to experience psychological and social attachments that achieve such awareness and responsiveness. These concepts relate to the humanistic ideas explored in chapters 1 and 2. Goleman (2006) has also explored similar abilities to deal with social situations and longer-term relationships.

Interventions that work on emotional and social intelligence include the following:

- Mindfulness—building a constant awareness of our impact on others and their reactions to us.
- Attachments—encouraging people to experience and build connections with other people.
- Talking therapies—enabling people to observe and review their connectedness in social interactions and relationships.

Many such approaches to helping rely on clients' sharing of observations—what happened in that situation—as well as rehearsing possible responses with practitioners, testing them out in further situations, and refining awareness and responses.

Case Study: Building a Response to Child Care Problems

Hannah had three children, each of whom had a different father, who left before she had each baby. She raised the children herself as a single parent, and eventually had difficulties managing the children's behavior and social relationships, partly because of poverty in the family, which meant that they were able to participate in only limited social and leisure activities. Felicity, a social worker with a children's project, discussed this history with Hannah. She found that Hannah felt that none of her previous partners was suitable as a lifetime partner. Accepting this, Felicity nevertheless pointed out that it was a pattern in Hannah's life and suggested that it also reflected Hannah's preference for independence and control over her living arrangements.

They worked together on the children's difficulties, teaching the children through reviewing what went wrong in their relationships, rehearsing alternative responses, and encouraging and supporting them to try these out as situations arose. As this process went on, Hannah began to identify that she had limited the children's contacts partly because of wanting to control their life experience and prevent them from having difficult experiences. However, she began to see that it was possible to help the children deal with problems in their relationships without being present. Felicity helped the children express how they found their mother to be too controlling at times.

Hannah asked Felicity to work with her on her own relationships, both with the children and with women friends, using some of the same techniques. She then began to use the same approach in testing out relationships with men, consulting with Felicity from time to time. Hannah found that she was able to build relationships and make friends without holding them at a distance, as she realized she had been doing.

SPIRITUALITY IS IMPORTANT FOR PRACTICE

If human beings are the focus of humanistic social work practice, what does this mean for spirituality? Secular humanism excludes religion, seeing it as superstition that the rational human mind can put aside. Christianity and other religions involve broader forms of humanist thinking by focusing on human rationality as an important responsibility in life. Transpersonal psychology and psychotherapy has developed approaches to dealing with spiritual issues, arguing that it is an important but hard-to-connect-with aspect of being human. This disagreement is an example of one of those painful aspects of human life and organization that stimulates human self and identity development and leads to organizational conflicts, discussed previously. Because it is painful and difficult, it leads organizations and practitioners into difficult areas of emotional conflict.

The difficulty of achieving engagement in spirituality suggests that it is at times important for humanistic practitioners. The first and most important reason for this is that most human beings see their spirituality as an important part of their identity. We have seen that self-actualization is in part about the development of our identity, and therefore, whatever is important to our clients is important in humanistic practice. It limits our practice to help develop another human being if we fail to engage with their spirituality. In this part of the chapter, therefore, I discuss ways of understanding spirituality that can inform how we incorporate it into our practice.

Second, human spirituality may be wholly personal and private, but spirituality is often expressed in public ways in and particularly through religion. Because religion is an important part of some people's lives, it should be included in our thinking about work with those people. It also generates important social institutions, so it affects people's social relationships and is part of the patterns of social power that affect people's lives. Moving on from thinking about spirituality in general, I also examine some issues about religion as part of social work practice. I suggest that we cannot engage with people's spirituality without examining the impact of religions and churches in the social patterns that both oppress and help develop individuals, families, communities, and societies.

Third, there is considerable evidence that having an explicit religious or spiritual commitment in life helps people deal with adversity. For example, they are more likely to be successful in overcoming major illness. Religious or spiritual commitment is often expressed in organizations, which often provide personal support networks. These may be a positive resource in helping people overcome difficulties in their lives. Therefore, the last part of this chapter looks at how we can assess spirituality and religion with our clients and in their families and communities, and how we might intervene with these issues.

ENGAGING WITH SPIRITUALITY

I have suggested that it is often hard to engage with spirituality and religion in social work and other helping practices. Our starting point needs to be, therefore, why this is difficult for us.

PAUSE AND REFLECT: Why Is Spirituality Hard to Engage With in Practice?

Review two or three people whom you have worked with, and try to pick some for whom spirituality or religion was important. If you cannot think of any, pick some clients whom you knew very well, and try to identify spiritual strands in their lives. What did you find were the difficulties of engaging with their spirituality? How did you deal with these difficulties?

Some Suggestions
Among the difficulties you may have found were the following:

■ Agencies are often explicitly nonsectarian (i.e., they are committed to serving and employing people from all religions or sects) or secular (i.e., they exclude religion as a focus of action). Many states explicitly require public services to be secular. That makes it hard to introduce and deal with religion.

■ Spiritual beliefs or faith is often connected to people's culture. Agency diversity or equal opportunities policies, which express important organizational values and that social workers are particularly committed to through their codes of ethics and practice, may seem to require acceptance without question of religious or spiritual beliefs. Therefore, it becomes difficult to engage with them critically as part of practice, such as when they seem to be getting in the way of human development or social care services.

■ Many people see issues of spirituality and religion as private, and it can be hard to introduce those issues into discussions.

■ Connected with this, it is hard to know how to assess such issues and how they may be helpful.

■ Because practitioners may have a commitment to their own religion, they find it hard to accept and engage with alternative religions (i.e., faith in another deity) or denominations (i.e., different organizational bases such as churches or temples for the expression of the same religion).

■ Connected with these points, they may fear being accused of inappropriately trying to convert a client to their own religion.

■ Connected with that again, they may not have a knowledge base that allows them to explore the other religion.

■ Practitioners may be agnostic (i.e., believing in the existence of unknowable forces in our life, without a commitment to a particular religion) or atheist (i.e., not believing in a god). Therefore, they disagree with the basis of all faiths and religions and find it hard to engage with those beliefs.

In this list, and in other issues that you might have identified as well, we can see a mixture of important individual reactions to spirituality and religion, as well as the complexity that arises as the organizations and society around us try to respond to these issues in a rational way. Part of the reason for the difficulty is that spirituality and religion are not rational, so rational responses cannot always help us deal with them. They are also concepts that are hard to explain.

UNDERSTANDING SPIRITUALITY PRACTICALLY

The title of this section can have different meanings. One meaning is that I discuss a practical way to look at the meaning of spirituality in a way that respects a vast and complex literature but that we can apply in practice. Another meaning is that I can get close enough to a useful account of spirituality without capturing every nuance of meaning that people might apply to it. This is like empathy—we can get close to what people might understand by their spirituality, but we probably cannot fully appreciate everything that spirituality might mean for them.

My starting point is that spiritual issues are about transcendence. Robinson, Kendrick, and Brown (2003) have defined transcendence as arriving at an overall personal view of the world outside ourselves by which we make important life decisions. Thus, there are two elements of a spiritual issue: how a person interprets the world and how this affects that person's thinking and reactions. I set these out in box 7.2. People may struggle with thinking out how they should react to a problem; I call these internally facing spiritual issues. Alternatively, they may be thinking about how they should interpret the world, or externally facing issues. We saw when discussing accountability in chapter 2 that many people's thinking may start from an innate intuition, which often develops into nonrational thoughts about how things happen, perhaps superstitions. We also saw, in discussing social construction ideas in chapter 4, that their thinking will inevitably be shaped by their social experience, which may include their family or community, religion or spirituality, or a particularly influential individual in their lives. Looking at the internally facing debate in someone, then, I conceive it as an interaction among formal religious ideas, social ideas imbibed from social relationships, and a person's own intuition and ideas, which I describe as their creativity. These interact as people deal with both internally and externally facing issues.

Box 7.2 Model of Spirituality

Two aspects of spiritual experience seem to be important. First, the spiritual is the opposite of the material, so spirituality is concerned with human life and experience that is different from, though perhaps connected to, physical experiences. It is also separate from material things in the world, such as money and wealth. Many religions emphasize poverty and charity as virtues; you give what you have to people if they need it more than you, and if you are poor and so are not able to be giving, you are sharing in their poverty.

Second, many people see the spiritual aspect of their self as providing energy and direction in their lives. It allows them to ascribe meaning to important experiences that they have, and it renders their lives intelligible. Thus, a spiritual awareness makes for accountability in one of the senses we discussed in chapter 2. It helps us achieve intelligibility about the world, about ourselves, and about others.

An important set of ideas is the connection among body, mind, and soul. Many spiritual ideas suggest that the identity of a human being exists during life in the form of a soul or spirit that continues to exist after death. During life, the soul is part of the body, giving it energy, direction, and meaning. When the body dies, the spirit continues in some form, maintaining the existence of the human identity. Different religions see this differently; some Eastern religions accept reincarnation, in which the spirit moves to inhabit another body. How is the idea of the soul or spirit connected to the concept of the mind? At first sight, they seem rather similar, as the intellect and thinking processes may offer human beings stimulation and direction. Is a soul just an old-fashioned way of talking about the mind?

The conventional view about this issue is interactionalism (Flew, 1964). This view sees the body and mind as different aspects of a person that interact and affect each other. Either physical states, such as chemical changes in the body that create emotional or cognitive changes, produce the mind, or the mind is autonomous and influences behavior. The interaction may be both ways, with the mind being influenced by physical states and in turn influencing physical actions by its thinking. The soul, however, is usually seen as different from mind, because it does not have such constant interaction with the body and is thought to have an existence outside the mind and body. However, we cannot scientifically observe or fully understand such an entity, if it exists. Debates about these ideas have swung back and forth across the centuries.

Because the human mind, spirit, and body interlock, how can we disentangle spirituality from other aspects of the human? Should we try, or do the connections make the differences unanalyzable? This may be particularly so when we think about the connections between the knowledge bases of professions working in psychology, social work, and divinity. Each profession focuses on meaning in human life. Psychologists might look at how the mind works to deliver intellectual understanding of the world through cognition. The social worker might work with how social influences create meaning for people. Religion and spirituality might try to identify how the overall meaning of the world in which we live affects our humanity as a whole person.

Many religious and spiritual approaches focus on personal understanding, providing ways of "working on ourselves," as Brandon (2000, p. 3) puts it. He includes in this "mind dancing," or accepting and appreciating incongruities and inconsistencies in life, not only seeking strength and resilience but also including vulnerability as a strength because it enables us to empathize with others and make connections with them. We cannot seek for everything to flow or to be easy; we cannot seek for it to release us from the disciplines of everyday life or of social expectations (Brandon, 2000). Although we can claim uniqueness for everyone, this does not mean that we can be individualistic in our approach, because we must use our uniqueness in social relationships, the work, leisure, and human roles that we accept in our connectedness with others. Several writers reject the idea that spirituality should be seen as something special or possessed only by elites who have the chance for extended meditation or special insights (Brandon, 2000; Lindsay, 2002).

To sum all of these points up, Moberg's (2005) review of conceptual research found that definitions of spirituality were found to focus on the following:

- Meaning and unity, that is, ideas that express ways people see the world as being consistent and themselves as being consistent within it; in this way, for many people, spirituality expresses an important aspect of self.
- A dimension of people that transcends their self and present experience.
- A motivating force or belief in a power beyond the person's existence.
- The connections with breath and its activities; that is, it connects with aspects of humanity that express or give life.
- Postmodern interpretations of an unobservable aspect of living that lies beyond empirical understanding.

RELIGION

Spirituality is often expressed through religion, and as we have seen, most societies have religions and religious organizations active in public life. Yet there are doubts about and often prohibition of religious expression as part of social work practice.

PAUSE AND REFLECT: Religion in Social Agencies

In many societies, public services and social agencies are required to be explicitly secular. Review the policies of your own social agency or an agency that you know well: Are there explicit rules requiring their approach to be secular, excluding religion from being expressed in the workplace or practice of the agency? Or are there informal practices that are designed to keep religion out of your work? What is your understanding of the reason for these formal or informal rules?

Some Suggestions
You may find that there are regulations that prevent staff from wearing symbols associated with particular religions; this is true even in countries where religion is important.

For example, there has been a lengthy history of controversy in the United States about a policy of separating the expression of religion from public life, as in the Pledge of Allegiance in schools and in public monuments that have religions connotations (Harvard University Pluralism Project, 2004). There are examples in other Western countries, as well. In 2006, a U.K. airline dismissed a check-in clerk for wearing a visible cross and claimed that many airlines had similar policies ("Woman loses fight," 2006). In France, there has been controversy because Muslim schoolchildren are not allowed to wear the headscarf because of an explicitly secularist policy ("Headscarf defeat," 2005). There may also be rules that prevent practitioners from expressing religion, such as praying, with clients or from taking into account religious observance when making decisions.

Among the reasons for policies like this are the following:

■ Religion is thought to be a nonrational faith, inconsistent with evidence-based practice and rational decision making in the agency.

■ Religion is a source of conflict between people and communities.

■ Religion may be excluded from public services and secular spaces because it has the potential or is believed by some to be at least potentially "oppressive, an obstacle to free speech, personal liberty and political democracy, and a threat to neutral public space" (Furbey, 2009, p. 21).

Religion and spirituality are important to many people, and therefore, in humanistic practice that is based on relationships between whole human beings, it cannot be ignored. Box 7.3 shows a listing of the number of adherents of major religions across the world, drawn from extensive statistical sources. Information from three English-speaking countries is compared with this. Of course, such summary information does not tell us how committed the adherence to these religions is, and we would have to go back to the sources for the precise definition of many of the categories. There would also be dispute about whether some of them might be considered religions. For example, the large group of secular or nonreligious people is very diverse, and many would explicitly reject the idea that they are part of a religion, although as we have seen throughout this book, secular humanists have a well-defined philosophical base, and some would distinguish themselves from atheists or agnostics for that reason. Another example is Scientologists; some countries explicitly refuse to define Scientology as a religion. However, it is part of the lives of many people who social workers will be dealing with, so it cannot be neglected.

A further concern arises about the reality that religion cannot be ignored in relationship-based practice. That is, because religion is an expression of spirituality, and spirituality is a way to connect our own identity and internal understanding with the outside world, religion is an important element of how people react to human situations that are important in their lives. That is why I incorporated religion as an element of internal debate when describing spirituality.

Box 7.3 Adherents of Major Religions Worldwide and in Three English-speaking Countries

Worldwide	Canada	United Kingdom	United States
Christianity: 2.1 billion	Catholic: 12,936,905	Christianity: 42,079,000	Christianity: 159,030,000
Islam: 1.5 billion	Protestant: 8,654,850	Buddhism: 152,000	Nonreligious or secular: 27,539,000
Secular, nonreligious, agnostic, atheist: 1.1 billion	Christian Orthodox: 479,620	Hinduism: 559,000	Judaism: 2,831,000
Hinduism: 900 million	Christian not included elsewhere: 780,450	Judaism: 267,000	Islam: 1,104,000
Chinese traditional religion: 394 million	Muslim: 579,640	Islam: 1,591,000	Buddhism: 1,082,000
Buddhism: 376 million	Jewish: 329,995	Sikhism: 336,000	Agnostic: 991,000
Primal indigenous: 300 million	Buddhist: 300,345	Other religion: 179,000	Atheist: 902,000
African traditional and diasporic: 100 million	Hindu: 297,200	*All religions: 45,163,000*	Hinduism: 766,000
Sikhism: 23 million	Sikh: 278,410	No religion: 9,104,000	Unitarian-Universalism: 629,000
Juche: 19 million	Eastern religions: 37,550	Not stated: 4,289,000	Wiccan/Pagan/Druid: 307,000
Spiritism: 15 million	Other religions: 63,975	*All no religion and not stated: 13,626,000*	Spiritualist: 116,000
Judaism: 14 million	No religious affiliation: 4,900,090		Native American Religion: 103,000
Baha'i: 7 million			Baha'i: 84,000
Jainism: 4.2 million			New Age: 68,000
Shinto: 4 million			Sikhism: 57,000
Cao Dai: 4 million			Scientology: 55,000
Zoroastrianism: 2.6 million			Humanist: 49,000
Tenrikyo: 2 million			Deity (Deist): 49,000
Neo-Paganism: 1 million			Taoist: 40,000
Unitarian-Universalism: 800,000			Eckankar: 26,000
Rastafarianism: 600,000			
Scientology: 500,000			
Source: Adherents.com (2009).	*Source:* Statistics Canada (2001).	*Source:* Office for National Statistics (2009).	*Source:* Kosmin, Meyer, & Keysar (2001).

SPIRITUALITY IN SOCIAL WORK PRACTICE

We can see that spirituality is an issue for social work practice for practical and theoretical reasons. This is because most people see themselves as spiritual people, and therefore spirituality affects how they behave and react. Religion is part of spirituality; for some people, it is their spirituality. Therefore, when social workers deal with people who are religious, they have to assess it and take it into account in their practice (Bullis, 1996; Canda & Furman, 1999).

The humanistic ideas discussed in chapter 1 suggest two important reasons for a concern with spirituality. Humanistic psychologies suggest that personal fulfillment is an important outcome of successful practice, and what Maslow called peak experiences came from some kind of transformational experience; they are energizing in the same way that creativity, discussed in chapter 6, is energizing for people. Transpersonal psychologies emphasize experiences that connect life experience with these experienced transformations. Human rights ideas emphasize the importance of freedom of religion and freedom to express religion through faith and organized religion.

Religion may also be an important factor in agency decision making. For example, in adoption and foster care, it can be important, and in some states is a legal requirement, that adopters or caregivers follow the same religion as children placed with them. With older people and others entering residential care, denominational care homes or hospitals can be an important resource.

Case Example: Ken's Divorce and His Children

Ken, a divorced man in his forties, talked about his contribution as a parent. One of his sons had supported his mother in the divorce. This son was estranged from Ken, who had more involvement with his daughter, who had stayed in touch with him after the divorce. Being a good parent was important to him. Looking at his life, he asked himself, "Where did I go wrong? Should I have stayed with my wife and made a better contribution to my son's personal development?" The externally facing issue was the importance of parenting as a part of life and a contribution to the community. The internally facing issue was how he should feel about himself in light of that view of the world. I spent a good deal of time talking through with him what had happened, whether he should see himself as having failed because of the estrangement and how important that was in the context of his many other contributions to the life of his family and community.

Some areas of health and social care practice have particularly focused on spiritual care, because they have a history of spiritual issues arising. This has often been where people experience major changes in life, for example, in maternity services, where people often face crises because of the death of either a mother or a child during or soon after childbirth, or disability, where there is a serious life-threatening illness or a major physical disability as a result of an accident. Another area of practice in which spiritual care has been important is at the end of life, when people are face-to-face with their own mortality.

An example of such a specialist area in which social work makes a contribution is palliative care, the multiprofessional practice of caring for people who are dying of an advanced illness. Palliative care identifies four elements of practice:

- Biomedical, which is divided into treatment and care
- Psychological
- Social
- Spiritual (Reith & Payne, 2009)

Making these distinctions draws attention to differences among the important focuses of practice. Biomedical care or treatment focuses on the body, psychological care on the mind, social care on relationships and social structures, and the spiritual on issues of meaning. However, several of these areas overlap, particularly because they focus on different aspects of meaning to human beings:

- Biological meaning is about how people interpret their perceptions of their bodies; are their bodies telling them that they are weak, strong, or vulnerable?
- Psychological meaning focuses on the consequences for mental functioning of differences in meaning.
- Social meaning focuses on issues that arise around different interpretations of events in a client's family, community, and society; often cultural differences and expectations affect these meanings.
- Spiritual meaning focuses on the integration of events into the person to achieve congruence and wholeness.

Case Example: Ken's Divorce Continued

In the consequences of Ken's divorce, we can see that the different reactions of his children might have a variety of consequences.

Biologically, Ken might become depressed, and as we saw when discussing the interaction of mind, body, and spirit, mental and physical reactions may affect one another. Ken's depression might lead to a perception that he is experiencing physical symptoms of illness.

The psychological meaning for Ken might be that he loses confidence in his ability to be a parent, so that when he marries again, he might feel that he does not want to have more children, and this might be distressing for his second wife. Conflict between Ken and his first wife might lead her to discourage the children from having a good relationship with him, and this might lead to conflicts in the wider family; for example, the children's grandparents might be deprived of relationships with the children, and friends and family in the local community might take sides with one or the other.

More broadly, if the legal system is adversarial in dealing with divorce and people learn that conflict gets them a better income after divorce and more power over the children, lawyers might be forced to advise parents going through a divorce to maintain a conflictual stance in their own financial and personal interests. This would give divorce a particular social meaning.

If Ken's church argued strongly that marriage was to last for life and that divorce was a failure in its members' lives, Ken might have more difficulty in incorporating into himself a feeling that he was a good parent and made important contributions to the community than if he were in a more accepting religious community. Therefore, the loss of church relationships from the failure of his marriage might affect his social relationships, and a particular religious view would be incorporated into his spiritual adjustment to his divorce.

We can see this in the political and social importance of human rights. Although the basic ideas of human rights thinking come from our experience of what is important to us as human beings, systems of human rights principles are developed by thinking rationally about social arrangements that are required to implement those principles. We can see this by exploring the historical context of the various systems of principles that are summarized in box 1.5. The causes that led the first American citizens to fight the Revolutionary War led to the emphases of the Bill of Rights; compare that with the need to establish principles of international mutual respect among nations in the Universal Declaration of Human Rights and the creation of a level playing field for social relationships in the European economies that are signatories to the European Charter of Fundamental Rights.

EXCLUDING OR INCLUDING SPIRITUALITY IN OUR PRACTICE

Because including spirituality in practice may seem difficult and may be questioned by agencies, clients, and others, it is important to think through the arguments for and against including or excluding it from our practice.

PAUSE AND REFLECT: Your Spirituality and Its Effects on Practice

As a starting point, think through your own spirituality. Note your views on its role and importance in your life and how this might affect your practice, and in turn other people's lives.

Some Suggestions

An almost-infinite range of possibilities opens up. You, the practitioner, may be committed to a particular form of formal spirituality or a religious faith or to atheist, agnostic, or secularist views in your life. Whether or not you are committed to a particular spiritual position or religion yourself, you may feel or your agency may require that social work be secular in its approach. Alternatively, you may feel that it is appropriate for services to allow or encourage workers to express their spirituality in their practice.

Whatever your personal commitment, you may feel you should respect the possibly different position of your clients. Respecting clients' positions may mean simply accepting the nature and expression of their spirituality. However, we saw in the discussions of congruence and genuineness in humanistic psychology (chapter 1) and of communication as an aspect of caring (chapter 3) that simple acceptance is not enough: we have to communicate that acceptance has an impact on how we behave; it must make a difference. There is a problem for practitioners in doing this if their own spirituality, or the expression of it through religion, is different from that of their clients. Do we openly disagree? Or do we agree to disagree (and if we try to do that, perhaps the client will not agree to disagree)?

To deal with all these issues, humanistic social work starts from its first principles. First, everyone has a human right to freedom of religion and spirituality; that means a right to believe what they believe and to practice and express it. Every human puts that belief and expression together in different ways, even if the stated spirituality, religion, or denomination is the same; their individual humanity will express it differently.

Case Example: Muslim Spirituality

A Muslim woman was admitted to hospital; asked to see the hospital chaplain, a Christian; and asked whether someone of her faith could visit to help her. The chaplain called his contact at the local mosque, who said, "Make sure she has a copy of the Koran and reads it regularly; that is the most important thing." The chaplain asked if someone from the mosque could visit, as he would have expected from a Christian church, but the mosque had no arrangements for this and said that her family would visit and help with her spirituality. Members of the family read passages from the Koran together at her bedside, and a brother told the chaplain that this had brought them closer together.

This case illustrates how religions approach issues in different ways. However, this may reflect cultural assumptions that may not be fulfilled in a new environment. For example, the assumption here was that the family would be available to help this Muslim woman, and that doing so was the appropriate course of action. However, affective inequality may mean that some people may not have access to the traditional sources of support. If we look back at Phuoc, the Vietnamese refugee whose case I discussed in chapter 3, we can see that some migrants or others in minority cultures may not be able to call on their families in the traditional way. Therefore, a way to deal with the issue in the majority culture may be incorporated for use in the minority culture. In this case, it may be useful to recruit Muslim volunteers who may be prepared to substitute for some of the missing affective opportunities. This adapts the traditional Western role of the volunteer to use in a different culture, where the actions required (e.g., reading the Koran—those in a health-care setting might be cautious about having volunteers read the Bible with patients) may be different but the volunteer role remains similar to the Western model.

This discussion also illustrates that rituals are important to preparing for reflection. Also, meditation and reflection are important to many ideas about how spirituality is expressed.

Case Example: Rituals and Reflection as Part of Spirituality

A group of practitioners in a day center for people who were recovering from cardiovascular accidents (e.g., strokes) had a discussion about ways they maintained strength and resilience in their work. A Roman Catholic Christian talked about the satisfaction of using the rosary to count her way through a number of standard phrases and prayers. A middle-aged volunteer who claimed to be agnostic talked about his worry stones, smooth, small stones collected on long walks that he carried in his pockets and touched. A minister of religion talked about kneeling at particular times of the day, holding his hands together, closing his eyes, and talking to God through prayers. A Buddhist described intoning non-sense syllables repetitively to distract him from the everyday before he began to meditate. Another member of the team described a number of physical exercises, some derived from yoga classes, as a way to begin a period of quiet reflection.

They agreed with the conclusion that they all in various ways used repetitive rituals to cleanse their minds and bodies of the everyday, and to focus on thoughts and issues in their minds. Although the Christians did not agree with this, some others thought that their interpretation of prayer was like the conversations that we all have with ourselves about what we are doing. To the more secular members, the idea of speaking to God and testing ideas out against the Christian concepts of what they thought God might say to them seemed very much like an externalization of the internal conversations that many people have. They also noted that many of the informal rituals of setting up team meetings, such as going to a special place, turning off phones, making drinks for one another, were also rituals in preparation for shared reflection.

Social work and religion are connected institutionally. Historically, social work agencies have often emerged from religious work (Lindsay, 2002). Many social work agencies are affiliated with different religions. Attempts have been made to provide joint divinity and social work courses so that practitioners from both professions may learn from and influence each other (D. Lee & O'Gorman, 2005). Political efforts have been made to increase the influence of faith groups in social affairs as a way to increase solidarity and gain the resources that come from the social commitment of many religious groups (Cnaan, Boddic, & Wineburg, 1999).

Spirituality may not be entirely about personal experience, but also about either achieving some personal perfection or personally satisfying understanding about the world (Lindsay, 2002). Liberation theology proposes that spirituality should engage us in searching for equality and freedom for poor and oppressed peoples (Gutiérrez, 1973). Similarly, feminist theology seeks to reclaim for women a female spirituality, distinguishing it from a patriarchal view in which the male conception of important meanings in the world has priority.

Can we address different spirituality by understanding alternative spiritual approaches or faiths? Many practitioners develop an interest in responding to spirituality for two reasons. One is that it seems important to develop understanding of important spiritual and religious principles by which clients live their lives. This is the objective of guides to the main beliefs of different religious traditions, such as those of Van

Hook, Hugen, and Aguilar (2001) and, in a specialist context, Neuberger (2004). It has also led to a substantial literature drawing on spiritual ideas to influence social work. For example, Chan and colleagues (Chan, 2001; Ng & Chan, 2009) have used principles drawing on Chinese medicine, and Cree and Maori ideas have also been applied in social work (Marsh & Crow, 1997; Nabigon & Mawhiney, 1996).

One weakness of this approach leads to criticism that we may be interested in minority religions because of their exotic or unusual features compared with the sources of spirituality in our own society. This interest may be because of the political and social importance of particular religions at a particular time, such as Islam (Crabtree, Husain, & Spalek, 2008), but it is sometimes just a searching for exotica or stimulation from the unusual, and it is important to make sure that use of spiritual ideas is relevant to the people that we are working with. Implementing multicultural guidelines in practice may, therefore, be complex and require judgments about the appropriateness of pursuing an interest in particular religions.

Case Example: Karim's Complaint About Discussing His Faith

Karim was a man in his thirties who had been diagnosed with multiple sclerosis, a progressive degenerative disease, which leads to increasing incapacity. He was a client of Joseph, a practitioner who was very committed to engaging with spiritual issues with clients. Karim found his Muslim faith very helpful in maintaining his motivation to deal with the many practice and relationship difficulties that had come with his condition, particularly the need to use a wheelchair for even short local journeys.

Joseph did not know about Islam, and he asked about Karim's religious observance and got him to explain how his particular beliefs helped him. He did this by focusing on particular events, judging that discussion of concrete examples of the benefits of religious faith would help him identify and incorporate the strengths of his faith into his resilience in the face of his condition. To maintain the sense of equality, and to demonstrate empathy, Joseph mentioned comparable experiences in his own Catholic Christian faith.

This took place on two occasions, but on the third occasion, Karim became angry and refused to have any further discussion about his faith and its role in his disability. Joseph was disconcerted about this, because he felt that he had been valuing Karim's faith and empowering Karim to use it as a positive in his life, thus strengthening his capacity to use it to enhance his resilience to adversity. He asked, "Where have I gone wrong?"

Joseph took this issue to his supervisor, who was also his manager, and who occasionally met Karim at a social club for disabled people, so he was able to talk to Karim about it. What emerged was that Karim, like many Muslims, saw his faith as integral to his identity and personality, and he saw his observances as a natural part of his culture; part of this was about the use of untranslatable concepts in Arabic. Although he could understand that ritual was a part of every religion, he did not see this as a separate element of his life. He felt that Joseph saw his Catholic faith as something done in church rather than as integral to his life.

Joseph explored with his supervisor the extent to which he had secured consent to engage in spirituality. Religion had been a part of the initial assessment, and Karim had been asked as part of the standard assessment how important his religion was to him and ways it had helped him manage his condition. However, he had not seen providing this information as giving consent to further exploration. Although he appreciated Joseph's support, he did not see it as his role or responsibility to help Joseph understand his religion. He did not see such understanding as possible without conversion. Part of his feelings were that Joseph ought to have some kind of intellectual understanding of major aspects of his religion anyway, as Karim did of Christianity, and if Joseph needed more information, it was his job to go and get it; it was not for Karim to provide it.

Another factor in Karim's feelings was that he saw no need to incorporate his faith as a rational resilience factor in his coping with everyday life. His view was that it was so central to his being that making it explicit and strengthening it was not relevant to what he wanted from the agency.

This case illustrates that practitioners need to seek explicit information from clients about the implications of their faith on a need-to-know basis. What do we need to know to carry out our responsibilities? In this case, for example, it might have been important to make sure that the routine of the day center did not interfere with Karim's religious observance. However, exploring the issue with his supervisor, Joseph saw that he was engaging in the religious discussion partly for his own interest rather than focusing on Karim's needs. This is a boundary in professional practice that we all need to be aware of. Also, if Joseph had followed an informed consent approach, as discussed in chapter 2, he would have gone beyond the basic information in the initial assessment and had an explicit discussion about how working on spirituality might help Karim's objectives. Instead, he had assumed, because of his own interest and commitment, that this would be a legitimate intervention.

ASSESSING AND INTERVENING WITH SPIRITUALITY

If we are to become engaged in clients' spirituality, we need to consider ways to identify spiritual issues and disentangle them from other issues. Narayanaswamy (2006) has suggested that spiritual assessment can include the following:

- Spiritual history
- Sensitivity to verbal and nonverbal cues, particularly about what is most important in their lives
- Observation of how they greet, meet, and interact with others to identify who is significant to them and why
- Observation of their immediate environment for religious or other spiritual symbols or for things that are important to them

- Three important factors in relationships: what and who gives them a sense of meaning and purpose in their lives, the extent to which they have means of forgiveness, and sources of love and relationships

Narayanaswamy and Narayanaswamy (2006) propose a series of seven spiritual needs that may be used as an assessment framework in health care, which I have adapted for wider use in Box 7.4. I would ask these sorts of questions or others covering these topics. I would start by asking, "How is it now?" and ask people to talk about how this has changed.

Some assessment frameworks focus only on formal religion, and this may be too limiting for social work. For example, Frame (2001) proposes an adaptation to a conventional genogram by adding religious commitments and roles to the family structure. However, her examples are limited to religious affiliations. This may be appropriate in particular settings, for example, a faith-based agency or a community in which only one faith is practiced but a wider range of ideas and conflicts need to be represented.

Hodge (2001) reviewed a range of qualitative modes of spiritual assessment and summarizes them into a framework for practice. This involves a narrative approach, similar to taking a family history, starting from the religious or spiritual tradition that a client grew up in, moving on to experiences and rituals that are important, and how their interpretation and use of those traditions and experiences has changed over time. He then developed an interpretive framework, looking at the impact of each of these ideas. This involves looking at the history using the following concepts:

Box 7.4 Framework for Spiritual Assessment

- Meaning and purpose—What gives people a sense of meaning and purpose in their lives?

- Sources of strength and hope—Who is the most important person to you? Who would you turn to when you need help? In what ways do they help?

- Love and relatedness—How do you relate to your family and relatives, friends, others, and your surroundings? What gives you peace or stimulation?

- Self-esteem—How do you feel about yourself?

- Fear and anxiety—Is there anything you are particularly anxious or fearful about? What helps with your particular fear and anxiety?

- Anger—Is there anything that makes you angry? How do you behave when you are angry? Do you try to control the anger? How?

- Beliefs and faith—Is there anything that helps you understand or think through what has been happening to you? What, if anything, has bothered or pleased you about what has been happening to you? What do you think is going to happen about this?

Source: Adapted and developed from Narayanaswamy and Narayanaswamy (2006).

- Affect—such as what experiences or traditions give pleasure or cause anxiety
- Behavior—which experiences and traditions you use and in what ways
- Cognition—which traditions and experiences have affected clients' thinking and planning
- Communion—how people describe their relationship with the ultimate being
- Conscience—the extent to which and the ways spirituality affects moral decisions about right and wrong, values, and forgiveness
- Intuition—the extent to which clients experience hunches, intuitions, and beliefs that affect their behavior

These assessment approaches offer ideas that practitioners can use to discuss spiritual issues with clients. It is often possible to use creative work or art to stimulate metaphors about spiritual experience (Stanworth, 2003), and Cascio (1998) has suggested a range of methods for stimulating discussion about spirituality, including keeping journals of meditation and reflection, writing stories, and discussing reading.

Faith is sometimes an issue, because many people think of it as the source of irrational thinking in religion: people have faith in the existence of a supernatural being who can affect their lives.

Case Study: Praying to Be Saved

A Pentecostal Christian man was admitted to a hospice for terminal care. His minister and members of the church visited his room in turns to pray for his recovery. Staff of the hospice felt that this inhibited their practice, because it meant that they could not help the man accept emotionally his terminal condition and make practical arrangements with his family for the care of his children after his death, because he and his church members believed fervently that he would be saved. A spiritual care adviser suggested that staff think about this in the same way as everyone "not knowing" what would happen in the course of an illness, and that helped staff encourage the man to make plans recognizing that, in the long-term, everyone dies.

This case study reminds us that we all have faith in many different things, much of which is based on evidence. For example, we believe (have faith) in the evening that the sky will become light the following morning and a new day will begin. In traditional faiths, this might have been thought to be the act of a supernatural being; currently, our faith is based on scientific knowledge. We may have faith in the evidence supporting a theory of intervention that we intend to use, because although its success is probabilistic (i.e., it works in a statistically significant proportion of cases), we have practice experience of its effectiveness with similar clients and its benefits, even if it is not fully effective in this case.

This takes us back to Hood's (2009) idea of supersense, an inborn, intuitive sense of what fits in the social situations we are familiar with. Thus, we can accept others' faiths because their faith connects with their innate and cultural experiences. Similarly, practitioners can accept their own faith, which may be spiritual, religious, or otherwise, but this does not need to control or influence their intervention with the self or spiritual nature of their client.

CONCLUSION

Working on the self and on religious and spiritual traditions and experience have an ambiguous and difficult role in social work practice; we have seen that they present difficulties in understanding and getting alongside the people we work with. However, I have argued in this chapter that, if practitioners fail to engage with the self as an objective, they will fail to define their practice objectives. Moreover, if they fail to engage with spirituality and religion, they will fail to engage with the whole person in the way that pursuing humanistic practice requires.

FURTHER READING

Howe, D. (2008). *The emotionally intelligent social worker*. Basingstoke, UK: Palgrave Macmillan.

An excellent text exploring a range of interventions for helping practitioners respond to emotions in themselves and others.

Jenkins, R. (1996). *Social identity*. London: Routledge.

A good, brief discussion of many aspects of social and personal identity.

Du Gay, P., Evans, J., & Redman, P. (Eds.). (2000). *Identity: A reader*. London: Sage.

A good collection of material that covers both psychological and social issues of identity.

WEB SITES

http://www.qolid.org/

To further investigate quality of life, the patient-reported quality-of-life instruments database provides descriptions of a wide range of health-related quality-of-life instruments, some of which are general and psychosocial in their content.

Developing Security and Resilience in Practice

CHAPTER AIMS

The main aims of this chapter are to establish the importance of a focus on building security rather than merely assessing risk or organizing surveillance and on building resilience rather than emphasizing problems.

After working through this chapter, readers should be able to

- Analyze critically the role of social work in managing risk and in enhancing surveillance of oppressed groups in their society
- Identify different kinds of security, including physical, legal, and self security
- Practice in ways that enhance clients' security within their social environment and contribute to a social order that enhances people's security
- Enhance dignity and support as ways to increase security in care settings
- Enhance resilience as a way to strengthen people's capacity to maintain their security

RISK: THE REASON FOR FOCUSING ON SECURITY

In present-day social work libraries, you will find a lot of books about risk and risk assessment but few about achieving security. Security is important to people and to societies. It is the opposite of risk, and social work has often concentrated on helping people who are at risk: children, older people, women at risk of domestic violence, anyone who is vulnerable to hurt. In this chapter, I argue that, rather than assess and manage risk, humanistic practice aims more positively to achieve security.

Risk is the likelihood of physical or psychological damage occurring. Risky situations or events threaten psychological or physical security. To focus on risk to people is another example of problem-focused social work using deficit language. It seems to clarify and set an objective in the situation: you can remove the factors in the situation that present risks, and the person is safe—problem solved. Or is it? Humanistic practice presents the more positive option to practice with a focus on security rather than risk. If practitioners think about risk all the time, they will concentrate on what may go wrong, and this may lead them to blaming if things go wrong: blaming the client, themselves, or their agency or society.

Macdonald and Macdonald (1999) point to several difficulties with the concept of risk in social work practice:

- As a concept, risk is probabilistic; that is, a risk is the likelihood of something happening, not the certainty of it happening. All we can say if we are assessing risk is that it is more or less likely.
- We are usually looking at a risk of harm rather than positive risks; there is often a benefit to taking a risk.
- People in different circumstances may assess risk differently.
- There is a difference between the objective probability of a risk and the subjective perception of those risks, harms, and benefits.
- If an assessment of risk brings a successful outcome, there will be no problem, but if things go wrong, hindsight allows people to identify all the things that might have been taken into consideration and to vary the judgment made at the time.
- We often worry more about preventing the risk of unlikely but morally reprehensible actions such as child abuse rather than concerning ourselves with preventing likely but blame-free actions, such as a child falling. So, we focus on the risk of dangerous human actions rather than the risk of dangerous places.

Macdonald and Macdonald (1999) also make several mathematical points. If we assess risk on a mathematical basis, for example, by saying that there is a 30 percent likelihood that something will happen, all the other possible outcomes must have a risk that sums to one. So if we decide that there is a 20 percent likelihood that an older person will fall, there is an 80 percent likelihood that he or she will not fall. Over what period are we talking about—each day or during the rest of her life? What is the evidence, because the risk is calculated only on what we know, not on what we do not know? And are we worried only about falls, or is there a range of worries, such as poor nutrition? Perhaps the fall matters less when we consider the risk that the older person might have a miserable quality of life in a care home, if that is the alternate to risk. Finally, Macdonald and Macdonald (1999) contend that Bayes's theorem in mathematics points out that people make judgments on the basis of their intuition and general assessment of likelihood before any rational mathematical assessment of the odds is calculated. We saw in chapter 2 that there is evidence that this is an important aspect of human behavior—most people do not work by wholly rational thinking. Included in that judgment is social knowledge, for example, that a daughter who appears loving and well organized in her household affairs is less likely to lose her temper with her elderly mother who is living with her than someone who is rough and ready and emotional.

SURVEILLANCE: ANOTHER REASON FOR FOCUSING ON SECURITY

Gilliom (2001) has made the point that, throughout history, welfare services, including social work, have been used to maintain surveillance of the poor and of groups in society that potentially present problems of social order and social disruption. One of the fears that social workers often have that leads to the focus on risk is that they will be criticized for things that go wrong. There are two things about such criticism: it is usually of people who are socially excluded or is seen as morally wrong. Patterns of social oppression mean that powerful groups and opinion formers in society use moral and social failings to reinforce their power. They also exercise power by blaming professionals for failing to prevent risks from materializing as actualities. Such criticism is always made with hindsight: the critics know that the situation actually went wrong, even though there was a low risk of the worst happening. Social workers and other officials dealing with risk develop approaches to protect themselves from criticism. One way to avoid someone with hindsight second-guessing you is to record all possible likelihoods that you can foresee and explain why they are unlikely; doing so forces a person with hindsight to think about what you knew as opposed to what they know later.

Another important response to fear of accusations about poor responses to risk is to increase surveillance of the poor. The modern state represents a shift from personal forms of social control toward bureaucratic and organizational control (Dandeker, 1990), in which social workers and all helping professions play a part. Foucault's (1979) work on prisons and the social control of sexuality made clear that helping and caring activities are often managed in such a way or seduced into ways of working that support the needs of the state for social order. Social order benefits many people, including those whose freedoms are limited, and people feel more secure in a socially ordered state. People who live in violent and physically deteriorating neighborhoods may well be strong supporters of surveillance and risk-avoiding practice. However, that order is always a balance between advantages and restrictions. This is particularly so when the restrictions are secret or partially concealed. One of the concerns about the social control achieved by helping and caring activities is that the benefits of caring may be outweighed by loss of autonomy and the fact that a caring attitude hides social restrictions that come along with it.

There are various ways to handle these issues. Humanistic psychotherapies seek to manage the controlling elements of their impact by sustaining a completely therapeutic focus for their activities. For many helping and caring professions, this is not possible; social work, for example, often participates in state services. Therefore, transparency of all the elements of social work actions is an important aspect of practice. Humanistic social work deals with this by informed consent, advance care planning, and the equality actions discussed in chapter 3. Because records are an important aspect of surveillance, making records accessible to enable clients to check them and put their interpretations into the records is an important aspect of due process. However, transparency with records can be a useful way to enter dialogue with clients about interpretations of their situation. Similarly, hearing their own interpretations through narrative and through creative work can also contribute to transparency.

S. Graham and Wood (2003) have suggested, in discussing the use of records and closed circuit television (CCTV) for surveillance in the modern state, that categorizing people, particularly according to the spaces that they occupy, and particularly where inequalities label them as potentially dangerous, difficult, or in need, are crucial aspects of surveillance. For example, if you go to the information service of your local government offices, you can often select your own information or receive leaflets and advice freely. If, however, you go to a social work agency, a record of your identity and some assessment of your needs is retained. If you live in or visit areas where there have been problems of disorder or crime, shops and the local police may be able to see CCTV records of your visit and your actions. Some of this may be helpful or desirable, but the use that agencies make of these records may disadvantage you or limit your freedoms.

SECURITY RATHER THAN RISK

Risk, therefore, has its limitations as a concept for doing social work by, but is security any better? Existential and microsociology ideas, in particular in humanistic practice, focus on ontological security. This means being able to maintain in our personal identities a thread of meaning and a stable sense of our self-identity (Thompson, 1996). Giddens (1991) refers to a "life politics" (p. 214) in which people seek a lifestyle that reflects their self-actualized identity in an ordered environment. Ferguson (2001) has proposed a social work based on helping people to make positive choices, and Webb (2006) has referred to trust and confidence as an important aspect of service provision and a significant aim in social work. C. R. Smith (2002) has pointed out, though, that the security of making our individualized choices in a relatively secure life environment means that we come to rely on the state or organized social institutions to maintain a wide social order that permits us to make these lifestyle choices. Thus, the development of our own secure self in our own secure environment requires a secure social order surrounding us.

This may be too idealistic when practitioners face demands for risk assessments when children or vulnerable adults need protecting. I do not object to this, but I suggest a focus on security as part of a risk assessment. Instead of looking only at factors in the situation that might present a risk, we can also look for factors that will offer security. This is for three reasons: one is that these may balance the risk factors, and perhaps be usable as an attractor in a very chaotic situation (see chapter 5). Second, looking at security might suggest positive factors that can be enhanced, positive behaviors to be strengthened by empowerment techniques such as support groups or by cognitive-behavioral techniques. Third, the absence of security and of possibilities for achieving it may strengthen the confidence we place in a risk assessment. Looking back at Yvonne and John's care needs, the case study in chapter 5, illustrates how positive factors can be built on and negative factors reduced.

I have argued that this requirement for a secure social order connects social work aimed at individuals' own psychological efficacy with a social work aimed at social agency within those individuals' wide social environment. If this requires a secure social order, social work needs to concern itself with what that order consists of.

Case Example: Ruth, a Disability Adviser

Ruth was a very intelligent married woman, paraplegic as a result of difficulties at birth. She progressed through a range of government posts and eventually was appointed as a disability adviser for the administration of an important city. Her independent lifestyle relied on family support and extensive equipment supplied by charitable donations and government grants to assist her in working. Thus, her lifestyle choices come partly from her own personal capacity and relationships with people in her social environment, family, and neighborhood. The possibility of living this lifestyle comes from many decades of campaigning for equality in life choices for disabled people, legal structures for equality, and supportive agencies and mechanisms in society. Her job focuses on maintaining and improving those mechanisms in the city she serves.

Insecurity limits our lives. We have seen in previous chapters that economic and psychological insecurity means that personal and family development cannot be fulfilled. An insecure child cannot grow; insecure people with mental illness or older people cannot take risks to improve their quality of life.

WHAT IS SECURITY?

Security is people's belief that they will be safe from harm and exploitation in their social environment and remain free to make choices that develop their self. Security is closely connected with the human rights that are integral to humanistic social work practice. This is partly because physical and legal security are also important dimensions of equality (Equalities Review, 2007). People who are insecure about their physical safety are oppressed by others; people who do not believe that they will be protected by the law against intolerance or by fair administrative procedures will feel insecure. Our self is closely bound up with the valuation of our personal identity, and we have seen in chapter 7 that developing and maintaining that identity is closely connected with national, family, and spiritual identities, some of the most important rights protected by human rights charters.

PAUSE AND REFLECT: What Makes You Feel Secure and Insecure?

Think about a time when you felt particularly secure and another when you felt insecure. Note down behaviors and experiences that made you feel secure and what made you feel insecure.

Some Suggestions

I recollect a time when I was under criticism by my employing agency after management difficulties with staff. I was helped by personal caring, physical closeness from friends, and a clear planned structure, as well as checks on what I was doing to improve the situation from my manager. I was made more insecure by threats to my job and family, who were themselves made insecure by the possibility that I might have to change jobs and possibly move to another town.

Not everyone will feel the same, but strengths-based and solution-focused ideas tell us to identify what worked for people on previous occasions and help them to reproduce those ideas.

Gilbert (2005) has explored the domains of human behavior associated with threat and defense, as against safeness, and has distinguished between active and passive safeness. He rejects the term *safety* because it may be associated with defensive behavior, such as aggression toward someone or something that is threatening or associated with running away. He sees safeness as a psychological state in which we feel safe, and from that position, we can explore how to meet our needs in a way that maintains our sense of feeling safe. As a consequence, he would say that you cannot become secure except from a safe situation; someone who has felt insecure for whatever reason will not be able to achieve safeness. Gilbert (2005) has suggested that social safeness "is co-created in relationships via a host of signals and exchanges that are fundamental to health and social well-being" (p. 22). In a safe situation, people can actively explore, become affiliated with people, and play; passively, they are tolerant and accepting. Where there is threat, people become distressed; seek reassurance; and more passively, appease or submit to others' wishes.

Gough (2004) has proposed that security is an issue in understanding and evaluating welfare regimes, the system of organizational arrangements, policies, and practices that lead to outcomes, whether positive or negative, for human well-being in different nation-states. He identified three broad groups of regimes on a continuum according to the overall level of security that the regime offers to citizens:

- Welfare-state regimes: people normally meet their needs for well-being by participating in formal labor markets and financial markets, and by finance of practical support from state machinery. In the Nordic welfare states, extensive public services are the main providers of social well-being if people are unable to work or provide pensions and insurance for themselves.

- Informal security regimes: people mainly rely on family, community, and patronage (e.g., benefits from employers or landowners). These regimes are hierarchical and asymmetrical. This means that social relationships are unequal, and poor people gain short-term security at the cost of longer-term insecurity and dependence on others. This is typical of many countries, but there are variations in the extent to which there is public responsibility for well-being or that responsibility is accepted.

- Insecurity regimes: social conditions have led to gross insecurity and block the emergence of informal mechanisms to mitigate and rectify conditions. In some countries, there has been a complete breakdown of law and order because of war or external interference in the economic systems.

PRACTICING SECURITY

The aim of humanistic social work is to increase people's control over their lives so that they can attain a quality of life that is important to them. Self-actualization implies overcoming psychological ambivalences and uncertainties in people's thinking so that they may aim for their own objectives (B. Smith, 1973). Goldson (2004) has pointed to an important ambivalence about children: we often see them as victims of the social order that adults create or as threats to it. A similar point might be made about vulnerable adults. We see and treat most adults most of the time as autonomous beings, capable of making their own security, whereas once we define them as vulnerable, they become liable to interventions to create security for them. When we see them as difficult, we ourselves become insecure and want to imprison or restrict them in other ways to protect ourselves.

Therefore, it is important to start from advance care planning based on the dialogue and narratives of clients and the people around them. These can then lead to a focus on what will make them feel secure. It is important to engage in dialogue about several different aspects of security:

- Physical security, for example, avoiding unwanted change, accidents, violence, or fear of them
- Legal security, for example, feeling that the law and administrative procedures protect them
- Self-security, or being respected and valued by others

Case Study: Securing a Man With Intellectual Disabilities

Joe was a middle-aged man with intellectual disabilities who had held down a job in a warehouse, which he found in his teens. The company was taken over by a large concern, and instead of receiving his wages in cash, he was required to open a bank account to receive electronic transfers. A social worker from an intellectual disability organization helped him through this process. In doing so, she took the opportunity to ask him whether he had any other worries about his work. He immediately said he was worried about losing his job, because a number of people had been made redundant in the takeover, and the manager who had employed him took early retirement.

She arranged an interview with his new manager, who, briefed by the social worker, took him through the positives of his working life, for example, that he was reliable, physically strong, and has a pleasant temperament in doing a routine job that other employees got bored with. The manager also drew attention to a newly introduced diversity and equal opportunities policy and pointed out that, because Joe was from a minority ethnic group and had a disability, he was protected by the policy and the law. He also pointed out that employing Joe meant that the company could demonstrate publicly if necessary that it was complying with its policy; Joe had not thought about this political advantage to the company of employing him.

This event supported Joe's legal and self-security, making clear to him his protections and valuation as useful in the eyes of the company. Advised by the social worker, the manager made sure to reinforce these points at regular intervals, and he picked up from her the idea of asking not "How are you?" when he saw Joe, but "Have you any particular worries at the moment?"—the sort of concrete question that may enable a person with intellectual disabilities to respond appropriately. This meant that, a year later, the manager picked up that Joe had debt problems, and it was found that this was because a neighbor who was a drug addict was taking Joe to the ATM and taking money from him. Again, calling on the social worker's advice, the manager called the police, who took action; this was another reinforcement, but this time of Joe's physical security.

It would be easy to see Joe as at risk, for example, of exploitation, as an employee in a warehouse and of social deterioration if he lost his job. However, by ensuring that different aspects of his security were assessed and responded to, the social worker improved the quality of his life at work and at home, at the same time creating relationships with the manager that enhanced security.

Dignity is another area of care provision that contributes to a feeling of security, particularly in long-term care of disabled or frail older people. A U.K. Dignity in Care project in 2006 undertook a public survey that identified ten major issues about dignity (Social Care Institute for Excellence, 2008):

- Clarifying what dignity is
- Making the complaints system more accessible and easy to use
- Being treated as individuals by finding out their needs and preferences, not talking to them as a child, not assuming that they need help with everything, and being patient in allowing them time (e.g., to finish meals and activities)
- Ensuring privacy
- Giving help with eating meals
- Ensuring that people had the right help to use the toilet
- Being addressed by staff appropriately, for example, not using demeaning terms such as *honey* or *love*, which treated older people as children
- Helping people maintain a respectable appearance
- Providing activities that are stimulating and offer a sense of purpose
- Ensuring that advocacy is available on behalf of people when making complaints

Minor issues were language barriers between staff and users and mixed-sex facilities.

The implementation of such concepts in practice is complex but has become a focus of professional interest also. Chan (2004), for example, proposed a human rights–based interpretation. He suggests that there are four elements to treating people with dignity:

- Behaving as though all people have equal human value, by valuing their views and wants, even if practitioners cannot follow all users' wishes
- Helping people have self-respect by helping them manage as much as possible their own affairs and remain in control of decisions

- Helping people have autonomy by helping them do things on their own and make choices where possible
- Promoting a positive mutuality, including supporting their relationships with others and encouraging positive attitudes to doing things with other people

Baillie, Gallagher, and Wainwright (2008) surveyed more than 2000 U.K. nurses about what enhanced dignity in care. They pointed to three levels of policy on dignity: governmental, organizational, and individual. The study argues that the individual responsibility and accountability of a professional can be fully carried out only where the other two contexts support the possibility of good practice. The overall recommendations are initial and continuing education focused on dignity, a concern for the physical environment and its adverse and positive effects on dignity, the role of the employing organization, professionals giving priority to dignity, and trying to make care activities dignified wherever possible. This connects with my analysis in chapters 2 and 3 on the importance of working on social agency and interpersonal equality alongside psychological efficacy and structures of social equality.

Support is another important aspect of practice offering security but is often underrated because it may be seen as a low-level activity, undertaken by paraprofessional rather than professional staff. We saw in the discussion of caring in chapter 7 that a cared-for person must experience the presence of the caregiver, but the caregiver does not have to be physically present, provided that the cared-for person is secure in the understanding that the caregiver is continuing to support even in his or her absence. Continuity is the most important factor in relationships because it demonstrates connectedness between caregiver and cared-for person. Therefore, important practical steps may include the following:

- Dialogue and narrative, which enable people to know that practitioners have built up an understanding of the situation as clients see it
- The security of knowing that regular checks will be made efficiently, for example, by maintaining regular telephone contact
- Demonstration of forethought and planning using advance care planning

Benner and Wrubel (1989) define caring as what matters to people; therefore, caring must be specific and relational. However, if people who are being cared for are vulnerable and at risk, then that leads to the temptation to set up safe places, which removes them from having the opportunity to have freedom and control what matters to them.

Case Example: Experiencing Abuse as a Child

Shankar was physically abused and neglected by his parents, who were prosecuted; he was cared for in residential care and then in a foster home. After about two years, he asked to be returned to his parents, whose income and housing had significantly improved, and they were functioning much better as a family. Although there was concern about his returning home and fear for the political consequences if the arrangement went wrong, his foster caregivers argued to his social worker that his feelings that moving back with his parents was the right move were very strong. Eventually, close supervision was put in place, and he returned home successfully. One factor in his thinking was the importance to him of his ethnic identity as part of his birth family, which the foster caregivers were unable to offer. His parents in turn worked very hard to support him, in part because they felt that the return home valued them as parents.

Again, in this case, physical security perhaps led to a concern for safeness, but caring, a safe environment, and emotional security were all signals that security was possible in this environment.

In looking for positive signs of security, we can seek evidence of the kinds of emotional and social intelligence discussed in chapter 7. Another positive factor that is becoming increasingly important in social work is resilience.

RESILIENCE

Resilience is the ability to bounce back from adversity. Knowing that they have resilience helps people to feel and to be more secure. Fraser, Richman, and Galinsky (1999) usefully define resilience as "unpredicted and markedly successful adaptations to negative life events, trauma, stress, and other forms of risk" (p. 136). This analysis points out that we talk about resilience only when people do better than expected at responding to adversity or to the risk of adversity. We do not refer to resilience when people react in a negative way to adversity. Ideas about resilience, therefore, assume that there will necessarily be adversities in people's lives, that things will not always go well. Resilience assumes a norm of reaction that some people, whom we see as resilient, will improve on.

The idea of resilience comes from attachment theory, which in turn comes from psychoanalytic ideas; Greene and Livingston (2002) also link it to humanistic psychology. Attachment therefore reflects the focus of psychoanalysis on the interaction of people's internal emotional responses and external experiences and on the impact of earlier on later experiences (Bower, 2005). Emotions are the way our bodies, brains, and minds react when aroused by external events that have meaning for us (Howe, 2005). Attachment theory assumes that, in close relationships, we build up a picture in our minds that explains other people's behavior (the term in attachment theory is *mentalize*); that is, we respond to how they behave according to our assumptions about their mental state. We base our assessment of their mental state on our previous experience, particularly with our parents and other people emotionally important to us, of how close relationships (attachments) work (Howe, 2005).

Resilience and attachment theory are bodies of ideas about human development and behavior, often used for therapeutic purposes. They connect with a recent policy focus on well-being and healthy living (Greene & Livingston, 2002). They have been widely used in work on child protection and in community work. One reason resilience is useful is that it is a positive idea that assumes that people have innate and learned capacities to respond to difficulties; a problem does not mean incapacity, and it may even stimulate strong and effective responses. In the context of the discussion of risk, it is interesting that the National Resilience Resource Center (2009) at the University of Michigan refers to people and communities being at promise rather than at risk.

PRACTICING RESILIENCE

We saw in chapter 2 that humanistic ideas suggest that we should focus both on individual capacities and on collective social agency. The conventional resilience approach looks mainly at individual and family resilience. A common approach, for example, in family work, is to develop mutual support and psychological strengths, such as by promoting more shared activities and supportive behaviors (Walsh, 2006). A strengths-based and positive psychology focus for practice may be allied with a resilience practice. Humanistic ideas appear in the resilience literature. For example, one study with adolescent girls, many of whom were sexually exploited, focused on listening carefully to their experiences, maintaining their integrity so that their behavior was not out of line with their moral preferences, and helped them negotiate more effectively to achieve their preferred outcomes in relationships (Watkins, 2002). Another useful approach in a school situation, with mental health or intellectual disabilities, may be to provide mentors to increase social support.

We may also identify many humanistic approaches in Walsh's (2006) account of resilience practice in families. It starts from three main family processes:

- The family's belief systems, that is, how the family achieves agreement about the meaning of adversity. Resilient families focus on resilience coming from their relationships and on developing a greater transcendent or spiritual meaning of their experiences of adversity rather than looking for rugged individuals to maintain a positive outlook.
- The family's organizational pattern, that is, their crisis shock absorbers. This includes their flexibility to change direction, their connectedness and mutual support, and their social and economic resources.
- The family's communication processes, that is, how they facilitate working together. These include clarity and consistency in the messages they give one another, the ability to share emotions openly, and a collaborative approach to problem solving.

In another perspective building on residential care practice, Ungar (2009) helpfully identifies accessibility to resources as the main focus of resilience. He includes the following:

- People's ability to navigate through society to resources that improve their well-being
- The ability of people's physical and social systems to provide resources for their well-being

■ The ability of people, their families, and their communities to negotiate culturally acceptable ways to share resources

Access to equality and social justice are important to this resource view of resilience. Not all resilience work is individual or family based. Another approach that focuses on resources in communities is an Australian tool kit (Hegney et al., 2008), which provides theoretically informed guidance. It draws on research findings on how to stimulate community strength. It identifies eleven resilience concepts:

■ Strengthening social networks and mutual support in communities.

■ Maintaining a positive outlook when presented with adversities, and viewing them as challenges rather than problems.

■ Focusing on accumulating learning from experience and seeking new learning to respond to new situations.

■ Identifying where your early experience might help or hinder progress; in a community setting, projects to coach children and young people to enhance their experience bring dividends in the long term.

■ Appreciating and strengthening contact with the natural environment and promoting engagement with valuing and improving the physical environment.

■ Infrastructure and support services should be examined to see where they can improve the resources available to a community; examples include transport for disabled people or ensuring that older people feel safe to go out and can use community resources.

■ Develop mission and a sense of purpose.

■ Promoting a diverse and innovative economy by encouraging new business to start.

■ Embracing and supporting difference and diversity of people and resources in the community.

■ Beliefs are important in strengthening individual responses to adversity and can form the basis of group support; public events such as concerts, environmental fairs, or book-reading groups that represent diverse beliefs and that support people in maintaining their beliefs can be helpful.

■ Leadership is important; identifying people who can lead different aspects of community endeavors and encouraging diverse people to take up some aspect of leadership can strengthen a community.

CONCLUSION

This chapter has focused on further positive elements of humanistic social work: the importance of people's physical, legal, and self-security. I have argued that social work is currently characterized by a negative focus on risk that presents many problems and leads to increased surveillance of people who are potentially at risk. It is better to enhance their security, dignity, and resilience. People's security is closely bound up with their equality and fair treatment in society; you do not feel secure if you are not treated as a person with value.

FURTHER READING

Carter, S., Jordan, T., & Watson, S. (Eds.). (2008). *Security: Sociology and social worlds.* Manchester, UK: Manchester University Press.

Hier, S. P., & Greenberg, J. (Eds.). (2007). *The surveillance studies reader.* Maidenhead, UK: McGraw-Hill and Open University Press.

These collections of articles are good introductions that will enable readers to extend their study of the issues raised in the chapter.

Greene, R. R. (Ed.). (2002). *Resiliency: An integrated approach to practice, policy and research.* Washington, DC: National Association of Social Work Press.

Hegney, D., Ross, H., Baker, P., Rogers-Clark, C., King, C., Buikstra, E., et al. (2008). *Building resilience in rural communities toolkit.* Toowoomba, Queensland: University of Queensland and University of Southern Queensland. Retrieved from http://www .scribd.com/doc/19348871/null.

These volumes offer a useful collection of articles focused on resilience work with traditional social work clients and a good practical tool kit for developing community resiliency, which is also theoretically informed.

WEB SITES

http://resilnet.uiuc.edu/index.html

Resilience Net at the University of Illinois at Urbana-Champaign is a good general site focused on early childhood and parenting.

Social Care Institute for Excellence. (2008). *SCIE Practice Guide 15: Dignity in Care.* London: Author.

http://www.scie.org.uk/publications/guides/guide15/index.asp

A regularly updated review of research on dignity in care.

Conclusion: Humanistic Practice Needs Developments in Research

CHAPTER AIMS

This chapter brings the book to a close by summarizing the main advantages of a humanistic model of social work, presenting differences between humanistic practice and conventional social work, and drawing attention to the direction of research that supports humanistic practice.

After working through this chapter, readers should be able to

- Distinguish the positive approach of humanistic practice from social work practice with conventional problem solving
- Discuss their view of the advantages of a humanistic model of social work practice
- Consider research directions for supporting humanistic practice

POSITIVE AIMS AS THE MAIN ADVANTAGE OF HUMANISTIC PRACTICE

Chapter 1 identified theoretical analysis of the importance of seeking positive achievements in humanistic practice. Several chapters followed this up. Our practice techniques should find ways to help people make progress in their lives. In looking at practice strategies in chapter 2, we saw that problem solving as a focus for social work means that we are always looking at deficits in the client or the problems that they cause other people or society. Instead, I argued that we should be looking for positives: positive personal efficacy and positive social agency in people's environments. Chapter 3 looked at positive practices that enhance equality both interpersonally and in social structures. Chapter 4 identified the positive advantages of flexibility by incorporating understanding and skills into our whole person in engaging with clients. Chapter 5 explored how to respond to complexity, not by seeking to oversimplify, but by dealing with the client and complexity all around. In chapter 6, we saw that the stand-back approach of the helping role means that practitioners' professional responsibility as a helper distances them from clients, whereas caring creates a connectedness in the relationships between caregiver and practitioners and clients. Chapter 7 pointed to how pursuing the important humanistic objective of self-actualization brought positive benefits in assisting people to develop a secure personal identity and spirituality. Chapter 8 suggested the disadvantages of the negative aspects of a focus on risk rather than the positives of security and resilience.

One of the research issues identified in chapter 2 was the tendency of social work techniques, such as task-centered and cognitive-behavioral practice, to emphasize a detailed definition of problems or aspects of their lives that clients want to change. I have suggested that this means that we concentrate on negatives in people's lives, not positives. This focus on the deficits, the problem-based mentality in social work, means that we do not focus enough on defining and theorizing the elements of the caring, service-providing aspects of social work. We have spent too much time researching the detail of problems and what we can do about them instead of defining positive objectives and service aims and what we can do about those things. We saw in chapter 1 that some positive psychology techniques, such as strengths-based, solution-focused techniques, have begun to shift in this way. Research on service effectiveness often emphasizes outcomes of service provision for clients rather than the detail of how to do the interpersonal job of assessment and decision making in service provision. We have tended to bureaucratize assessment and decision making instead of researching how to do this job interpersonally.

RESEARCH TO DEVELOP HUMANISTIC SOCIAL WORK:
DETAIL AND DEFINITION

In this book, I have tried to present ideas in humanistic practice in concrete ways that are amenable to research.

Looking at chapter 2, we can ask, What are the markers of psychological efficacy and social agency? Can people identify the group around them that will help their effectiveness in life and the people who do not? When do people feel confident that their social group can help them move forward? How do they define moving forward? After this, I examined dialogue and narrative, both rich sources of testable human experience. Finally, I developed the importance of informed consent and advance care planning in very specific ways. I think we can look to research for services that do and do not contain these elements, and see what the differences are in people's reactions and the success of these services. We can also look at services that introduce these elements into practice and research the changes that take place. Then we can look at reactions to specific elements of well-defined practices. We can also look at the guidelines that bring together accounts of and ideas about good practice and test out the various elements of what those accounts say is important.

The crucial element in all this is deconstruction: taking concepts apart in enough detail that we can understand what they consist of and test out the elements. In chapter 6, on caring, the model of care drawn from Montgomery's work enables us to look at what kinds of environments might be caring, what qualities of a caregiver and what specific acts create their caring, what the characteristics of a caring relationship are, and what transitions caring leads to.

Many elements of humanistic social work might be criticized, like the humanistic psychologies, because they seem to set idealistic, even ideological, goals. These seem generalized and open to many interpretations. It is easier to define what a problem is or what is wrong with a society than to think positively about how we achieve well-being, respect, or happiness. If we think about equality, we saw in chapter 3 how complex that concept is. However, we also saw that it was not only a high-level abstract concept but also one that needed to be pursued in everyday practice. If we say we are going to *do* equality, we can research practice acts to identify those that are said to improve equality, and test through research whether they do. We also saw that equality did not stand on its own as an objective; it is part of other issues in people's lives that we are helping with and caring about.

Moreover, we understand from complexity and social construction ideas explored in chapter 5, that achieving results is not an either-or situation in which we can say that outcomes are achieved or not at a particular point; both psychological and social states emerge over time and have complex and ambiguous characteristics. Many social and personal achievements are provisional: they lead to the next thing. Our research needs to have the complexity and quality that can understand and explore such ambiguity.

Humanistic social work research turns our minds toward careful and detailed distinctions and definition of what we are doing in practice so that we can look at the full complexity of what is happening in interactions among the human beings involved in caring practice. This detailed observation and analysis must take the place of oversimplifying assumptions of intervention research.

HUMANISTIC SOCIAL WORK:
THE FUTURE IS RESEARCH INTO HUMAN EXPERIENCE

An example of the sort of work that might be possible is an interesting study into the impact of psychological and social experience on the extent to which people survive cancer. Stephen, Rahn, Verhoef, and Leis (2007) pointed to many years of surmise and anecdote suggesting that the mind and social experience affect whether people survive cancer. Traditional healing systems emphasize the power of the mind over the body, thus enabling people to see illness as an opportunity for personal growth. There may be complex, not-fully-understood interactions among mind, body, behavior, external factors, and illness. Techniques try to enhance the power of the mind to influence the body through a wide variety of techniques such as meditation, mindfulness, and similar approaches. Many people have experiences of illness in the lives of themselves or their relatives and friends that support such ideas.

Some early research seemed to show that psychosocial risk factors affect whether people develop cancer and intensive psychological efforts and changes in lifestyle enabled them to combat the illness, but these were not replicated. So the position remains unclear. Stephen et al. (2007) argued that researchers moved too quickly to looking at the effectiveness of particular interventions. Instead of seeking to test rigorously that one technique or another "works," they argued instead for a wider range of research techniques focused on understanding people's behavior and experience, including the following:

- Whole systems research, which looks at the processes of change that are going on in whole human beings. Instead of subjecting people to isolated and testable interventions, we should try to understand the choices and pathways that people follow. Instead of focusing on interventions that professionals use in isolation, we should see those as part of people's life choices and self-care.
- Aptitude × treatment designs, which look at characteristics of individuals and social factors that affect them alongside the various interventions that professionals attempt.
- Participant-centered analysis, which gathers a wide range of data about individuals and assigns them to categories, such as people who responded or did not respond to intervention, so that we may look at all the human factors that might have affected their response.

Social work practice research in the future could similarly, and usefully, take several such approaches. This might enable us to say far more about what is going on in the experience of clients and the families and communities around them, before we try to isolate and test the effectiveness of particular interventions.

The crucial research that social work needs is about how social workers incorporate, express, and perform knowledge and evidence. Practitioners and students need this research to connect the world of theory that gives them ideas and the real world that gives them situations to act in and tasks to carry out.

We saw in chapter 3 the importance of research into people's narratives as a way to gain access to their experience of their lives. Related to this, in chapter 6, we saw the value of reminiscences and life review as a way to help people gain access to important events in their lives. In such endeavors, research techniques interact with practice techniques. In this way, research and practice connect with humanistic ideas because humanistic practice seeks to base its work on people's own understanding of their experiences, and practice is based on congruent practitioners' empathic appreciation of those experiences.

Humanistic practice is this: act interpersonally, learn interpersonally, research interpersonally, and live interpersonally, because we all share the same human possibilities and freedoms.

Bibliography

Adam, B. (1990). *Time and social theory*. Cambridge, UK: Polity Books.

Adams, R. (2008). *Empowerment, participation and social work* (4th ed.). Basingstoke, UK: Palgrave Macmillan.

Adherents.com (2009). *Major religions of the world ranked by number of adherents*. Retrieved from http://www.adherents.com/Religions_By_Adherents.html.

Alcoff, L. M., & Mendieta, E. (Eds.). (2003). *Identities: Race, class, gender, and nationality*. Malden, MA: Blackwell.

Allen, P. B. (1995). *Art is a way of knowing: A guide to self-knowledge and spiritual fulfillment through creativity*. Boston: Shambhala.

American Humanist Association. (2004). *Humanism and its aspirations*. New York: Author. Retrieved from http://www.americanhumanist.org/who_we_are/about_humanism/Humanist_Manifesto_III.

American Medical Association. (2009). *Informed consent*. Chicago: Author. Retrieved from http://www.ama-assn.org/ama/pub/physician-resources/legal-topics/patient-physician-relationship-topics/informed-consent.shtml.

Andersen, D. K., Furman, R., & Langer, C. L. (2006). The poet/practitioner: A paradigm for the profession. *Journal of Sociology and Social Welfare*, *33*(3), 29–50.

Andersen, R. M. (1995). Revisiting the behavioral model and access to medical care: Does it matter? *Journal of Health and Social Behavior*, *36*(1), 1–10.

Appel, K. J. (1980). Metaphor as experience in psychotherapy and sorcery. In S. Boorstein (Ed.), *Transpersonal psychotherapy* (pp. 44–56). Stanford, CA: Science and Behavior Books.

Archer, M. S. (1995). *Realist social theory: A morphogenetic approach*. Cambridge: Cambridge University Press.

Assagioli, R. (1990). *Psychosynthesis*. Wellingborough, UK: Crucible.

Austin Health. (2007). *Respecting patient choices: Advance care planning guide*. Heidelberg, Australia: Author. Retrieved from http://70.87.111.98/~rpccom/images/stories/pdfs/acpguide/advance_care_planning_guide_a4.pdf.

Australian Association of Social Workers. (2002). *AASW Code of Ethics*. Canberra: Author. Retrieved from http://www.aasw.asn.au/document/item/92.

Baillie, L., Gallagher, A., & Wainwright, P. (2008). *Defending dignity: Challenges and opportunities for nursing*. London: Royal College of Nursing.

Baker, J., Lynch, K., Cantillon, S., & Walsh, J. (2004). *Equality: From theory to action* (2nd ed.). Basingstoke, UK: Palgrave Macmillan.

Barbalet, J. M. (2001). *Emotion, social theory, and social structure: A macrosociological approach*. Cambridge: Cambridge University Press.

Barnes, M. (2006). *Caring and social justice*. Basingstoke, UK: Palgrave Macmillan.

Barrett-Lennard, G. T. (1985). The helping relationship: Crisis and advance in theory and research. *Counseling Psychologist, 13*, 279–294.

Benner, P., & Wrubel, J. (1989). *The primacy of caring: Stress and coping in health and illness*. Menlo Park, CA: Addison-Wesley.

Berger, P., & Luckmann, T. (1971). *The social construction of reality*. Harmondsworth, UK: Penguin Books.

Biestek, F. P. (1957). *The casework relationship*. Chicago: Loyola University Press.

Blumer, H. (1969). *Symbolic interactionism: Perspective and method*. Englewood Cliffs, NJ: Prentice-Hall.

Boehm, A., & Staples, L. H. (2002). The functions of the social worker in empowering the voices of consumers and professionals. *Social Work, 47*, 449–451.

Bower, M. (2005). Psychoanalytic theories for social work practice. In M. Bower (Ed.), *Psychoanalytic theory for social work practice: Thinking under fire* (pp. 3–14). London: Routledge.

Brandon, D. (1976). *Zen and the art of helping*. London: Routledge and Kegan Paul.

Brandon, D. (2000). *Tao of survival: Spirituality in social care and counselling*. Birmingham, UK: Venture.

Brandon, D., & Brandon, T. (2001). *Advocacy in social work*. Birmingham, UK: Venture.

British Association of Social Workers. (2002). *A Code of ethics for social work*. Birmingham, UK: Author. Retrieved from http://www.basw.co.uk/Portals/0/CODE%20OF%20 ETHICS.pdf.

Bugental, J. F. T., & Sapienza, B. G. (1994). The three R's for humanistic psychology: Remembering, reconciling, reuniting. In F. Wertz (Ed.), *The humanistic movement: Recovering the person in psychology* (pp. 273–284). Lake Worth, FL: Gardner.

Bullis, R. K. (1996). *Spirituality in social work practice*. Washington, DC: Taylor and Francis.

Burge, F. J., Lawson, B. J., Johnston, G. M., & Grunfeld, A. (2008). A population-based study of age inequalities in access to palliative care. *Medical Care, 46*, 1203–1211.

Burnside, I., & Haight, B. K. (1992). Reminiscence and life review: Analyzing each concept. *Journal of Advanced Nursing, 17*, 855–862.

Cameron, N., & McDermott, F. (2007). *Social work and the body*. Basingstoke, UK: Palgrave Macmillan.

Canadian Association of Social Workers. (2005). *Guidelines for ethical practice 2005*. Ottawa: Author. Retrieved from http://www.casw-acts.ca.

Canadian Hospice Palliative Care Association. (2009). *What is advance care planning?* Ottawa: Author. Retrieved from http://www.chpca.net/projects/advance_care_planning/ acp_what_is_advance_care_planning.html.

Canda, E. R., & Furman, L. D. (1999). *Spiritual diversity in social work practice*. New York: Free Press.

Canda, E. R., & Smith, E. D. (2001). *Transpersonal perspectives on spirituality in social work*. New York: Haworth.

Carkhuff, R. (2000). *The art of helping* (9th ed.). Amherst, MA: HRD Press.

Carkhuff, R. R., & Berenson, B. C. (1967). *Beyond counseling and therapy* (2nd ed.). New York: Holt, Rinehart, and Winston.

Carnaby, S., & Cambridge, P. (Eds.). (2006). *Intimate and personal care with people with learning difficulties*. Philadelphia: Kingsley.

Cascio, T. (1998). Incorporating spirituality into social work practice: A review of what to do. *Families in Society*, *78*, 523–511.

Castells, M. (1997). *The power of identity*. Malden, MA: Blackwell.

Chan, C. (2001). *An Eastern body-mind-spirit approach: A training manual with one-second techniques*. Hong Kong: Department of Social Work and Social Administration, University of Hong Kong.

Chan, C. K. (2004). Placing dignity at the centre of welfare policy. *International Social Work*, *47*, 227–239.

Chandler, K. (2009). Turning tricks. *Therapy Today*, *20*(3), 14–17.

Child, I. L. (1973). *Humanistic psychology and the research tradition: Their several virtues*. New York: Wiley.

Cnaan, R. A., Boddie, S. C., & Wineburg, R. J. (1999). *The newer deal: Social work and religion in partnership*. New York: Columbia University Press.

Connolly, M. (2006). Practice frameworks: Conceptual maps to guide practice in child welfare. *British Journal of Social Work*, doi: 10.1093/bjsw/bc1049.

Corcoran, K. J. (1981). Experiential empathy: A theory of a felt-level experience. *Journal of Humanistic Psychology*, *21*, 29–38.

Crabtree, S. A., Husain, F., & Spalek, B. (2008). *Islam and social work*. Bristol, UK: Policy Press.

Craib, I. (1998). *Experiencing identity*. London: Sage.

Csikai, E., & Chaitin, E. (2006). *Ethics in end-of-life decisions in social work practice*. Chicago: Lyceum Books.

Cunningham-Burley, S., & Backett-Milburn, K. (1998). The body, health and self in the middle years. In S. Nettleton & J. Watson (Eds.), *The body in everyday life* (pp. 142–159). London: Routledge.

Dalrymple, J., & Burke, B. (2006). *Anti-oppressive practice: Social care and the law*. Maidenhead, UK: Open University Press.

Dalrymple, J., Payne, M., Tomlinson, T., & Ward, S. (1995). *"They listened to him": Report to the Gulbenkian Foundation*. Manchester, UK: Advice and Advocacy Service for Children and Manchester Metropolitan University.

Dandeker, C. (1990). *Surveillance, power and modernity: Bureaucracy and discipline from 1700 to the present day*. Cambridge, UK: Polity Books.

Daniels, M. (1988). The myth of self-actualization. *Journal of Humanistic Psychology*, *28*(1), 7–38.

David, T. S. (2007). Mapping patterns of perceptions: A community-based approach to cultural competence assessment. *Research on Social Work Practice*, *17*, 358–379.

Department of Constitutional Affairs. (2007). *Mental Capacity Act 2007: Code of practice*. London: The Stationery Office. Retrieved from http://www.publicguardian.gov.uk/docs/mca-code-practice-0509.pdf.

Dobbs, S. (2008). Art therapy. In N. Hartley & M. Payne (Eds.), *The creative arts in palliative care* (pp. 128–139). Philadelphia: Kingsley.

Emerson, D., Taylor, R., & Payne, M. (1996). *Report on the Warrington Mental Health Advocacy Project*. Manchester, UK: Department of Applied Community Studies, Manchester Metropolitan University.

Engebretson, J. (2000). Caring presence: A case study. In M. Robb, S. Barrett, C. Komaromy, & A. Rogers (Eds.), *Communication, relationships and care: A reader* (pp. 235–247). London: Routledge.

English Community Care Association. (2007). *Mental Capacity Act 2005: What you need to do to ensure compliance*. London: Author. Retrieved from http://www.decha.org.uk/doc_up/1_99_Best-Interests-Assessor-Award-MCA-2005.pdf.

Epstein, L. (1992). *Brief treatment and a new look at the task-centered approach*. New York: Macmillan.

Equalities Review. (2007). *Fairness and freedom: The final report of the Equalities Review*. London: Cabinet Office.

Etzioni, A. (1993). *The spirit of community: Rights, responsibilities and the communitarian agenda*. New York: Crown.

European Union. (2000). The Charter of Fundamental Rights of the European Union. *Official Journal of the European Communities* (2000/C 364/01-22). Retrieved from http://www.europarl.europa.eu/charter/pdf/text_en.pdf.

Fairclough, N. (1992). *Discourse and social change*. Cambridge, UK: Polity Books.

Ferguson, H. (2001). Social work, individualization and life politics. *British Journal of Social Work*, *31*(1), 41–56.

Finch, J., & Mason, J. (1993). *Negotiating family responsibilities*. London: Routledge.

Firman, J., & Vargui, J. (1980). Personal and transcendental growth: The perspective of psychosynthesis. In S. Boorstein (Ed.), *Transpersonal psychotherapy* (pp. 92–115). Stanford, CA: Science and Behavior Books.

Fitzpatrick, T. (2005). *New theories of welfare*. Basingstoke, UK: Palgrave Macmillan.

Fjelland, R., & Gjengedal, E. (1994). A theoretical foundation for nursing as a profession. In P. Benner (Ed.), *Interpretive phenomenology: Embodiment, caring and ethics in health and illness* (pp. 3–25). Thousand Oaks, CA: Sage.

Flaskas, C., McCarthy, I., & Sheehan, J. (Eds.). (2007). *Hope and despair in narrative and family therapy*. London: Routledge.

Flew, A. (1964). Introduction. In A. Flew (Ed.), *Body, mind and death* (pp. 1–28). New York: Macmillan.

Foucault, M. (1972). *The archaeology of knowledge*. London: Tavistock.

Foucault, M. (1979). *Discipline and punish*. Harmondsworth, UK: Penguin Books.

Frame, M. W. (2001). The spiritual genogram in training and supervision. *Family Journal, 9*(2), 109–115.

Fraser, M. W., Richman, J. M., & Galinsky, M. J. (1999). Risk, protection, and resilience: Toward a conceptual framework for social work practice. *Social Work Research, 23*, 129–208.

Furbey, R. (2009). Controversies of "public faith." In A. Dunham, R. Furbey, & V. Lownes (Eds.), *Faith in the public realm: Controversies, policies and practices* (pp. 21–40). Bristol, UK: Policy Press.

Garfinkel, H. (1967). *Studies in ethnomethodology*. Englewood Cliffs, NJ: Prentice Hall.

Geller, L. (1982). The failure of self-actualization theory: A critique of Carl Rogers and Abraham Maslow. *Journal of Humanistic Psychology, 22*(2), 56–73.

Gibbs, L., & Gambrill, E. (2002). Evidence-based practice: Counter-arguments to objections. *Research in Social Work Practice, 12*, 452–476.

Giddens, A. (1979). *Central problems in social theory: Action, structure and contradiction in social analysis*. Los Angeles: University of California Press.

Giddens, A. (1991). *Modernity and self identity*. Cambridge, UK: Polity Books.

Gilbert, P. (2005). Compassion and cruelty: A biopsychosocial approach. In P. Gilbert (Ed.), *Compassion: Conceptualizations, research and use in psychotherapy* (pp. 9–73). New York: Routledge.

Gilligan, C. (1993). *In a different voice: Psychological theory and women's development*. Cambridge, MA: Harvard University Press.

Gilliom, J. (2001). *Overseers of the poor: Surveillance, resistance and the limits of privacy*. Chicago: University of Chicago Press.

Glassman, U., & Kates, L. (1990). *Groupwork: A humanistic approach*. Newbury Park, CA: Sage.

Gleick, J. (1998). *Chaos: The amazing science of the unpredictable*. London: Vintage.

Goffman, E. (1968a). *The presentation of self in everyday life*. Harmondsworth, UK: Penguin Books.

Goffman, E. (1968b). *Stigma: Notes on the management of spoiled identity*. Harmondsworth, UK: Penguin.

Goffman, E. (1972a). *Encounters: Two studies in the sociology of interaction*. Harmondsworth, UK: Penguin.

Goffman, E. (1972b). *Interaction ritual: Essays on face-to-face behaviour*. Harmondsworth, UK: Penguin.

Goffman, E. (1972c). *Relations in public: Microstudies of the public order*. Harmondsworth, UK: Penguin.

Goldson, B. (2004). Victims or threats? Children, care and control. In J. Fink (Ed.), *Care: Personal lives and policy* (pp. 78–109). Bristol, UK: Policy Press.

Gold Standards Framework. (2009). *Thinking ahead: Advance care planning discussion.* Walsall, UK: Author. Retrieved from http://www.goldstandardsframework.nhs.uk/content/guides_and_presentations/ACP%20General%20version%20Oct08%20v%2017.pdf.

Goldstein, H. (1984). A cognitive-humanistic approach to practice: Philosophical and theoretical foundations. In H. Goldstein (Ed.), *Creative change: A cognitive-humanistic approach to social work practice* (pp. 3–32). New York: Tavistock.

Goleman, D. (1996). *Emotional intelligence: Why it matters more than IQ.* London: Bloomsbury.

Goleman, D. (2006). *Social intelligence: The new science of human relationships.* New York: Bantam Dell.

Gough, I. (2004). Human well-being and social structures: Relating the universal and the local. *Global Social Policy, 4,* 289–311.

Gould, N., & Taylor, I. (Eds.). (1996). *Reflective knowledge in social work.* Aldershot, UK: Arena.

Graham, J. R., & Barter, K. (1999). Collaboration: A social work practice method. *Families in Society, 80,* 6–13.

Graham, S., & Wood, D. (2003). Digitizing surveillance: Categorization, space, inequality. *Critical Social Policy, 23,* 227–248.

Greene, R. R., & Livingston, N. C. (2002). A social construct. In R. R. Greene (Ed.), *Resiliency: An integrated approach to practice, policy, and research* (pp. 63–93). Washington, DC: National Association of Social Workers Press.

Greening, T. (2006). Five basic postulates of humanistic psychology. *Journal of Humanistic Psychology, 46,* 239.

Guillemard, A.-M. (2005). The advent of a flexible life course and the reconfigurations of welfare. In J. G. Andersen, A.-M. Guillemard, P. H. Kensen, & B. Pfau-Effinger (Eds.), *The changing face of welfare: Consequences and outcomes from a citizenship perspective* (pp. 55–73). Bristol, UK: Policy Press.

Gutiérrez, G. (1973). *A theology of liberation.* Maryknoll, NY: Orbis.

Hall, S. (1992). The question of cultural identity. In S. Hall, D. Held, & T. McGrew (Eds.), *Modernity and its futures* (pp. 273–316). Cambridge, UK: Polity Books.

Halmi, A. (2003). Chaos and non-linear dynamics: New methodological approaches in the social sciences and social work practice. *International Social Work, 46*(1), 83–101.

Hartley, N., & Payne, M. (Eds.). (2008). *The creative arts in palliative care.* Philadelphia: Kingsley.

Harvard University Pluralism Project. (2004). Research report: Religious symbols in the American public square. http://pluralism.org/research/profiles/display.php?profile=73493.

Headscarf defeat riles French Muslims. (2005). BBC News. Retrieved from http://news
.bbc.co.uk/1/hi/world/europe/4395934.stm.

Healy, K. (2005). *Social work theories in context: Creating frameworks for practice.* New
York: Palgrave.

Hegney, D., Ross, H., Baker, P., Rogers-Clark, C., King, C., Buikstra E., et al. (2008). *Building resilience in rural communities: Toolkit.* Toowoomba: Centre for Rural and Remote
Area Health, University of Southern Queensland, University of Queensland.

Henry, C., & Seymour, J. (2008). *Advance care planning: A guide for health and social care
staff* (Rev. ed.). London: Department of Health. Retrieved from http://www.endoflife
careforadults.nhs.uk/eolc/files/F2023-EoLC-ACP_guide_for_staff-Aug2008.pdf.

Heron, J. (2001). *Helping the client: A creative practical guide* (5th ed.). London: Sage.

Hodge, D. (2001). Spiritual assessment: A review of major qualitative methods and a new
framework for assessing spirituality. *Social Work, 46*, 203–214.

Hoffman, M. L. (2000). *Empathy and moral development: Implications for caring and practice.* Cambridge: Cambridge University Press.

Holden, K. (2004). Personal costs and personal pleasures: Care and the unmarried woman
in inter-war Britain. In J. Fink (Ed.), *Care: Personal lives and policy* (pp. 44–76). Bristol,
UK: Policy Press.

Holopainen, R. (2009). *Humanism in action: The work of Gora and the Atheist Centre in
India.* Hagen, Germany: Internationaler Bund der Konfessionslosen und Atheisten.
Retrieved from http://ibka.org/en/articles/ag02/ratna.html.

Hood, B. (2009). *Supersense: From superstition to religion—the brain science of belief.* New
York: HarperOne.

Howarth, D. (2000). *Discourse.* Buckingham, UK: Open University Press.

Howe, D. (2005). *Child abuse and neglect: Attachment, development and intervention.*
Basingstoke, UK: Palgrave Macmillan.

Howe, D. (2008). *The emotionally intelligent social worker.* Basingstoke, UK: Palgrave
Macmillan.

Illouz, E. (2007). *Cold intimacies: The making of emotional capitalism.* Cambridge, UK:
Policy Press.

International Federation of Social Workers. (2000). *International definition of social work.*
Zurich, Switzerland: Author.

International Humanist and Ethical Union Congress. (2002). *Amsterdam Declaration
2002.* London: Author. Retrieved from http://www.iheu.org/amsterdamdeclaration.

Jacobs, P., & Rapoport, J. (2003). *The economics of health and medical care* (5th ed.). Sud-
bury, MA: Jones and Bartlett.

Jenkins, R. (1996). *Social identity.* London: Routledge.

Johnson, C., & Webster, D. (2002). *Recrafting a life: Solutions for chronic pain and illness.*
New York: Brunner-Routledge.

Jordan, B. (1978). A comment on "Theory and practice in social work." *British Journal of Social Work, 8*(1), 23–25.

Keith-Lucas, A. (1972). *Giving and taking help.* Chapel Hill: University of North Carolina Press.

Kondrat, M. E. (2002). Actor-centered social work: Revisioning "person-in-environment" through a critical theory lens. *Social Work, 47,* 435–448.

Kosmin, B. A., Meyer, E., & Keysar, A. (2001). *American Religious Identification Survey 2001.* New York: Graduate Center of the City University of New York. Retrieved from http://www.gc.cuny.edu/faculty/research_briefs/aris.pdf.

Krill, D. F. (1978). *Existential social work.* New York: Free Press.

Kumar, H. (1995). *Theories in social work practice.* New Delhi: Gitanjali.

Lee, D., & O'Gorman, R. (Eds.). (2005). *Social work and divinity.* Binghamton, NY: Haworth.

Lee, J. A. B. (2001). *The empowerment approach to social work practice: Building the beloved community.* New York: Columbia University Press.

Lindsay, R. (2002). *Recognizing spirituality: The interface between faith and social work.* Crawley: University of Western Australia Press.

Lynch, K., Baker, J., & Lyons, M. (2009). *Affective equality: Love, care and injustice.* Basingstoke, UK: Palgrave Macmillan.

Macdonald, K. I., & Macdonald, G. M. (1999). Perceptions of risk. In P. Parsloe (Ed.), *Risk assessment in social care and social work* (pp. 17–68). Philadelphia: Kingsley.

Mallick, M. D., & Ashley, A. A. (1981). Politics of collaboration: Challenge to advocacy. *Social Casework, 62,* 131–137.

Marsh, P., & Crow, G. (1997). *Family group conferences in child welfare.* Oxford, UK: Blackwell.

Maslow, A. H. (1971). *The farther reaches of human nature.* New York: Viking Press.

Maslow, A. H. (1999). *Toward a psychology of being* (3rd ed.). New York: Wiley.

Mayeroff, M. (1971). *On caring.* New York: Harper and Row.

McBeath, G. B., & Webb, S. A. (1997). Community care: A unity of state and care? In R. Hugman, M. Peelo, & K. Soothill (Eds.), *Concepts of care: Developments in health and social welfare* (pp. 36–51). London: Arnold.

McDougall, G. J., Blixen, C. E., & Suen, L.-J. (1997). The process and outcome of life review psychotherapy with depressed homebound older adults. *Nursing Research, 46,* 277–283.

Mead, G. H. (1934). *Mind, self, and society.* Chicago: University of Chicago Press.

Mearns, D., & Thorne, B. (2007). *Person-centred counselling in action* (3rd ed.). London: Sage.

Misiak, H., & Sexton, V. S. (1973). *Phenomenological, existential, and humanistic psychologies: An historical survey.* New York: Grune and Stratton.

Moberg, D. O. (2005). Research in spirituality, religion, and aging. In H. R. Moody (Ed.), *Religion, spirituality and aging: A social work perspective* (pp. 11–40). Binghamton, NY: Haworth.

Montgomery, C. L. (1993). *Healing through communication: The practice of caring*. Newbury Park, CA: Sage.

Morrison, T. (2007). Emotional intelligence: Emotion and social work; context, characteristics, complications and contribution. *British Journal of Social Work, 37*, 245–263.

Moss, D. (2001). The roots and genealogy of humanistic psychology. In K. J. Schneider, J. F. T. Bugental, & J. F. Pierson (Eds.), *The handbook of humanistic psychology: Leading edges in theory, research and practice* (pp. 5–20). Thousand Oaks, CA: Sage.

Murdach, A. D. (2009). Discretion in direct practice: New perspectives. *Social Work, 54*, 183–186.

Nabigon, H., & Mawhiney, A.-M. (1996). Aboriginal theory: A Cree medicine wheel guide for healing first nations. In F. J. Turner (Ed.), *Social work treatment: Interlocking theoretical systems* (4th ed., pp. 18–38). New York: Free Press.

Narayanaswamy, A. (2006). Reflections and conclusion. In A. Narayanaswamy (Ed.), *Spiritual care and transcultural care research* (pp. 176–198). London: Quay.

Narayanaswamy, A., & Narayanaswamy, M. (2006). Spirituality and health care. In A. Narayanaswamy (Ed.), *Spiritual care and transcultural care research* (pp. 15–41). London: Quay.

National Association of Social Workers. (1999). *Code of ethics*. Washington, DC: Author. Retrieved from http://www.socialworkers.org/pubs/code/default.asp.

National Resilience Resource Center. (2009). *National Resilience Resource Center*. St. Paul: College of Continuing Education, University of Minnesota. Retrieved from http://www.cce.umn.edu/National-Resilience-Resource-Center/index.html.

Neimeyer, R. (2001). The language of loss: Grief therapy as a process of meaning reconstruction. In R. Neimeyer (Ed.), *Meaning reconstruction and the experience of loss* (pp. 261–292). Washington, DC: American Psychological Association.

Neuberger, J. (2004). *Caring for dying people of different faiths* (3rd ed.). Oxford, UK: Radcliffe.

Ng, S.-M., & Chan, C. (2009). Alternative intervention: A Chinese body-mind-spirit perspective. In R. Adams, L. Dominelli, & M. Payne (Eds.), *Social work: Themes, issues and critical debates* (pp. 271–280). Basingstoke, UK: Palgrave Macmillan.

Noddings, N. (1984). *Caring: A feminine approach to ethics and moral education*. Berkeley: University of California Press.

Office for National Statistics. (2009). *Religion in the UK*. London: Author. Retrieved from http://www.statistics.gov.uk/cci/nugget.asp?id=293.

Office of the Public Guardian. (2009). *Lasting powers of attorney*. London: Author. Retrieved from http://www.publicguardian.gov.uk/arrangements/lpa.htm.

Parker, J. (2000). *Structuration*. Buckingham, UK: Open University Press.

Pawson, R., Boaz, A., Grayson, L., Long, A., & Barnes, C. (2003). *Types and quality of knowledge in social care*. London: Social Care Institute for Excellence.

Payne, M. (2000). *Anti-bureaucratic social work*. Birmingham, UK: Venture.

Payne, M. (2005). *Modern social work theory* (3rd ed.). Chicago: Lyceum Books.

Payne, M. (2006). *What is professional social work?* (2nd ed.). Chicago: Lyceum Books.

Payne, M. (2007). Performing as a "wise person" in social work practice. *Practice, 19*(2), 85–96.

Payne, M. (2008a). Complexity and social work theory and practice. *Social Work Now, 39*, 15–20.

Payne, M. (2008b, Summer). Religious and spiritual issues at the end of life. *National Association of Primary Care Review*, 262–263.

Payne, M. (2009a). Knowledge, evidence and the wise person of practice: The example of social work and social care in palliative care. In H.-U. Otto, A. Polutta, & H. Ziegler (Eds.), *Evidence-based practice: Modernising the knowledge base of social work?* (pp. 77–94). Farmington Hills, MI: Budrich.

Payne, M. (2009b). Practice theory: Ideas embodied in a wise person's professional process. In B. Borden (Ed.), *Reshaping theory in contemporary social work: Toward a critical pluralism in clinical practice* (pp. 234–254). New York: Columbia University Press.

Payne, M. (2009c). *Social care practice in context*. Basingstoke, UK: Palgrave Macmillan.

Payne, M. (2009d). Understanding social work process. In R. Adams, L. Dominelli, & M. Payne (Eds.), *Social work: Themes, issues and critical debates* (3rd ed., pp. 159–174). Basingstoke, UK: Palgrave Macmillan.

Payne, M., Adams, R., & Dominelli, L. (2009). On being critical in social work. In R. Adams, L. Dominelli, & M. Payne (Eds.), *Critical practice in social work* (2nd ed., pp. 1–15). Basingstoke, UK: Palgrave Macmillan.

Payne, Martin. (2006). *Narrative therapy: An introduction for counsellors* (2nd ed.). London: Sage.

Pembroke, N. (2004). *Working relationships: Spirituality in human service and organizational life*. Philadelphia: Kingsley.

Pithouse, A. (1998). *Social work: The social organisation of an invisible trade*. Aldershot, UK: Ashgate.

Pratt, J. W., & Mason, A. (1981). *The caring touch*. London: HM+M.

Priestley, P., & McGuire, J. (1983). *Learning to help: Basic skills exercises*. London: Tavistock.

Rawls, J. (1971). *A theory of justice*. Cambridge, MA: Harvard University Press.

Reid, W. J. (1978). *The task-centered system*. New York: Columbia University Press.

Reith, M., & Payne, M. (2009). *Social work in end-of-life and palliative care*. Chicago: Lyceum Books.

Roach, S. (1992). *The human act of caring: A blueprint for the health professions* (Rev. ed.). Ottawa: Canadian Hospital Association Press.

Roberts, B. (2006). *Micro social theory*. Basingstoke, UK: Palgrave.

Robinson, S. (2008). *Spirituality, ethics and care*. Philadelphia: Kingsley.

Robinson, S., Kendrick, K., & Brown, A. (2003). *Spirituality and the practice of healthcare*. Basingstoke, UK: Palgrave Macmillan.

Rogers, C. R. (1951). *Client-centered therapy: Its current practice, implications and theory*. London: Constable.

Rogers, C. R. (1961). *On becoming a person: A therapist's view of psychotherapy*. London: Constable.

Rogers, C. R. (2007). The basic conditions of the facilitative therapeutic relationship. In M. Cooper, M. O'Hara, P. F. Schmid, & G. Wyatt (Eds.), *The handbook of person-centered psychotherapy and counselling* (pp. 1–5). Basingstoke, UK: Palgrave Macmillan. (Originally published 1982).

Rowan, J. (1993). *The transpersonal: Psychotherapy and counselling*. London: Routledge.

Schön, D. A. (1983). *The reflective practitioner: How professionals think in action*. New York: Basic Books.

Sheppard, M., Newstead, S. di Caccavo, A., & Ryan. K. (2000). Reflexivity and the development of process knowledge in social work: A classification and empirical study. *British Journal of Social Work, 30*, 465–488.

Sheppard, M., & Ryan, K. (2003). Practitioners as rule using analysts: A further development of process knowledge in social work. *British Journal of Social Work, 33*(2), 157–176.

Sherwin, S. (1992). *No longer patient: Feminist ethics and healthcare*. Philadelphia: Temple University Press.

Shorrock, A. (2008). *The transpersonal in psychology, psychotherapy and counselling*. Basingstoke, UK: Palgrave Macmillan.

Sibeon, R. (1990). Comment on the structure and forms of social work knowledge. *Social Work and Social Sciences Review, 1*(1), 29–44.

Smith, B. (1973). On self-actualization: A transambivalent examination of a focal theme in Maslow's psychology. *Journal of Humanistic Psychology, 13*(2), 17–33.

Smith, C. R. (2002). The sequestration of experience: Rights talk and moral thinking in "late modernity." *Sociology, 36*(1), 43–66.

Smith, E. R. (2001). Alleviating suffering in the face of death: Insights from constructivism and a transpersonal narrative approach. In E. R. Canda & E. D. Smith (Eds.), *Transpersonal perspectives on spirituality in social work* (pp. 45–61). New York: Haworth.

Smithbattle, L. (1994). Beyond normalizing: The role of narrative in understanding teenage mothers' transition to mothering. In P. Benner (Ed.), *Interpretive phenomenology: Embodiment, caring and ethics in health and illness* (pp. 141–166). Thousand Oaks, CA: Sage.

Social Care Institute for Excellence. (2008). *SCIE Practice Guide 09: Dignity in care.* London: Author.

Solomon, B. B. (1976). *Black empowerment: Social work in oppressed communities.* New York: Columbia University Press.

Stanworth, R. (2003). *Recognizing spiritual needs in people who are dying.* Oxford: Oxford University Press.

Statistics Canada. (2001). *Population by religion, by province and territory.* Ottawa: Author. Retrieved from http://www40.statcan.gc.ca/l01/cst01/demo30a-eng.htm.

Stephen, J. E., Rahn, M., Verhoef, M., & Leis, A. (2007). What is the state of the evidence on the mind-cancer survival question, and where do we go from here? A point of view. *Supportive Care in Cancer, 15,* 923–930.

Stevens, I., & Cox, P. (2008). Complexity theory: Developing new understandings of child protection in field settings and in residential child care. *British Journal of Social Work, 38,* 1320–1336.

Stroebe, M., & Schut, H. (1999). The dual process model of coping with bereavement: Rationale and description. *Death Studies, 23*(3), 197–224.

Tasker, M. (2008). Digital arts. In N. Hartley & M. Payne (Eds.), *The creative arts in palliative care* (pp. 113–127). Philadelphia: Kingsley.

Taylor, C., & White, S. (2000). *Practising reflexivity in health and welfare: Making knowledge.* Buckingham, UK: Open University Press.

Taylor, C., & White, S. (2006). Knowledge and reasoning in social work: Educating for humane judgement. *British Journal of Social Work, 36,* 937–954.

Thompson, N. (1992). *Existentialism and social work.* Aldershot, UK: Avebury.

Thompson, N. (1996). *People skills.* Basingstoke, UK: Palgrave Macmillan.

Thompson, N. (2000). *Theory and practice in human services.* Philadelphia: Open University Press.

Thorndike, E. (1921). Intelligence and its uses. *Harper's Magazine, 140,* 227–235.

Trevithick, P. (2005). *Social work skills: A practice handbook* (2nd ed.). Maidenhead, UK: Open University Press.

Truax, C. B., & Carkhuff R. J. (1967). *Toward effective counseling and psychotherapy: Training and practice.* Chicago: Aldine.

Ungar, M. (2009, August). Resilience practice in action: Five principles for intervention. *Social Work Now,* 32–38.

United Nations. (1948). *Universal Declaration of Human Rights.* Retrieved from http://www.un.org/Overview/rights.html.

United States. (1791). *Constitution of the United States.* Retrieved from http://www.usconstitution.net/const.html.

U.S. Department of Health and Human Services. (2008). *Advance directives and advance care planning: Report to Congress.* Washington, DC: Author. Retrieved from http://aspe.hhs.gov/daltcp/reports/2008/ADCongRpt.pdf.

Van Hook, M., Hugen, B., & Aguilar, M. (Eds.). (2001). *Spirituality within religious traditions in social work practice.* Pacific Heights, CA: Brooks Cole.

Walsh, F. (2006). *Strengthening family resilience* (2nd ed.). New York: Guilford.

Walter, I., Nutley, S., Percy-Smith, J., McNeish, D., & Frost, S. (2004). *Improving the use of research in social care practice.* London: Social Care Institute for Excellence.

Watkins, M. L. (2002). Listening to girls: A study in resilience. In R. R. Greene (Ed.), *Resiliency: An integrated approach to practice, policy, and research.* Washington, DC: National Association of Social Workers Press.

Watson, J. C. (2001). Re-visioning empathy. In D. J. Cain & J. Seeman (Eds.), *Humanistic psychotherapies: Handbook of research and practice* (pp. 445–471). Washington, DC: American Psychological Association.

Webb, S. A. (2001). Some considerations on the validity of evidence-based practice in social work. *British Journal of Social Work, 31*(1), 57–79.

Webb, S. A. (2006). *Social work in a risk society: Social and political perspectives.* Basingstoke, UK: Palgrave Macmillan.

Weick, A. (1999). Guilty knowledge. *Families in Society, 80,* 327–332.

White, M. (1995). *Re-authoring lives: Interviews and essays.* Adelaide, Australia: Dulwich Centre Publications.

White, M., & Epston, D. (1990). *Narrative means to therapeutic ends.* New York: Norton.

Wilbur, K. (2000). *Integral psychology: Consciousness, spirit, psychology, religion.* Boston: Shambhala.

Wiles, E., Heath, S., Crow, G., & Charles, V. (2005). *Informed consent in social research: A literature review.* Southampton, UK: ESRC National Centre for Research Methods. Retrieved from http://www.ncrm.ac.uk/research/outputs/publications/methods review/MethodsReviewPaperNCRM-001.pdf.

Woman loses fight to wear cross. (2006). BBC News. Retrieved from http://news.bbc .co.uk/1/hi/england/london/6165368.stm.

Index